Maroon Heritage

Maroon Heritage

Archaeological
Ethnographic and
Historical Perspectives

edited by

E Kofi Agorsah

Canoe Press

●BARBADOS ●JAMAICA ●TRINIDAD AND TOBAGO

Canoe Press
The University of the West Indies
1A Aqueduct Flats, Kingston 7, Jamaica
© 1994 by Canoe Press. All rights reserved
Published 1994
Printed and bound in Canada
99 98 97 96 95 94   6 5 4 3 2 1

ISBN (pbk) 976 8125 10 1

Cataloguing in Publication Data

Maroon heritage: archaeological
ethnographic and historical
perspectives / E. Kofi Agorsah, ed.;
with foreword by B.W. Higman.

p. cm.
Papers presented at a symposium on Maroon
heritage held 18-19 October 1991 at the
University of the West Indies, Mona, Jamaica.

Includes bibliographical references.
ISBN 976 8125 10 1
1. Maroons – Jamaica – Congresses.
2. Maroons – History – Congresses.
3. Maroons – social life and customs
– Congresses. I. Agorsah, E. Kofi
F1893.M3M37 1994   972.92
                 dc 20

Maps: p. 38 – Courtesy National Library of
Jamaica; p. 66 – Courtesy UWI Mona Archaeological
Research Project (UMARP)
Photo credits: p. 115 – Courtesy National Archives of
Jamaica; pp. 174-75, 177-80 – Courtesy E Kofi Agorsah

Book and cover design by Prodesign Ltd, Jamaica
Text set in 9/12 Palatino and Dauphin display
Printed on acid-free paper: 50lb Husky Offset

Table of Contents

List of Figures

 *Foreword*

The papers published in this volume had their origin in a conference on Maroon Heritage held at the University of the West indies, Mona, 18-19 October 1991. That conference was memorable for a number of reasons.

Scholars often choose to keep a distance between themselves and their subjects of study. The conference on Maroon Heritage was therefore unusual in the manner in which it brought together observer and observed on an equal, mutually reinforcing basis. Academic researchers came from Jamaica and other parts of the hemisphere, and Maroons came from their main bases in Jamaica— Accompong, Moore Town and Scott's Hall. Papers were delivered by both Maroons and academics, and dialogue flowed freely.

Maroons have never been marooned in the sense of being lost, cast up in some isolated, desolate place, without networks to the wider world. They have always been in the world and of the world. An acceptance of this past and present interactive relationship is essential for the future preservation of Maroon heritage as well as the study of Maroon peoples and their history.

Maroon communities have been studied frequently and intensively by the outside scholarly world. What scholars have said and written about them finds its way back into the culture, one way or another. This in turn adds to the store of knowledge, whether it be right or wrong, and can enter the oral tradition. Students of oral historiography call this the problem of feedback. The big question here is how far what scholars think they are learning from people as their oral tradition is really a product of exposure to the wider world, including the scholarship of that wider world. No oral tradition is pure, and no written document offers an unblemished record of experience. Scholars working with written documents, however, are almost always reading accounts created by the oppressors rather than the oppressed. This carries its own special dangers, as papers in this volume indicate, complicating the problem of feedback. The interface between the oral and the written becomes extremely busy, and it becomes increasingly difficult to identify and separate the source-origins of the heritage.

The conference on Maroon Heritage was particularly significant in facing up to these questions, even if in the deliberations the issues were more often implicit than explicit. It was not just a matter of healthy dialogue, but an encounter at close quarters that provided a clearer view of the present state of understanding and some notion of how research and dissemination should proceed in the future.

In this volume, the essential character and spirit of the conference has been retained successfully. There are papers by Maroons and papers by academic scholars, papers from individuals with a wide variety of disciplinary alliances. For ensuring this achievement, full credit must go to Kofi. I had the privilege of serving as Head of the Department of History at Mona at the time of the conference, but Kofi was the initiator and the essential energy behind all of the arrangements. It was his contact with the Maroons, established through his archaeological and cultural studies, that provided the basis for the fruitful exchange that characterized the conference. Beyond any selfish scholarly concerns, there was also the spirit of sharing, the desire to give something back. Kofi was also responsible for seeing that the published proceedings, the contents of this book, maintained this spirit. I am proud to have been his associate.

Finally I wish to thank all of the participants to the conference, and particularly the authors of the papers contained in this volume, for their contribution towards a widening and deepening of our understanding of Maroon history and culture.

B W Higman
University of the West Indies
Mona, Jamaica

 *The Place of the Maroons in Jamaica*

I feel honoured by the fact that you recognize that as the resident representative of Africa on the island, it is appropriate to associate me with this symposium. I want to commend the organizers of this symposium for their foresight and I have special commendation for the Maroons for their active participation in the analyses and discussion of research results on their heritage. This is a practice that should be encouraged because it provides the opportunity also for community participation in research ventures at all levels.

I am informed that this symposium was originally planned as a local University activity but has now turned out to be an international event with participation of panelists from such places as the Smithsonian Institution and New York University, the Institute for Policy Studies, Washington DC, the Cave Hill campus of the University of the West Indies, and other areas. I am also informed that most of the participants paid their way to come to this conference. There is, therefore, a clear challenge to Jamaicans to sustain this interest.

When the British conquered this island in 1655 it soon became clear to them that the freedom-fighting Maroons were a force to be reckoned with. Apart from the later rise in the number of black slaves and its attendant complex organizational needs, as a result of colonial economic policy, the colonial power recognized the escapee community as a legacy that was to determine or rather influence the course of events. This is supported by the fact that the British, from the time of Charles 11 in 1658 to George 111 in 1795, had to ceaselessly grapple with the desperate fight of the slaves, who were struggling for their freedom, and escapees also struggling to maintain their freedom. A close examination of the cultural history of Jamaica indicates clearly that the Maroon society provided a cultural link between the indigenous societies of the island and the Spanish settlers on the one hand, and the English on the other. Historically, this is significant because it indicates that the history of the Maroons of Jamaica is not only a link, but has become and remains in its entirety a part of the historical period. The importance of Maroon heritage as a major cultural element that runs through the historical period in the cultural development of Jamaican society is thus incomplete without retracing the course of this major thread.

Many accounts in history misrepresent and misinterpret the Maroons. They are considered as rebels rather than as freedom fighters. I am told that so far only one author has had the courage to use a title for his book which emphasizes the point of the fight for freedom. The book is entitled *The Fighting Maroons*, and I am pleased to learn that the author will be actively participating in this symposium. I salute this scholar, and hope that the message of the freedom-fighting people will be driven deep into the minds of people to correct a wrong notion that has held sway for centuries.

I have heard criticisms whispered against the real motives of the Maroons in their campaigns against the British. I notice that there is still a bad feeling in the Jamaican community about events surrounding attempts by a part of the community trying to establish an alternative life style to that of the plantation system on the one hand, while on the other acting as informants against others of their own community trying to rebel against the same system. Many people find it contradictory, but this is not new in history. Examination of events in other places, for example amongst the Egyptians, the Greeks, the Romans, reveals similar contradictions. Even modern day political and military situations abound with repetitions of this kind of thing observed in Jamaica. It must be borne in mind too that the further back we go in history the closer we come to divergences of language and culture amongst the ethnic Jamaicans, many of whom still retained their tribal languages and customs which often cut across national identity, if it is correct to apply this term to those periods in history.

However, as a country trying to establish a national identity, these issues need some more serious examination and discussion to pave the way for reconciliation and peaceful co-existence. It is for this reason that my High Commission has, over the years, provided strong support for all efforts geared towards issues of cultural importance such as this symposium will be addressing.

Allow me to acknowledge the important role played by my predecessor, Prof Adefuyehimself a historian, who maintained a strong link with the Maroons. I am going to maintain, strengthen and diversify this link during my tour of duty.

Ladies and gentlemen, allow me to congratulate the University research committee, and specifically the Department of History of the University, and specially Dr Kofi Agorsah and the Faculty of Arts and General Studies for this fine initiative. Let me use this opportunity to extend a hand of fellowship to the History Department and the Faculty of Arts in any and all matters pertaining to the teaching of African history and culture.

It is, in my view, important that Jamaica consider Maroon life as a positive sharing experience and examine the implications of learning from this experience to build more positively at the community level. This includes sharing Maroon values with the younger generation. The Maroons themselves must also realize that the old enemy is gone but that a new and more serious one lurks around the corner. The new enemy, economic servitude, must be fought by all Jamaicans as one people, everyone contributing their bit.

The programme for the symposium is clear in its objective. One effective way to carry on the search that would provide a clearer appreciation of the need for the much desired peaceful co-existence is the inter and multi-disciplinary approach. Why and how have Maroon communities kept their values alive over all these years? How have these values helped them and for how long will they remain distinctive? What are the implications for assimilation? These are the questions that ought to be uppermost, in addition to the purely academic examination of the issues of this symposium. It is important to examine the past Maroon heritage. It is equally important to examine it as it is today. But it is even more important to speculate about its future because that is the time when future generations will need to understand and know the true nature of their heritage.

(Abridged version of the Opening Address by Professor E.N. Ugochukwu, High Commissioner of the Federal Republic of Nigeria to Jamaica, at the Symposium on Maroon Heritage held 18-19 October 1991 at the University of the West Indies, Mona)

 *Preface*

Two things are clear. First, all contributors emphasize the significance of the Maroon heritage in the Caribbean as an indispensable element within and of the cultural history of the region. Secondly, all contributors stress the significance of the need for a deeper analysis of "resistance" history in the New World. A third theme raised by many contributors to this volume identifies and discusses the phenomenon of "resistance" as an important element in the shaping of the history of the New World, and the geographical distribution of Maroon resistance groups in the Caribbean and adjoining areas. In addition, the implications of maronage and its associated developments in the New World such as guerrilla warfare, the treaties, the impact on colonial policy directions, the environment and environmental adaptation, art and artistic expressions are discussed.

Resistance is a phenomenon that cannot be separated from slavery or oppression—as has also been repeatedly stated by several scholars such as Singleton [1985] Beckles and Shepherd [1991], Heuman [1986]—and therefore remains an inseparable part of New World History and particularly Caribbean History [Augier and Gordon 1962]. The development of resistance groups was a direct response to the cruel torture devices on slave ships and on the plantations, such as the whips and guns, posses of soldiers and dogs sent after escaping slaves, horrible punishments and executions of "troublemakers" [Beckles 1986; Brathwaite 1977; Price 1992; Robinson 1969]. These experiences were life-threatening enough for the enslaved to resort to defensive violence. Archaeological and historical studies recognize the significance of "resistance" as an important element in the shaping of New World History [Agorsah 1993, Beckles 1986, Price 1973]. This is even more important for the Caribbean where the best examples of resistance to slavery can be obtained [Augier and Gordon 1962, Hall and Beckford 1960].

On their arrival in the New World, in their lust for power and precious metals and other wealth, the Spaniards encountered many local ethnic groups such as the Lucayanos living in the Bahamas [Keegan 1987; Keegan, Stokes and Nelson 1990;

Loven 1935], the Borequinos in Puerto Rico [Alegria 1980], and the Tainos in Cuba [Barroso 1984], the Dominican Republic and Haiti [Arrom and Aravelo 1986] and much of the eastern Caribbean inhabited by the Caribs whose ferocity prevented European colonization of islands such as Grenada and St Lucia. Parry and Sherlock [1965], record that there were "negroes" on board the vessels that brought the Spanish adventurers to the New World. As the Spaniards forced the Indians and their slaves on board their vessels they escaped, sometimes in small groups, into hiding. For example, it is reported that as early as 1502 an African slave escaped from his enslaver into the interior hills of Hispaniola and that during the early parts of the 16th century strongholds established by escaped African slaves already existed on one of the islands referred to as Samana, off the coast of Hispaniola [Price 1973]. These groups eventually developed into Maroon communities who were certainly not the only resistance group in the Caribbean but whose activities have recurred throughout, and shaped the history of the colonial period in the New World.

Looking into the future of the research on Maroons has relied on observations of the modern way of life of the Maroons. Maroon Chiefs very proudly recount some of these traditional practices that serve as authentic indication of cultural continuity from their past. Ethnographic evidence indicates some continuities of the life of the days of marronage and its attendant wars of resistance. The study of the traditional systems of West Africa is particularly important for the Caribbean not only because of the link with the slave trade but also because West African social systems such as those extant in Africa before and after colonial contact present several authentic characteristics of general development that form the basis of observed continuities in the Caribbean. Maureen Warner-Lewis and Marjorie Whylie provide very good examples of such links in the form, style and content of Maroon music.

Although transformations have been observed in several aspects of the technological [Goucher 1991] and social systems [Kopytoff 1973; Alleyne 1988] and even in physical types [Watters et al. 1992], there still remain many detailed aspects of these and other related areas that could indicate the trend, as well as the force, of the impact of the various changes which have occurred over time. Ethnographically, many aspects of the West African cultural traditions before European contact could help to identify transformations resulting from that contact, particularly after AD 1500 and they are critical for explaining cultural continuities in the Caribbean. Family systems, language, ethnicity, religion, festivals, marriage patterns, art, music and dance are some of the areas with evidence of observed continuities. However, the nature of the impact from Africa on any cultural practices in the New World will depend to a very large extent on the part of the African continent from which they derived. Personal names such as Cudjoe, Cuffee, Quao, Sambo; place names such as Konkonsa Ceitful, Accompong and Abeokuta; the use of the side blown horn (bugle) known by the name *abeng* among the Akan of Ghana; names and techniques of drums and drumming; hunting techniques; musical and religious forms; names such as *prako* for pig and *nsuo* for water, known among the Akan of Ghana; and even the approach to settling disputes at the local level —these and many such examples should provide good bases for identifying continuities and explaining the nature and mechanism of the functional adaptations of the Maroons. Colonel C.L.G. Harris and Kenneth Bilby provide numerous examples of this kind of evidence of continuity in language and expressions. Together, these indications suggest that research into Maroon heritage must consider both sides of the Atlantic.

The Maroons can be credited with many achievements. They became the frontline fighters in the struggle against slavery in all its various forms. Before any known struggles for independence in the New World, Maroon communities had developed strong ideas and strategies of self-sufficiency, self-help and self-reliance and fought with great skill and courage for the right to self determination. Also, the communities managed to unite people who had come from diverse backgrounds and regions of the world, speaking different languages and practising diverse customs and traditions. African traditions featured prominently in the formation and transformation of the ways of life of these groups throughout the entire period of their struggle. It is, however, difficult to clearly identify all aspects of the African elements retained by the Maroons. Although the majority of the Maroons consisted of slaves derived from West Africa whose cultural traditions should help to identify any retention and how these may have contributed to the survival of the Maroons, the fascination with the stories about the Indian in the New World which persists among scholars today on a variety of levels needs to be taken into consideration. For example, among scholars of Caribbean archaeology the Indian has been the recipient of the credit for many, if not all, of the Caribbean prehistoric cultural traditions. It is speculated that this cultural background both constituted the basis of what early Maroons developed and survived, emphasizing the cultural link [Price 1976, 1973; Campbell 1990; Agorsah 1993].

Results of recent research in Caribbean archaeology demonstrates that the development, growth and survival of Maroon societies provided a cultural link between the indigenous societies and the Spanish on one hand, and the English on the other. Historically, this is significant because it indicates that the history of the Maroons of Jamaica is not only the most important link, but has become and remains in its entirety a part of the historical period. The importance of Maroon heritage as a major cultural element that runs through the historical period in Jamaica can, therefore, not be over-emphasized. A reconstruction of cultural development in the Caribbean and particularly in the Jamaican society is thus incomplete without retracing the course of this major thread.

The study of some contemporary Maroon societies provides some indications of aspects of the nature and mechanism of cultural continuities among them. New ways of life using the old ways of the Amerindian and the African were utilized. Hunting, fishing and farming methods recapitulated old practices. For example, among Suriname Maroons (the Djuka), methods used to prepare cassava which was the staple food, remained the same although one could also liken that method to preparation of the *gari* or *yakeyake* of the Anlo of modern Ghana and *eba* among modern Yoruba of Nigeria in West Africa. This may indicate both Amerindian and

West African connections. Similarly, a special food made from corn (maize) and called *dukunu* among Jamaican Maroons is prepared in the same way and bears the same name as in modern Ghana, again showing African influence. *Suffki* or *toli*, two very popular dishes of the Seminole Maroons of Oklahoma and Texas, also appear to have been inherited from native Americans. Contemporary fishing and trap-setting techniques as well as traditional herbal medicine among the Maroons in Suriname and Jamaica in particular reflect Amerindian, African and European sources. It is observed that in their attempt to survive the struggle to maintain freedom, the Maroons devised methods of subsistence, military strategies, systems of shared authority, shared languages, compromising on each other's different ways of religious practice, speaking, marriage systems, birth and death rites, ownership and property control, music and dance, utilizing the wide range of African, European and Amerindian cultural resources available to them.

According to Kenneth Bilby (writing in this volume), the music, verbal arts and spiritual traditions of contemporary Maroons remain predominantly African. As in Africa, these features of Maroon culture are not separated. They form parts of everyday life in activities that weave one into another. However, certain other elements have been identified in dance, for example: such as an Amerindian-style dance—called Seminole Stomp. among the Seminole Maroons; and in songs to the dean—considered among the Aluku of Guiana to be of native American origin. Maroon cultural development has thus been formation and transformation of a mixture of diverse cultural elements from both sides of the Atlantic. Through Maroon activities the heritage of Mexico, Suriname, Jamaica, Cuba, Colombia, North America and many parts of the New world are linked to others of the Old World. They provide not only the thread but also the context.

The greatest successes of the Maroons are recognized in their military ability and leadership. Very able and charismatic leadership enabled them to attain their goals in their struggle. Among the Maroons of Jamaica, Nanny, Cudjoe, Quao and Accompong are names to remember. Among those from other Maroon societies there were leaders of exceptional qualities, such as Yanga of Mexico, Boni of Suriname, Bayano of Panama, Ganga Zumba of Brazil, Benkos Bioho of Colombia, and John Horse (sometimes referred to as Juan Caballo or Gopher John) of Southern USA and Mexico. Political organization appears to imitate traditional systems of Africa. For example, in Jamaica the head of the group is referred to as Colonel (also called Chief) of Maroons, and then a Major and Captains in that order, each with specific roles to play in the administration and policy making with the help of a Council of Elders (*Kamati*) (committee?). Similarly, Maroon groups in Suriname and Guyana have paramount chiefs known as Ganman or Gaama. He wields a considerable amount of power and authority and respect. He is followed by *Ede Kabiteni* (head chiefs) and *Kabiteni* (village chiefs) and *Basia* (sub-chiefs)— comprising women and men—in that order. Meetings (*kuutu*) are held for several different issues as required—for administration of justice, policy formulation and settlement of disputes.

Family organization (matrilineal or patrilineal) continues to be the core of the family system. At Accompong one observed a reflection of the importance of the family in its extended form even in the location and distribution of family residential areas. This follows a rule of family relationships—a pattern established for many parts of West Africa [Agorsah 1985, 1990].

Wood and calabash carving, body scarification, decorative art on walls, named hair styles, as well as rituals of all kinds clearly represent continuities from Africa although one can hardly identify the specific areas from which many of the traditions were derived. The use of drums and side-blown cow horns as means of communication—some of these bearing the same names as used among some African societies—clearly emphasize the point that Maroon cultural traditions possess a remarkable number of direct and sometimes spectacular retentions. The verbal arts such as play languages, folktales, proverbs and speeches and spirit possession are also rooted in a wide variety and range of styles based on everyday languages. Richard Price concludes that these "keep alive a large number of distinctive esoteric languages used only in special ritual settings".

Carolyn Cooper and Kamau Brathwaite should be commended for presenting in the small space available in this volume information on the Great Nanny of Jamaica that could fill volumes. Carolyn's statement that "marronage should be recognized as the natural response of free people to dehumanizing attempts to restrict and restructure them" contends, and rightly so, that "Caribbean historiography needs to place the resistance science of the Maroons along a broad ideological continuum of cultural autonomy that manifested itself, however guardedly, even within the very belly of the plantation. Indeed, the well-documented conflicts of interest between the Jamaican Maroons and the slaves marooned on the plantations clearly resulted from a too narrow definition of who constituted the community of essential political affiliation".

Nanny is one of the most celebrated females in the resistance history of the New World. It is not surprising that almost all the contributions refer to her achievements. There may have been more than one Nanny, but Nanny of the excavated Nanny Town (the subject of Kofi Agorsah's chapter on archaeology in this volume), epitomizes the true spirit and role of the Caribbean woman in the fight for freedom and human dignity. Cooper further quotes a poem by Louise Bennett, *Jamaican Oman*, and suggests how "it establishes in the opening two verses . . . the cunning Jamaican woman and then proceeds in the third verse to summons Nanny, wittily suggesting the unexpected complementarity of the militant, magico-religious powers of the ancestor figure":

> *Jamaica Oman cunny, sah!*
> *Is how dem jinnal so?*
> *Look how long dem liberated*
> *An de man dem never know!*
> *Look how long Jamaican oman*
> *– Modder, sister, wife, sweetheart –*

Outa road an eena yard deh pon
A dominate her part!
From Maroon Nanny teck her body
Bounce bullet back pon man,
To when nowadays gal-pickney tun
Spellin-Bee champion.

Nanny symbolizes the pride of the Caribbean woman. Brathwaite, Bilby, Cooper, Harris, and Edwards make this point very strongly. Her role as a true model of the true Caribbean woman may be summed up in Cooper's words:

> *The ambiguous image of domesticity and militancy that the combole embodies is replicated in Reid's presentation of the function of women in Maroon culture. Nanny is the prototype of all less celebrated, unnamed Maroon women who excelled at both the domestic arts of nurturance and the military arts of survival. Maroon women, as much as men, were warriors actively defending their communities. If slavery was the first equal opportunity for employers of black men and women—to cite Johnnetta Cole—the free societies of Jamaican Maroons also provided equal opportunities for men and women to engage fully in the double-sided life of the community.*

Other writers such as Awang [1991], Beckles [1989], Bush [1990], Goveia [1970], Mavis Campbell [1990], Green [1992] Terborg-Penn [1986] have most recently demonstrated in their studies how continuities of the Nanny example may be identified as a significant one in the history of freedom fighting not only in the Caribbean, but in the New World as a whole.

Maronage *(petit or grand marronage)* had a residual effect on the plantation system and was not just a bargaining strategy for better treatment on the plantation but also the main basis for the formation of Maroon societies who eventually took the leadership in the fight against slavery. Maroon history provides a very good example of how colonial people played oppressed off against oppressed. Both the "black shots" employed (as a kind of gendarmerie) to help curb Maroon activities in the early 18th century, and the Maroons who later helped colonial people (as on-hand militia) to control those marooned on the plantations as mentioned in contributions by Pereira, Brathwaite and Cooper, were ignorant of the fact that they were being played off against each other in order to sustain the plantation economy. The events of this aspect of Caribbean history have had serious implications for the unity and understanding of the common heritage shared by all Caribbean people. Continued reference to incidents after the peace treaties continues to cause bad feeling among Caribbean societies as demonstrated by Robinson. For the African historian this strategy would not be considered as new. Playing oppressed groups off against each other is a historical phenomenon known in every part of the world and continues to be part of today's politics. It is in consideration of this that researchers should begin to identify similarities or continuities in the struggle against slavery and human degradation. Understanding the nature and mechanism of the functional adaptation of Maroons and marronage and the intricacies of human survival is of utmost importance for a meaningful re-creation of cultural development in the Caribbean and indeed in the New World.

An abundance of ethnographic data is available. The archaeology is just at the initial stages. Maroon experience is a truly African and American experience and its nature and mechanism of formation and transformation need to be explained and understood. Why ? As Ken Bilby and N'Diaye [1992] have put it: because

> Not only were the Maroons in the forefront of resistance to slavery, they were among the first pioneers to explore and adapt to the more remote, unsettled spaces in both American continents and the Caribbean. Maroons were among the first Americans in the wake of 1492 to resist colonial domination, striving for independence, forging new cultures and developing solidarity out of diversity — processes which only later took place, on a larger scale, in emerging nation-states. The cultural uniqueness of Maroon societies rests firmly on their fidelity to "African" cultural principles . . .whether aesthetic, political, or domestic, rather than on the frequency of their isolated "retention" of form. Maroon groups had a rare freedom to develop and transform African ideas from a variety of societies and to adapt them to changing circumstances. With their hard-earned freedom and resilient creativity they have built systems that are at once meaningfully African and among the most truly "alive" among African-American cultures.

I consider this volume a humble beginning. Its development and birth, as is usually the case, rested on the heads of the contributors who, I would say, deserve every credit. I pay special tribute to our Maroon Chiefs whose contributions make this volume the only one of its kind in Maroon heritage studies, for here we are with the researched and the researcher engaged in a dialogue with a common goal.

 *Acknowledgements*

Now the volume is born. Helping to give birth to it has not been easy, and topping the list is the Institute of Caribbean Studies (ICS), particularly its Chairman, Mr Joe Pereira, senior lecturer in the Department of Spanish and a contributor to this volume. Thank you, Joe, for your support, hard work and dedication toward the publication of this work. The support of the Embassy of Mexico and the Nigerian High Commission in Kingston is respectfully acknowledged with many thanks. I wish to express sincere gratitude to the Institute of Jamaica and particularly Mrs Beverley Hall-Alleyne, the Jamaica National Heritage Trust, particularly Mr Ainsley Henriques, Chairman of the Board of Directors and Dr Patrick Bennett, Executive Director; to the president and members of the Archaeological Society of Jamaica, particularly Mr Basil Reid, Mr Dorrick Gray, Mr Samuel Bandara, Ms Elaine Grant, Ms Marcia Pitt, Mr Albert Edwards (a contributor to this volume), and Ms Audrey Francis; to the Chiefs and people of Accompong and to the Moore Town Maroons, particularly Colonel Martin-Luther Wright and Colonel C.L.G. Harris (contributors to this volume), and Major Aarons. To Professor Mohammed Wader (Political Science), Professor Candice Goucher (Black Studies), and Dr Francis Wambalaba (Black Studies and Department of Economics), all of Portland State University, Oregon, USA, as well as Professor Chris Decorse (Department of Anthropology, Syracuse University), I express deepest appreciation for the invaluable contributions to this publication.

If this volume is readable and becomes a welcome addition to your libraries it is because of the hard work and expert advise and support of Ms Linda Cameron, Director of The Press UWI, and all the staff of that institution. I also wish to thank Donny Miller, Manager of the University Printers Ltd, UWI, and his staff, as well as Beresford Callum (the Jamaica National Heritage Trust), Karen Thompson (the Archaeology Laboratory), Arlene Barnes (Office of Disaster Preparedness), and Sharon Niemczyk (Portland State University) for the illustrations. My sincerest gratitude goes, not least of all, to Mrs Hope Senior and Ms Julliet Williams and fellow members of staff of the Department of

History—particularly Professor Barry Higman—for the encouragement and support and for sponsoring the symposium on Maroon heritage the result of which is the material of this volume. It is impossible to list all who contributed to this volume, for to do so would be to include the names of all the participants of the symposium, particularly those whose papers, for several reasons, could not be included in this volume, as well as the members of the Maroon cultural groups. To each and every one of "the unknown contributors" I wish, on behalf of all of us who present the material in this volume, to say — as the Ewe of Ghana would put it — "*akpe na mi kataa!*" (Thank you all!).

Kofi Agorsah

June 1994

 *Maroon Heritage*

one

Background to Maroon Heritage

E. Kofi Agorsah

Introduction

Lust for power and precious metals attracted Columbus and the Spaniards farther and farther into the New World where they encountered many local ethnic groups, such as the Lucayanos, living in The Bahamas [Keegan 1987; Loven 1935], Borequinos in Puerto Rico [Alegria 1980], and Tainos in Cuba [Corso 1988], Jamaica, the Dominican Republic and Haiti [Arrom and Aravelo 1986].

Much of the eastern Caribbean was inhabited by the Caribs, whose ferocity prevented European colonization of islands such as Grenada and St Lucia. Parry and Sherlock [1965] record that there were "negroes" on board the vessels that brought the Spanish adventurers to the New World. Some of them reportedly escaped to freedom to join the local groups in the interior and inaccessible regions [Guillot 1961].

As the Spaniards forced the Indians and their Spanish slaves on board their vessels they escaped individually or in small groups into hiding. For example, it is reported [Price 1979] that in 1502 an African slave escaped from his enslaver into the interior hills of Hispaniola and that during the early parts of the sixteenth century, strongholds established by escaped African slaves already existed on one of the islands referred to as Samana, off the coast of Hispaniola. These groups eventually crystallized into communities today referred to as Maroon. From their settlements they fought back against their pursuers to retain their freedom.

Resistance is a phenomenon that cannot be separated from slavery or oppression [Singleton 1985; Beckles and Shepherd 1991; Heuman 1986]. The development of resistance groups was a direct response to the cruel torture devices on slave ships, the whips and guns, posses of soldiers and dogs sent after escaping slaves, horrible punishments and executions of "troublemakers" [Beckles 1986; Brathwaite 1977; Price 1992; Robinson 1969]. These life-threatening experiences were enough for the enslaved to resort to defensive violence. For example, it was the Maroons who spearheaded the Haitian revolution which resulted in the declaration of that country as the first black republic in the New World.

Although there were many such communities between the sixteenth and nineteenth centuries, today they have been absorbed into the larger communities especially after peace treaties were signed.

Some of the known Maroon communities include those of eastern and western Jamaica; the Paramaka, Saramaka, Matawai and Kwinti of Suriname; the Aluku of French Guiana; the Palenqueros of Colombia; the Garifuna of the Atlantic coast of Central America; the Maroons of the Costa Chica region of Mexico; the Quilombos of Brazil; the Cimarrones of Cuba and the Seminole Maroons of Oklahoma, Texas, Mexico and The Bahamas.

Richard Price [1979:1] indicates various terms used to describe these societies, such as *palenques, quilombos, mocambos, cumbes, ladeiras,* or *mambises*. Owing to the different circumstances and areas in which the societies were formed, different definitions have been used to refer to the people making up those societies and the general references that could be made to them as identifiable socio-cultural groups or groupings.

Generally, the Maroons consisted of groups or communities of enslaved indigenous and African peoples who escaped from bondage and established viable communities in various parts of their territories, and fought to maintain their hard-won freedom.[1]

There still remain Maroon societies in various parts of the New World, which have preserved their identities as the creation and embodiment of the spirits of the heroic freedom fighters [Bilby and N'Diaye 1992; Garcia 1965; Genovese 1979] (see Fig. 1.1).

The Maroons of Jamaica have been very well known because of their long struggle with the British colonial authorities, who had to pass more than forty laws in frantic attempts to control them. These communities are now located around the main towns of New Nanny Town (Moore Town) and Scott's Hall in the east, and Accompong in the west of the island of Jamaica. Archaeological evidence [Agorsah 1992] indicates that the nucleus of the Maroons in the east consisted of various groups who lived in the inaccessible areas of the Blue Mountains, before, or certainly during the period of Spanish domination, when a large number of slaves escaped into the hills. Documentary evidence [Morales 1952; Bryan 1971] indicates that in the early sixteenth century, the Spanish government attempted to flush out some of the slaves who went into "maronage" (flight) into the Blue Mountains, where they had established themselves.

In Suriname there are the Saramaka who escaped from plantations in the early seventeenth century, fought against the Dutch for more than a century and finally signed a treaty in 1762 giving them the right to control the rain forest region of the

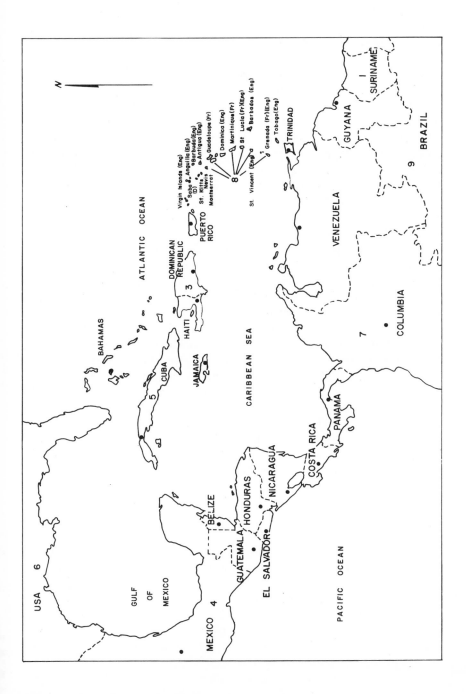

Fig. 1.1 Locations of New World Maroons

basin of the Suriname River. In addition there are the Okanisi (Aukaners), popularly known as the Djuka, who signed their peace treaty with the Dutch colonizers in 1760 which gave them control of the Tapanahoney and the Cottica basins. The Aluku or Boni, having come over from Surinamee into French Guiana and having struggled to maintain their freedom, sealed by a treaty in 1860, now live across the Maroni and Lawa rivers in French Guiana.

During the seventeenth century, slaves who escaped from Spanish plantations in Colombia established their community at Palenque de San Brasilio near the port of Cartagena. They gained recognition and permanent control of the area after several attempts to exterminate them failed. The result was a peace treaty signed with the colonial government in 1717. Many of the slaves who went into flight in the Costa Chica area of Guerrero and Oaxaca in Mexico, had escaped from Spanish cattle ranches on the Pacific coast. Their retreat into most inaccessible areas made it impossible for the colonial government to subdue them. The conflict ended after the abolition of slavery in Mexico in 1829.

The Seminole Maroons consisted of groups of slaves who escaped from South Carolina and Georgia and sought refuge in Spanish Florida, in the southeastern United States where they established their earliest settlements. They established good relationships with the indigenous groups who came to be known later as Seminole Indians. They are now divided and settled in Oklahoma, Texas, The Bahamas and the northern Mexican state of Coahuila. Together with their Indian allies, these Maroons were deported to Oklahoma after the Seminole wars and some of them later moved to Mexico where they are referred to as *Negros Mascogos*. A century later, some of them again moved back to Texas where they were engaged to serve as a special military unit referred to as Seminole Negro Indian scouts.

Indian escapees (*indios bravos*) were the first known Maroons to be referred to as "cimarrones" in Cuba. They were later joined by others of African descent. Attempts to wipe out the cimarrones in Cuba, like those in other Maroon areas, failed. In 1868, a decree which abolished slavery recognized the existence of the *palenques*.

The Maroons, clearly, became the frontline fighters in the struggle against slavery in all its forms. Before any known struggles for independence in the New World, Maroon communities had developed strong ideas and strategies for self-sufficiency, self-help and self-reliance and fought with great skill and courage for the right to self determination. The communities managed to unite people who had come from many different backgrounds and regions of the world, speaking different languages and practising diverse customs and traditions. African traditions featured prominently in the formation and transformation of the way of life of these groups throughout the period of their struggle. It is however difficult to clearly identify all aspects of the African elements retained by the Maroons. It is recorded that the majority of the Maroons consisted of slaves derived from West Africa, whose cultural traditions should help to identify any retentions and how these may have contributed to the survival of the Maroons.

Although devoid of remote mythologies and evidence of great antiquity of the origins of man and the development of his early cultural traditions, as is characteristic of the Old World, evidence exists which indicates that the Caribbean region has a pre-history that dates back several thousand years before the Christian era [Kozlowski 1974; Rouse 1986]. These early traditions provided the background and the basis for the traditions from which Maroon societies initially emerged. The following questions are therefore relevant: What was the impact of the basic traditions on those of the Maroons? What are the main features that provide the link between the old and the new?

The emerging complexity of the archaeological record that is coming to light in the Caribbean [Rouse 1986; Singleton 1985; Drewet 1991; Tabio and Rey 1985] indicates a pattern of cultural transformation in the New World that appears to have been mosaic in character. Added to this difficulty is that the identification of its component features is very elusive.

New World foundation

The treatment of subjects of human movements and developments through time and space, as if they occurred in a linear evolutionary sense, as implied in chronological schemes proposed by Rouse, Kozlowski and others, is misleading [Agorsah 1993].[2] The cultural categories used by archaeologists in their interpretations must make distinctions between technological and chronological evidence, or between these and other facets of culture. The philosophy behind the drawing of these schemes should be geared towards the reconstruction of past human behaviour, using the schemes as means to an end. In other words, although the concept of time is of singular importance in archaeology, it constitutes a tool towards facilitating interpretation of temporal variability as well as synchronic and diachronic patterning and changes or transformations. These cannot be achieved except on the basis of chronological considerations that objectively eliminate all biases and use analytical approaches suitable for the evidence available.

So far, it appears that the chronological schemes for the Caribbean seem to have been constructed only on strict lithic typology for the prehistoric and early part of the historical period. But the problem is that these typological constructions—whether stylistic, functional or cognitive—although important tools used in archaeological analysis, are of archaeologists' making and are abstractions and therefore should not be equated to human movements or cultural traditions, except where evidence clearly identifies such movements or traditions. Failure to do this might imply that all traditions in the New World, particularly the Caribbean, had a single common origin. A discussion of the early background cultural traditions should clearly demonstrate that many different cultural traditions played a part in laying the foundation for the development of these early freedom fighters.

The prehistoric period

The prehistoric period in the Caribbean is divided into two: Early Prehistoric Age and Late Prehistoric Age. This period covers the times of the earliest human beings in the Caribbean and adjoining areas where Maroon societies took seed. It covers the periods termed Palaeo-Indian I and II and Meso-Indian by Kozlowski [1974] and Rouse and Allaire's [1978] Lithic period. The main features of this period, from available evidence, include bifacially-chipped stemmed projectile points, choppers, scrapers and leaf-shaped (tanged) arrowheads, all made of stone. The societies may have been hunting and gathering groups in varying degrees and intensity over time. The earliest evidence known so far comes from Venezuela, where this assemblage is dated to 7,000 years ago [Rouse and Allaire 1978] at the sites of Caroni in the Middle Orinoco basin area (5000 BC) and El Jobo.

Finds from the site of Blanchisseuse in Trinidad [Harris 1989] are thought to belong to this period as well. The only Lithic Age finds in the Lesser Antilles consists of what has been described as workshop debris off the coast of Antigua on Long Island and flint flakes and shell celts found in a shell mound at the site of Jolly Beach, dating to approximately 2000 BC [Nodine 1990]. From the Greater Antilles the Early Prehistoric Age evidence comes from the Dominican Republic where dates to between 3000 and 2000 BC have been obtained from the sites of Casimira [Cruxent and Rouse 1969], and from Haiti from the sites of Cabaret and Mangones. Evidence comes from Cuba in the presence of highly developed lithic industries which have been observed [Nunez 1948, 1963] and dated at the sites of Seboruco to about 4000 BC, Residuario Fuenche to about 2050 BC and Guayabo Blanco to 1300 BC.

Kozlowski [1974] has often referred to a combination of the lithic material from Seboruco in Cuba [Moure 1984] and Mordan in the Dominican Republic as representing a dominant lithic tradition in the Greater Antilles, calls it the Seboruco-Mordan Culture (in which case the new scheme will call it a cultural complex). It may be observed that the dating of the earliest period in Caribbean chronology decreases in time, as one draws a line from the northern coast of South America across the Lesser to the Greater Antilles. This is often the basis of the diffusionist theories regarding human movements which constitute a whole subject that cannot be discussed here.

The second stage of the prehistoric period which continued from the earliest signs of settlement and the advent of ceramic traditions also saw the earliest development of agriculture in the Caribbean. It covers what Kozlowski [1974] refers to as Formative period, or what Rouse and Allaire [1978] refer to as Archaic and Ceramic. The last part of this Late Prehistoric Age is considered as the period of agricultural societies, the earliest part being considered as the transitional period between them and the hunting and gathering societies predominantly non-food producers. The Late Prehistoric Age therefore includes Kozlowski's Neo-Indian period.

Numerous Late Prehistoric Age ceramic manufacturing and early agricultural sites have been identified in the Caribbean. Again, the earliest evidence comes from

Venezuela, where sites include La Gruta dating to between 1585 and 2140 BC, Los Merecurotes 1020 BC, Parmana 700 BC, Saladero 920-850 BC and Los Barrancos AD 580 [Sanoja and Vargas 1983]. Often, finds from these sites have been considered as representing specific ethnic groups or populations by the use of terms such as "Saladoid" or "Barrancoid", "series", "people" [Rouse and Allaire 1978], or the more preferable term, "Saladero complex". An attempt has been made by Rouse to correlate the distribution of the Saladero cultural complex with the linguistic evidence that shows the divergence of the Maipurau and the known proto-Arawakan language groups. This cannot be discussed fully because of an inability to check for details at this time.

Evidence of the Late Prehistoric Age in Trinidad comes from the site of Banwari [Harris 1989] dating to approximately 5000-4000 BC and Pitch Lake (500 BC). From the Lesser Antilles evidence of cultural material that dates to the early centuries AD has come from the site of Jolly Beach in Antigua [Nodine 1990]. Other sites in the Lesser Antilles include Chancery Lane and Silver Crest among others in Barbados [Drewet 1991], Banana Bay in the Grenadines, as well as Toumassee, Girandy and Lavoulte in St Lucia. However, the earliest date for the area seems to point to the times the Jolly Beach finds in Antigua.

The Late Prehistoric Age in the Greater Antilles shows chipped and pecked stone tools, grinding stones and pestles alongside pottery and several midden sites. Sites in the Virgin Islands include Krum Bay (880 BC), Cancel Hill (870 BC) and Aboretum (AD 50). Puerto Rico is represented by the sites of Cayo Hondo (1060 BC), Cayo Cofresi (325 BC) and Hacienda Grande (AD 120). Mordan (2610 BC), El Porvenir (1030 BC), El Caimite (180 BC) and San Juan de Maguana (AD 695), are the main sites in the Dominican Republic representing the Late Prehistoric Age; while White Marl (AD 877) and Bottom Bay (AD 650) provide the earliest known tradition in Jamaica [Robotham 1980]. Sites of this age in Cuba include Residuario Fuenche (2050 BC), Damajayabo (1200 BC), and Mogote de la Cueva (AD 330).

One feature of the Late Prehistoric Age is the regional diversification represented by a gradual shift from the broad base of cultural complexes to regional or zonal traditions.

The reason is that as the traditional societies gained greater control over the environment, the adaptive mechanisms began to crystallize into distinct traditions. While it appears that developments in some areas followed roughly parallel courses, in other areas, as expected, these processes followed completely different courses. This regional diversification is a phenomenon observed for cultural traditions reaching that stage of development in various parts of the New World as well as in Europe and Africa. The reason may be found in the environmental resource differences. For example, Cuba, with a land area comprising more than half the total area of Antillean islands has terrestrial, marine, freshwater and estuarine environmental conditions which are significantly different from those of the smaller islands, particularly in the eastern Caribbean. Even among islands in close proximity, such as the low-lying limestone islands of Barbuda and the volcanic island of

Montserrat (only 100 kilometres apart), differences exist in the environmental conditions and resources. Evidence also shows that while some of the traditions became more complex and grew faster, others developed slowly until very recent times.

The historical period

The historical period is a convenient division in Caribbean chronology that attempts to deal with the contact of the region with cultural traditions from outside. Specifically, the period refers to the earliest contact with European cultural traditions and starts at different times in different parts of the region, although by and large such contacts cover the last 500 years in the greater part.

Two sub-periods are proposed for the period [Agorsah 1993], the first one being the transitional period with the end stages of the Late Prehistoric Age which concerns evidence of the contacts with the cultural traditions of the Mesoamerican area such as the Mayan traditions and the Andean cultural areas, as well as the earlier cultural traditions of the northern South American coast that interacted with the other Caribbean and adjoining areas.

The second historical period begins with the contact between European and Caribbean traditions. In Jamaica, for example, this last sub-period could be broken down into (a) the Spanish era and (b) the English era. These may be further sub-divided, depending on the preferred grouping of the events of the general period. It appears that it is during this period that the formation of Maroon societies started in earnest.

The difficulty in archaeological reconstruction of the historical period does not lie with the chronology because of the support it has from documentary evidence, such as public records [Garrow 1986], census materials [Moran 1986], maps [Higman 1986], missionary records [Whiteman 1986], and travellers' accounts such as the report by Columbus on his first encounter with the people he met in the area. The main issues needing attention continue to include:

- the identification of the archaeological proof of the ethnic elements carried over from the prehistoric into the historic period, artifact patterns and how they lead to the identification of socioeconomic lifestyles;
- "Afro-Caribbean traditions" and the identification of the elements of continuity in traditions, and the processes that led to their transformation [Armstrong 1982, 1985].

These and other issues, more than the chronology, are vital to the study of the period, but cannot be discussed here.

It is unfortunate, however, that Caribbean historians have accepted the erroneous claim of early scholars that relates the early populations of the Caribbean to those "observed" for northern America—"Palaeo-Indians", "Indian groups", as well as even those casually referred to in travellers' report. Fascination with the story about the Indian persists among scholars today on a variety of levels. Among scholars of Caribbean archaeology, the Indian has been recipient of the credit for many, if not all, of the Caribbean prehistoric cultural traditions. Rouse [1982] in tracing continuities in norms in ceramic stylistic features in the Caribbean during the later stages of the prehistoric period, drew the conclusion that "styles and their series are analogous to languages and their families"—a statement that he may not accept in totality today. However, this view demonstrates the basis for many of the pioneer chronological schemes drawn for the Caribbean. Although the historical period can be clearly identified in many areas of the New World as beginning with European contact, the true picture of a transitional period—between the prehistoric and historical—is still unclear with respect to whether it is referred to as "preColumbian" or "protohistoric". However, it is the African background that has been emphasized in much of the discussion of the formation and transformation of Maroon societies.

African foundations

The development and growth of societies and social organizations of West Africa are closely linked with those of the African continent.[3] So are the links of African with Maroon societies of the New World, particularly the Caribbean. The study of the traditional systems of West Africa is particularly important for the Caribbean, not only because of the link with the slave trade, but also because West African social systems present several authentic characteristics of general development (such as systems extant in Africa before and after colonial contacts) that form the basis of observed continuities in the Caribbean.[4] Although transformations have been observed in several features of the social systems, there still remain elements that indicate the trend as well as the force of the impact of the various events that have occurred over time.

Many aspects of the West African cultural traditions before the European contact could help to identify transformations resulting from that contact, particularly after AD 1500, and are also critical for explaining cultural continuities in the Caribbean. Family systems, language, ethnicity, religion, festivals, marriage patterns, art, music and dance are some of the issues of relevance that need to be discussed. These aspects of the West African cultural systems related closely to political, economic and technological systems of the area. Fortunately, with the increase in scholarly studies and with the aid of new scientific research methods and techniques, many of the misconceptions about the African, his continent and its past have been corrected. For example, Africa has been viewed as a homogenous cultural entity with a single stream of cultural development. This is now proven to be erroneous. It must be noted at the outset that as a result of the combination of its long history, size and very varied environmental setting, Africa has developed a highly heterogeneous society, more than can be found elsewhere. With such heterogeneity came the development of varied traditional forms of social organization and institutions. It is also important to associate the ethnic groups of social systems with specific geographical areas or social groups which constituted the context in which we observe cultural practices and transformations that possibly cut across ethnic areas and boundaries. But one thing is clear about Caribbean culture, and that is the fact that it developed from a mixture of cultural traditions of which African culture was an important component. This is an issue that needs to be discussed much more seriously.

Archaeological and historical evidence available indicate that the earliest forms of social organization in West Africa date back to prehistoric times. The turning point of this development occurred in many parts of West Africa in the wake of European and other outside contacts. But the foundation had been established prior to that.

The prehistoric period

Approximately 10,000 years ago, in many parts of Africa, the fundamental change of utmost importance was the origin of agriculture. Implicit in this was the early beginnings of controlled food supply and development of more permanent settlements [Phillipson 1985; Clark, 1982]. The pioneering technology and new settlements of the Stone Age man were closely linked with the need for food as well as social organization. Societies moved and cooperated not only because of the love of adventure but much more because they wanted fresh pastures or fields to cultivate. With increased supplies of food provided by farming and improved tool types, settlements grew larger and larger causing the "splitting-up" of groups, and as the centuries passed new groups began to spread. Social relations became more complex, languages increased not only in number but in complexity and individuality as well, resulting in the hundreds of languages and dialects observed today. Developing along with these have been strong and viable *family groupings*, *clans*, *villages*, *cities*, *kingdoms* and *traditional industries* such as potting and metal working. Good examples of the evidence come from ancient Nigeria and the Sudanic areas of West Africa.

Other developments included customs related to birth, initiation, marriage, purification and funerals. In addition, there came *traditional religious*, as well as *harvest*, *reunion* and *thanksgiving* festivals; social relationships and taboos; and various aspects of art and craft such as *sculpture, architecture, painting* and *basketry, ceramic, textile* and *metal industries*—all of which began to develop towards the diversity that characterized the West African culture at the time of European contact. Our limited sources include archaeology, travellers' accounts, ethnography, linguistics and historical documents.

The historical period

Kamau Brathwaite [1988], a leading West Indian cultural anthropologist, points out that West Indians seeking their identity require an objective study of the transatlantic trade period, and especially the background folk culture of the slaves. The

West African slave must be seen as coming from quite a far distance away from the original area of his tradition and planted in a new environment to which he must adapt, using the available tools and memories of his traditional heritage. The slave set something new—something Caribbean—but something recognizably African. Clearly, like the study of other cultures, understanding the root African heritage as it evolved before and during slavery is especially important to an understanding of present-day Caribbean societies.

One may well ask if there is any justification for this. Although they are not always totally reliable, available figures suggest that throughout the entire period of the slave trade, the Caribbean was the recipient of the largest number of slaves imported from Africa, receiving over 43 per cent of all slave imports [Postma 1990]. Jamaica, Haiti, Cuba, the Leeward Islands and Barbados were the islands that received the largest number of these slaves. An estimate of about six million is provided for the slaves imported. Given the vast number of Africans imported, there can be no doubt that Africans made an important contribution not only to the population of the Caribbean region but also to the culture of the region.

At the time of the intensification of the slave trade in the seventeenth and eighteenth centuries, important social and economic systems were already established in West-Central Africa. Agriculture was the basis for most of the economic activity in this region. Slash and burn and crop rotation were the main techniques used in crop production. Hoes and axes were the most important tools used. The main crops grown were millet, sorghum, maize, beans and cowpeas. While agriculture was the main economic activity, not all the Africans living in West-Central Africa were farmers. Those who lived in areas where grass or savanna lands existed were for the most part pastoralists. They reared cattle, goats, chickens, ducks and pigs.

Apart from agriculture and animal husbandry, at the time of the slave trade Africans in West-Central Africa were also skilled craftsmen and craftswomen. They produced iron goods such as knives, arrowheads, axes and bracelets. The pottery industry was also well developed. Items such as cooking utensils, vessels for storing corn and beans and for brewing beer were also made. Africans in this region were also skilled in mat-making, leather work and woodcarving. Woodcarvers were responsible for the production of chairs, mortars, handles for iron implements and tables. As far as occupations were concerned, it is clear that the slaves who came to the West Indies from the West-Central African region possessed a variety of skills.

In contrast to West-Central Africa, the slaves who were taken to the West Indies from West Africa came from a region which had greater variety in climate and geography and belonged to different ethnic groups (Fig. 1.2). The slaves came from two major climatic zones in West Africa: the forests and the grasslands. The forest region stretches across West Africa; from Sierra Leone in the west to the Cameroon in the east. It reaches from the coast for about 200 miles. For much of the period prior to the development of the Atlantic slave trade the forests of West Africa were sparsely populated. This was mainly because of the hot, humid conditions, the density of the vegetation and the presence of the tsetse fly (an insect which kills

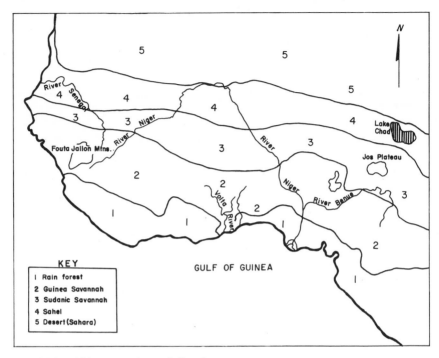

Fig.1.2 West Africa: vegetation and climatic zones

animals and causes sleeping sickness in humans). Nevertheless, by the time the slave trade developed, Africans such as the Yoruba and Ibo (Nigeria), the Fon (Togo), and the Ashanti (Ghana) had succeeded in overcoming some of these barriers and had settled in various parts of the forest.

As a result of the threat posed to animals by the tsetse fly, the majority of slaves drawn from the forest region would have been involved in some form of agriculture. The main crops cultivated included yams and oil-palm (which were indigenous to the forests) together with rice, cassava and maize which were introduced as a result of West Africa's contact with areas in the Americas and Asia. Africans of the forest regions of West Africa were for the most part agriculturalists.

Despite its importance, agriculture was not the only means through which Africans who lived in the forest region earned their livelihood. Those who lived in the Akan forests would have had some knowledge of gold mining, smelting and forging [Goucher 1990, 1991] because in Akan states such as Gyaman, Bono and Banda gold mining and processing were major economic activities. In addition, the Akan speaking people of the forest region were also skilled at pottery [Crossland 1989], the spinning and weaving of cloth and manufacture of soap.

Women played an important role in specialized occupations among the Yoruba and Ibo people who dwelt in the forests of West Africa. For example, Yoruba (Nigeria) and Brong (Ghana) women made dyes, manufactured shea butter and produced palm-oil and cosmetics. They also dominated occupations such as hairdressing and tattooing. Among the Ibo, women tended to dominate the same type of occupations, one of the exceptions being that they were responsible for decorating houses and building and plastering walls. In addition to these occupations, the forest dwellers were also skilled at making pins, stirrups, horse-bits, bells, chains, bangles, hoes, cutlasses and in the production of musical instruments such as drums and flutes. Slaves drawn from the forest region of West Africa were well equipped to make a significant contribution to life in the West Indies.

Savanna or grasslands cover a substantial portion of the land area called West Africa. The species of grass would have varying height of between five to ten feet as one moves north to south. However, in parts such as the Guinea Savannah they could grow as much as fifty feet in height. The tsetse fly is prevalent in this area and as a consequence animals cannot be reared in order to make a livelihood. This area was sparsely populated and agriculture formed the basis of economic activity.

In other parts of the Sudanic grasslands, especially the areas around the headwaters of the Niger River, the practice of agriculture was the main means through which Africans here earned their livelihood. The crops cultivated included pearl millet, sorghum, cowpeas, bambara groundnut and cotton. In other areas to the north and east of the main river systems, especially the extensive open plains, the rearing of animals—especially cattle, donkeys, horses and camels—is the most important occupation. Because of the need to find land to graze their herds, most of the pastoralists in the Sudanic zone were nomads.

In general, therefore, slaves drawn from the savanna or Sudanic zones came from a region in which agriculture and pastoral farming were the dominant means by which people earned a livelihood. Agriculture was particularly important among the Mandingo speaking people such as the Soninke, Malinke and the Bambara; the Mossi, the Songhai and the Hausa (Fig. 1.3). Pastoral farming was very important to people such as the Fulani, the only people in West Africa to whom it became a fundamental way of life.

Despite their overall importance, agriculture and animal husbandry were not the only means through which Africans in the savannah or Sudanic zones earned a livelihood. Some people earned a living as blacksmiths; others were skilled in the production of textiles and a variety of leather goods (including hides, shoes and bags), the making of boats and canoes, and in fishing. Like their counterparts in the forests, Africans in the Sudanic savanna zones also made musical instruments such as drums, flutes and rattles. Like their counterparts in the forest zone, therefore, the slaves who were drawn from the savannah or Sudanic zones came from occupations which would have enabled them to make an important contribution to life in the West Indies.

The majority of Caribbean slave imports came from two main areas in Africa—the Lower Guinea coast and West-Central Africa, in particular Angola. In the Sudanic zone in areas such as Hausaland, parts of the Senegambia and lands lying to the north of the Akan forests, foodstuff such as rice, groundnuts, millet, sorghum, dried

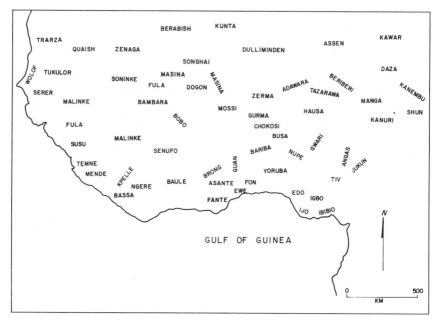

Fig. 1.3 Ethnic groups of West Africa

fish and fruits and vegetables were the main items of trade. An important feature of these markets was that the bulk of the trading was conducted by women.

Apart from catering to local needs, the domestic market also provided an opportunity for traders of various regions to exchange their goods. States in the forest zone purchased large quantities of goods produced in the Sudan and the Sahara such as salts of various kinds, cattle products and cloth. States in the Sudan purchased gold, kola nuts and iron goods which were produced in the forest zone. The inter-regional aspect of the domestic trade was dominated by two major groups of West African merchants — the Juula (also known as the Wangara and the Dyula) of the Western Sudan and the Hausa of the Central Sudan. Both terms refer to the languages spoken by the traders which, in each case, is that of the largest local savanna cultivator group, the Mandingo in the west and the Hausa farther east. The Dyula were the first group of merchants to emerge. They began as gold traders. The Hausa merchants emerged later and have always concentrated on the internal market. However, they sometimes dealt in ivory and slaves for trans-Saharan export trade.

Social factors

Social groupings in West Africa have been identified on the basis of linguistic affiliations. The geographical distribution of these groups was often wrongly referred to as "tribes". Fig. 1.3 is, in fact, a very simplified map of these "major" ethnic groups, as it includes only groups that have been historically documented rather than the real existing groups. The concept of "ethnic" only appeared in the historical literature in the past fifty years and has been considered as "named, bonded units of people who identify themselves or others as different; they have distinctive patterns of social, economic and political organization, but strictly social-based".

In West Africa, for most of its history social behaviour and value systems such as language and religious affiliations have been important but not essential markers of "ethnic" identity. However, owing to the fluidity and multidimensionality of ethnicity as well as the frequency with which it is differently used, it has been extremely difficult to clearly demarcate their geographical distribution. By design and partly through ignorance, political boundaries initiated by colonial powers after AD 1500, cut across these groups unevenly, resulting in the separation of families, clans and other social affiliations. The impact of this arbitrary separation is too well known to be further discussed here. The main effect of this action on ethnic groups was the undermining of the unity that was the backbone of the socio-cultural institutions and entities. More divisions meant less interaction and greater differentiation in the trend of cultural development. Of course, differentiations caused by environmental conditions are well known—the pastoral ethnic groups occupying much of the savanna while the agricultural ethnic groups occupy the forest lands for obvious reasons.

West African family and clan systems are directly connected with ethnic grouping. This aspect of the social system has remained until today among many groups, despite the negative impact on them from outside contacts. In modern Ghana, Nigeria, Benin (Dahomey), Burkina Faso, Mali and Cameroon the relationships may be summarized as follows, although local names for these divisions vary from place to place:

- Individual
- Family
- Clan
- Major clan
- Ethnic group

In descending order, the family usually forms the nucleus of all the units along the line, each being so defined that members belonging to each have common bonds and traditions that differentiate them from non-members. One feature of these relationships is the extended family system — whether patrilineal or matrilineal. Changes in the size and composition of these domestic groupings are brought about mainly by the births, marriages and deaths within them. The impact of the slave trade and the recent job hunting in urban areas by the rural people have also caused changes in the size and composition of the family and clan units. However, kinship and family relations continue to play important roles in the ownership and transmission of property and the productive capacity of many West African societies, and forms the basis of political and economic institutions such as kingships.

Time and seasons

The African concept of time is one that has never been properly understood. The reason is that time is considered to be tied in to activities of the season, day or night. In many parts of West Africa, time is thought of as periods in a chain of events gradually culminating one into another. Time is seen as a sequence of activities such as planting, sowing and harvesting. Among some societies, such as the Guan and Akan of Ghana, there has been the tradition of the six-day week. For the Tallensi of Ghana, for example, the year starts in mid-October and the number of days in each month varies from year to year. In the periods after European contact in most of West Africa, seasons or periods have built the calendrical system of seven days in a week and twelve months in a year. In areas influenced by Islam, the Islamic calendar is used side by side the solar calendar.

Despite the influence of western contact on the timing of events among many societies in West Africa, most areas still operate the traditional system. In fact, festivals and festivities are still observed on the basis of the traditional seasons in many parts of West Africa.

Names and naming systems

In many West African societies, systems of family names, given names and other identification procedures have been used by traditional societies with specific meanings that identify places, persons, families, clans or individuals, objects or concepts. Names may also have religious connotations. The name of a person or traditional phenomenon must also reveal a little of the history of the person or his ancestors. Day names such as those used in Ghana—Kofi for males born on Friday, Kwame for Saturday, etc.—are also common and usually refer to the deity or the local god of the day on which a person was born.

Among the Ewe of Ghana, for example, several names are linked to the overwhelming authority of *Se* (*Mawuga*), the Supreme being and ruler of the universe. Names such as *Senyo* (meaning *Se* or God is good), *Senanu* (*Se* or God gives); *Senagbe* (*Se* or God is giver of life) are examples. Names may also be associated with life (*agbe* in Ewe or *nkwa* in Akan), or after different local gods, or the circumstances of birth. Fond names are also common.

In the Islamised areas, people have adopted Arabic names since the first millennium AD. These relate mainly to names in the Koran or to the great practices of Mohammed. *Saidu, Alidu, Tahiru, Abdallah,* Iddi are examples. Contrast this with other traditional names such as *Agyei, Adefuye, Agorsah, Boateng, Bonsu, Ogwuchuku, Ogun, Oudraogo, Okai, Musonda, Abebe, Addae, Gyima, Gyeffour* and *Diop*.

Since the fifteenth century, through contact with Europeans and missionaries, names in West Africa have tended to be Europeanized or Christianized or even in some cases completely changed to foreign names. Many of these changes were effected through baptism into a Christian church. Non-Moslem groups were the main victims. For example, a name such as *Kofi Dua* became

Kofi Wood; *Kwame Ansa* became Quansah or Quansa, and we find names ending in *-son* indicating the son of someone (e.g. Johnson, Addison, Forson, Kamason, Lawson, etc.). While some of these names were consciously changed, others changed gradually over time. Some West Africans adopted names of their colonial masters and some of them still exist. Some of the changes were adopted either as a means of identification or for the prestige of bearing European names. Other names became established by the Europeans because they could not pronounce West African names such as *Agbemabiase*, *Agbemafle* or *Amematekpor*, *Oloruntimihin*, *Bemenebenya* or *Kuntukununku*.

Generally, there have been more changes in names in the southern forest areas of West Africa than in the northern Sudanic areas, where Islamic influences have more strongly persisted over a long period of time. Names of places (towns, village towns) and of physical features such as rivers and mountains have also been affected by European contact. In local settings, traditional names existed for such rivers as Volta, Niger, the Gambia. The changes recently effected in Burkina Faso and Togo in personal names are deliberate attempts to change this situation back to the *status quo*.

Religious practices

Anthropologists generally think that human societies belong to two worlds. One is the mundane and practical in which man recognizes what is going on. The other is the world of the strange, the unseen and the unpredictable, i.e. the supernatural. In the context of West African religious practice, both worlds flow together and disharmony between the two is attributed to man's general behaviour. African religious practices have been extensively discussed as they formed the reason and medium of colonization. Among the significant aspects discussed are:

(1) The concept of God as the creator and maker of the universe. The Yoruba of Nigeria, the Kpelle of Liberia, the Limba and Yalunka of Sierra Leone, the Mossi of Burkina Faso conceive of the Supreme Being in the same fashion.

(2) The belief in spirits of the dead—hence ancestor veneration. Ancestors are considered as the saints of the communities to which they belonged.

(3) Associated rituals, observances such as libation, taboos and spirit possession. Although these issues are central to religious practices in West Africa, they do not by any means constitute any single thing that can be termed "one West African religion", because there are different mechanisms or approaches to these practices in different areas.

Festivals and festivities

Festivals in West African tradition consist of the most significant and richest forms of art and cultural practice. Often ritually based, West African festivals consist of socio-political events, heroes and heroic events and also serve as a strategy for political or social control, or they may be purely memorial. Each festival has a special message such as the Olimi festival of the Ukpila of Nigeria, which is a festival of the dead; the festival of the bull of the Kirdi of North Cameroon called Maray; the Aboakyir festival of the Efutu of Ghana (animal-hunting festival); the Homowo festival of the Ga of Ghana; the rain-making festival of the Mossi of Burkina Faso called Tengana and the Tedudu festival of the Ewe of Togo and Ghana; the Damba festival of the Dagomba of Ghana; and the Odwira festival (cleansing festival) of the Akwamu of Ghana. There are military elements in some of these festivals that are related to the organization of para-military groups to recount the struggle of the past.

The coming of Europeans to West Africa has affected the timing of these festivals and modifications have been made to suit the new religious and political order. Some of these festivals have changed in character while others still survive with almost no changes. The Aboakyir (hunting) festival of the Winneba of Ghana, for example, has added European military costumes and names that make them appear foreign. Masquerade festivals have added faces that are strictly foreign. But the most important point is that many of these festivals maintain their traditional artistic forms and ritual characteristics. The effect of European influences on these festivals varies and can only be discussed on an individual basis, as each has specific traditional features that offer specific responses to the influences from outside the ocalities.

Marriage systems

In West Africa, like many parts of Africa, marriage goes far beyond the bounds of mere relationship between man and woman. It creates alliance between groups, because in addition to involving sexual and economic union between two people, marriage establishes reciprocal rights and obligations among husbands, wives, families and their offspring. However, in some groups such as the Kpelle of Liberia, a wife is considered a husband's financial asset, so that the more wives a man has, therefore, the stronger his labour force in terms of their offspring. This has led to the development of the tendency to be polygamous among some groups who are strictly subsistence-based. It is for this reason that many scholars have considered African marriages as merely a means for reproduction. Marriage in Africa has also been a means for fostering bonds of unity and friendship. Among the Tiv of Nigeria, in pre-colonial times a man may exchange one of his sisters for the sister of another man, thus mutually binding their families together. This is rare today.

Another important aspect of West African marriage is premarital moral education. The process of such education varies from society to society, but generally the process ends with initiation and puberty rites. While premarital moral education is very formal among societies such as the Nchumuru and Krobo of Ghana, it may be quite informal in others. Such education involves the teaching of housekeeping skills, the fundamentals of subsistence practices such as farming, cattle keeping and fishing, or craftwork such as weaving, carving or smelting. Some emphasis is also placed on morality in greeting, obedience of and respect for elderly people, food preparation, human relations and knowledge of local traditions, as well as sanctions related to these modes of behaviour.

In recent times, especially since the colonial era, the aesthetic aspects of initiation rites for the youth have been emphasized. However, the moral value is still maintained. To the Krobo of Ghana, for example, the puberty rite referred to as *dipo* is the first qualification of a girl towards marriage. Its main goal is to regulate the marriageable age of girls and to make sure that they are properly schooled in the rudiments of married life. Similarly the *Gbotowowo* of the Ewe of Ghana and Togo aim for detailed premarital education about good housekeeping and moral behaviour.

Another important aspect of marriage in West Africa is the exchange of gifts or payment often referred to as brideprice or bridewealth or dowry. These involve the transmission of gifts or property. In pre-colonial days and even until recently among the Gonja of northern Ghana, such a price consisted of a calabash or cowry shells and 12 kola nuts. Later, in colonial times, it was 12 shillings and 12 kola nuts. Among the Lowilli of the same geographical and cultural area, the payment was 350 cowries, in addition to kola nuts. The terms of bridewealth differ from group to group and is influenced in recent years by the religious practices. The wedding ceremonies also differ from society to society, but generally are community affairs down the line. The main stages are:

a) knocking the door and betrothal

b) family negotiations and consultation

c) bridewealth payment

d) the wedding ceremony and ritual

e) the final blessing and public declaration of the marriage.

All these have their accompanying ritual and other performances. Excision (the removal of certain portions of the female genitals as custom) is a controversial issue related to marriage in Africa. In West Africa it was quite popular in parts of the Ivory Coast, Mali, Niger, Burkina Faso, Benin and Togo. It is said to protect virginity, or is seen as a rite of passage to adulthood to assure fertility (as claimed by the Bambara, Dogon and Mossi) or as a means of purification. Its medical effects are well known and have been the main reason for discouraging this custom. It still persists in some communities.

Many of the marriage rites and practices have been affected by new ideas coming from both Christian and Islamic religions. In the urban areas in particular, traditional marriage has been overshadowed by new forms introduced through colonial contact. The extent of effect also varies from society to society and from one geographical area to another.

Art, music and dance

Art plays a vital role in helping to bind men together in organized groups. Nowhere is this better manifested than in Africa. The best examples are derived from West Africa where one can trace a clear continuity in the development of art from prehistoric times. Art in West Africa carries the sharpest imprint of the peculiar genius of each family, clan or larger society. Although many scholars speak of "African art", "African culture", or "African philosophy", etc., it would be a serious error to assume that African art forms are characterized by a unique style and that all art forms are identical in scope and orientation. However, one can recognize similar currents that flow through them. One important characteristic is that many art forms in West Africa are related to a social or religious content. For example, masks are not to be contemplated as works of art *per se*, but for use in connection with religious or social rituals or ceremonies.

Similarly, while art forms such as dance, spoken drama or concerts, and music are generally practised as separate forms in the western world, there is no such distinction in the African context. Of course, there are instances of dance displays or musical performances that are practised in isolation. Music, dance and ritual are often linked in a single framework related to a specific, religious or social ceremony. This is not to say, for example, that the mask carver is not guided by any formal aesthetic considerations or does not strive for stylistic perfection. It only means that the aesthetic value is not the end in itself, but a means to an end.

Art forms generally found among West African societies range from sculpture (in wood, stone, bronze, terracotta, etc.) to weaving, basketry, architecture, body decoration, music, dance, ritual performances embodying dramatic elements, oral literature, etc. The decorative and symbolic representations in all these cannot be fully discussed here. The proverbial symbols linked with the "adinkra" cloth of the Akan of Ghana as well as the gold weights of Ghana are good examples of how symbolism, concepts about the universe and art are linked to the social system in West Africa.

There have been considerable ranges of artistic freedom and improvisation within the larger framework of communal beliefs and conventions in Africa. It is for this reason that much of the art, music and dance of West Africa has accommodated much of the external influences. Another problem is that most of the thinking and writing about African art, music, and dance have been done by non-Africans or westernized African scholars, most of whom simply see outdated, substandard religious practices, initiation symbols, ill-assorted and purely functional cult and art objects, folktales and proverbs, music, superstition and magic. Nevertheless, many of the art, music and dance forms still maintain their traditional sense and value within individual West African social systems, for which good examples still exist in Benin, Ghana, Nigeria, Ivory Coast, Mali, Burkina Faso and Togo.

This chapter cannot be said to have done full justice to the historical development and transformations within West African social systems. Rather, only a few significant specific aspects have been enumerated and discussed, the reason being the heterogeneity of the societies in the region. Important changes have occurred in the social systems since prehistoric times, but the most significant ones occurred in the colonial era, during which the most widespread contact opportunity was available. These can only be identified on an individual basis. The purpose of this chapter has been to raise issues related to individual social systems that could be transferred to the Caribbean. It is essential to identify the transformations within individual social practices as the slaves arrived in the Caribbean from the West African region. The development of post-colonial societies such as the Krio societies of Liberia and Sierra Leone, have provided additional dimension to the understanding of the transformation aspects which we see today in many parts of the region.

The significant aspects of the social systems of West Africa have changed since colonial times. Evidence can also be adduced to demonstrate that many of the social practices, organization and institutions that characterized much of the sub-region of Africa have persisted to today and, also that some elements have been carried over to areas that later became occupied by Africa-derived populations such as the Caribbean.

Clans or lineages are maintained by a congregation of elders whose status was determined by their "rank" or an age-set system. It is because of the high level of political development of some of the empires and kingdoms, that some earlier observers tended to believe that the institutions may have been imported — a notion that has now been found to be unacceptable. But it is not possible to go into the details of the causes of the rise and fall of these states.

In western Africa, by AD 300 the ancient Sudanic empire of Ghana had taken root, probably stimulated by the trans-desert trade in gold and other goods. It rose to considerable prominence by AD 1000 but gave way 200 years later to Mali, which also gave way to Songhay by AD 1600. Also important were the Kanew-Bornu states, the Mossi states, Oyo and Benin states that flourished during the second part of the first millennium AD. The early states of the Egypt land, Axum and Ethiopian areas are well known. Thus we see the long history of Africa culminating in viable political entities. During the same period, we also see foreign contacts both inland and along the coast. But the history of Africa was to take a new turn: fast development—structural and social—but at the same time, exploitation by foreign elements.

Political factors

The last 1,000 years have seen a faster and more elaborate cultural development in Africa. African history records not only the importance of metallurgy and population movements but more importantly the rise of states or urbanization. In many areas of Africa the creation of states was fundamental to the gradual development of societies. The question of the development of the centralized state and its related institutions of kinship or chieftaincy, had been bedevilled by theories about the spread of divine kinship from other areas. Centralized states have developed through many processes:

(1) conquest of a majority by a minority such as happened with many West and East African groups;

(2) defence needs requiring a society to demand a leader at a time of attack or invasion;

(3) control of trade leading to acquisition of wealth and political power — this probably happened with the Zimbabwe of eastern Africa;

(4) group migration or groups on the move often requiring leaders;

(5) the emergence of charismatic leaders;

(6) natural instinct;

(7) strategic location.

In some cases, the origins of African states were not intimately linked to the remote prehistoric past. For some regions such as the Sudanic belt of West Africa or the Swahili coast of eastern Africa, written sources (often in Arabic) concerning the rise of states exist from the last few centuries BC. Scholars have often proposed two basic kinds of traditional political organization:

• centralized states with political authority vested in the hand of hereditary rulers

• the more egalitarian decentralized communities where political power was regulated by interactions between kinship groups.

Colonization and independence

Another factor of significance to this later part of the history of Africa, was the impact of Islam and Christianity, in both cases for better or for worse. Islam, according to scholars, is not just a religion. It is a culture, a state or vast economic complex, a common market. Founded by the Prophet Mohammed (AD 570-632), it spread quickly over the Arabian Peninsula and Syria and many other places including Africa—by soldiers, then settlers and then traders.

In Ethiopia, for example, it was first introduced by Muslims, i.e. "those who accept Islam"—refugees from the Arabian side of the Red Sea. It soon became deeply rooted, answering to the spiritual and cultural needs of millions of people and, within a few centuries, large numbers of Africans. These people were not only in North Africa but also further south across the Sahara and along the East African coast. Islam in West Africa has a clear link with Islam in North Africa. The large states of Ghana, Mali and Songhai which developed as a result of gold and slave trade links became increasingly Islamised.

Islam in East Africa was built on old foundations laid by pre-Islamic Arabs from South Arabia and the Persian Gulf who had been engaged in slave and ivory trade

—a factor to which Mohammed referred in the following way: "The merchant is the favourite of Islam". Islamic culture and ethics were therefore clearly compatible with commerce, reflecting the fact that early Islam was often the religion of urban merchant classes. Thus long distance trade, seaborne trade and the trans-Saharan trade must have brought many Africans in touch with Islam, permanently or temporarily. The impact of Islam on the social and political life of Africans is clearly recorded in settlements along the coast of eastern Africa and importantly, in settlements in various parts of the interior of western Africa.

Christianity, on the other hand, came to Africa with many more identifiable elements. It came through explorers (so-called civilizing agencies, traders and later colonizers). The dual purpose of the contact with western societies is exemplified in one of the castles (Elmina) where part of the structure includes a chapel on top of a room where slaves were locked up: religious missionary work over the slave trade, or what I call the R/ST factor (Religious factor over Slave Trade factor) of social analysis in colonial Africa. This is to introduce the results of the contact with respect to African history.

- Slave trade
- Urbanization and initiation into international trade
- Partition of Africa
- Depletion of economic resources of gold

These issues are quite well known to many and will not be discussed here. The desire for organization resulting in the establishment of lines of authority, patterns of behaviour and a code of conduct is a basic instinct common to all human societies. West Africans have from time immemorial designed systems of social and political organization through which the values of the society are enforced and individuals are guaranteed their safety and well-being.

But the character of the social and political organization is influenced by a number of factors. As mentioned earlier, the history of the society, the geographical environment in which particular groups were located, and their modes of earning a livelihood were crucial. Before the coming of the Europeans, West African societies had developed social and political organizations which were highly dynamic—adjusting to changes as they occurred. Similarly, the political institutions were being transformed—modifying and adapting.

The manner in which West African societies first evolved had much to do with the nature of the environment in which the societies were located. There were three major zones defined earlier — the coastal, the forest and the savannah zones were significant for the adaptations of the time; each had its own distinctive terrain, climate and vegetation. But it was much more than that. In many areas, people had similar livelihoods, as well as similar forms of political institutions and religious patterns. Languages transcended geographical or political boundaries.

The coastal zone is the area closest to the Atlantic Ocean. It extends inland for a distance of twenty to eighty miles. It is a low-lying land of plains in the Senegambia and mangrove swamps in Portuguese Guinea and the Niger Delta area. People in this area appear to have spoken common branches of the Kwa language. Originally, some lived nomadic lives, others settled permanently and took part in fishing, hunting, and gathering wild fruits andm vegetables. But with time, they acquired better knowledge of farming techniques, fish storage and salt refining and the settlements grew larger.

The forest zone stretching from Sierra Leone to the Cameroon is an area of heavy rainfall between June and November. With tall trees and thick vegetation, this area was largely uninhabitable until West Africans learnt how to forge iron tools. The forest was inhabited by people who lived in wandering bands which gathered wild crops and hunted. They lived in small villages ruled by the headman. The dense forest prevented contact between groups. By AD 1000, the forest people experienced what is called the neolithic revolution during which they learnt how to make polished stone tools, with which they cultivated the soil. They also learnt how to domesticate animals. The gradual improvement in agricultural techniques—especially with the acquisition of better tools—enabled some people to have a food surplus which they traded. Initially, most forest units were small, fairly isolated and politically independent. Within each village, the main political and social bond was kinship which is blood relationship. The heads of families, the kin group elders, led their people and ensured that law and order were maintained. In cooperation with the priests of the local cults, they saw that customs were followed and the year's activities planned in advance. Small states and chiefdoms were the characteristic form of political organization until the eighteenth century. There were, however, two major exceptions to this general rule, namely Benin and Oyo. In both cases, growth on a commercial scale began to take place from the fourteenth century onwards. Oyo and Benin kingdoms had been in existence from about the twelfth century.

The Sudan belt which stretches across West Africa from the Atlantic Coast to Lake Chad and beyond is a region of tall Savannah grass and open woodland, covering the vast fertile plains that lie between the tropical forest and the Sahara. It is the home of numerous people mostly referred to as "negroid stock" among whom are the Wolof, Jukun and Fulani who speak the West Atlantic languages [Dakubu 1973; Ehret and Posnansky 1982]. The Fulani are widely dispersed and had been the main apostles of Islam in this area. Although there were communities run by village elders and priests, the typical political unit was a kingdom. One man appointed by established traditional laws of succession was the Chief Executive. With the advice of his principal officers, he governed an area containing a number of settlements of his people and his authority was bolstered by his headship of the local religion.

With the improvement of traditional technology [Goucher 1985, 1991; Vansina 1984], people in the different zones interacted and through activities such as trade network, introduction of new political ideas and migration of people from one zone to the other, custom and culture intermingled. One major result was the emergence of political units which were much larger than those in existence by AD 1000. Small political units based on kinship and headed by lineage elders were absorbed by larger units thus leading to the emergence of kingdoms. Among the kingdoms that emerged were Benin, Oyo, Dahomey, Mossi, Gonja, Asante, Kanem Bornu, Kom and the Sokoto Caliphate.

The manner of the emergence of the kingdoms dictated the nature of their social and political organization. Many of the kingdoms of West Africa grew out of the desire of a core group to extend its frontiers and incorporate into its fold neighbouring groups which were usually smaller and lacking in elaborate political systems. Thus in all the kingdoms, there was always the easily identifiable core group which controlled much of the political and economic power. In Oyo the Yoruba constituted the core group. In Benin the Edo held sway. In the Gold Coast it was Asante, and Dahomey was dominated by the Fon. The Kom and the Mossi had the kingdoms named after them while the Fulani dominated the Sokoto Caliphate. The core group usually took advantage of such factors as advantageous location with its attendant economic privileges, the existence of a strong military force and the presence of outstanding individuals who used diplomacy and/or force to weld together people from diverse origin. Security was another means by which one neighbouring group dominated another. Oyo, for examples, took advantage of its strategic location between the coast and the Savannah to establish trading contacts and build up its power; Asante exploited the fear of a threat from Denkyra to incorporate the smaller communities. The history of Oyo would not be complete without the mention of Alafin Orompoto, while the Agadja contributed much to the rise of Dahomey. Osei Bonsu and Osei Tutu of the Gold Coast were hero leaders of Asante. In some cases the process of state formation was enhanced by religious factors such as the emergence of a spirit cult, which tended to compel obedience to whoever held religious authority. The result was that between 1400 and 1800, political entities made up of people of diverse origin emerged in West Africa, and administrative structures that coped with situations created by the emergence of these kingdoms evolved.

The system of government which eventually emerged was to a large extent a product of the experience to which the various peoples that made up the empire had been subjected. It is, however, clear that in case of a clash, the experience of the core group would dominate. In some parts of Africa, the mode of conquest sometimes influenced the relationship between the capital and the provinces—as, for example, Shaka's Zulu kingdom and Mosheh's Basuto empire. However, in West Africa the distinction did not seem to matter much. The core people made use of a combination of force and/or diplomacy to establish control over the other groups. There is always a form of marriage and other links between the capital and the provinces so as to ensure the loyalty of the provinces.

The head of the political entity was the king who was usually referred to by several names and titles in the different traditional areas. He often belonged to the ruling dynasty. In every African kingdom, a tradition regarding the origin of the ruling dynastyis preserved. This tradition asserts the claim of a single descent line to sole right to rule. It is what some social scientists have called "a mythical charter"—an account of the past that serves to justify the present. The first rulers were sometimes believed to be endowed with miraculous power and their claim to authority and obedience had the element of the supernatural. The unity of the several towns and settlements which eventually made up the Asante kingdom was symbolized in the institution of the Sidakwa—the Golden Stool—which was regarded as having descended from the sky and which compelled obedience to the Asantehene.

What usually happened was that individuals who played important roles in the emergence of other kingdoms had their leadership role acknowledged by being conferred with the headship of the kingdoms. Such roles involved leading the campaign to incorporate small groups into the kingdom; leading the group during the course of migration; these individuals probably influenced critical decisions such as place of settlement. The "mythical charter" also influenced appointments to other positions of authority, in that important offices of state within the capital and the provinces could only be inherited by people from a particular lineage or family. There was the belief that ritual power and the ability to perform certain tasks were hereditary and therefore the monopoly of particular lineages.

The king, in theory, held sway in the kingdom. His authority could not be challenged. All activities were carried out in his name, but in actual practice there were certain rules and regulations that governed his conduct of affairs. The king was expected to listen to the views of specified groups of people forming councils which often had their distinctive names. In most kingdoms, there were specified persons with the right and responsibility of nominating the successor to a dead king, and even where succession was regulated by strict rules, the people in charge of the installation of the new ruler had considerable influence. In many kingdoms, the ruler depended on the cooperation of priests whose ritual powers derived their validity from sources outside the control of the king. Although the Oyo recognized a common ritual head in the Alafin, he did not exercise much political control and no one Alafin controlled a very extensive domain. And, in many other kingdoms, the power of the king was limited by the need to take the army commander and the chief justice into his confidence. What is being stressed is that the organization of the kingdoms was such that it was difficult, if not impossible, for any one king to be dictatorial or tyrannical. Institutional checks against such excesses existed and were frequently applied.

In Nigeria, for example, there were two important sections of the kingdom: the capital and the provinces. The king lived in the capital which comprised a greater complex of buildings and a larger population than could be found elsewhere in the king's domain. There were categories of officials concerned specifically with its organization and provision. The kings had elaborate regalia, for the upkeep of each of which, again, a specific official was responsible. In addition, members of the highest political authority under the king had their residences at court or the capital.

In the provinces, the highest authority was exercised by an individual, the provincial ruler, whose relationship with the king at the capital was determined by a number of factors, the most important of which was the manner in which the political entity came into being. In some cases (in Benin, for example), the provincial rulers were sons of the reigning Oba in the capital. In others (Mossi, for example), they were leaders of the communities incorporated into the kingdom. They were allowed to continue to exercise authority so long as they acknowledged the authority of the capital by sending annual tributes and going to the king in the capital in celebrating important festivals. This served to emphasize the province's subjection to and dependence on the capital.

The relationship between the Asantehene, king of the Asante and the Omanhene (provincial ruler) is typical of what obtained between the centre and the periphery. Each Omanhene held his own annual religious political festival during which his subjects reaffirmed allegiance to him. But the Omanhene would not hold his festival until he himself had attended the Asantehene's in Kumasi and thereby confirmed his allegiance to the king. The Omanhene maintained his own treasury and raised revenue by taxing his subjects. But from his treasury, the Asantehene could demand contributions for use in the overall interest of the kingdom.

Each Omanhene maintained his own courts, but from such courts a right of appeal to the Asantehene could be exercised. Finally, an Omanhene possessed his own military organization and was responsible for mobilization and demobilization, and could command the use of his army in the national interest and could restrict the use of his forces when it was considered inimical to the overall interest of the kingdom—as, for example, in the case of a conflict between one Omanhene and another personality of the traditional area or one of his sub-chiefs.

The political structures described above were not without their weaknesses. Most of the West African kingdoms existed for centuries. The amount of political stability that they enjoyed was affected by factors such as the quality of their leadership and the resilience displayed by the kingdom in coping with fundamental weaknesses. Most of the kingdoms were too large for effective administration. Against the background of poor communication, the ability of the king at the capital to effectively monitor events in the provinces was limited. In Oyo, for instance, state officials were inefficient, corrupt and exploited the weaknesses in the political system for personal gain. There was the example of the council of king makers who, in exercise of their right to force the king to abdicate, forced six successive rulers to commit suicide. There were also many instances in which the provinces refused to honour their economic obligation to the capital in the form of tribute payment, and the process weakened the kingdom.

But the most important factor which caused the decline of these kingdoms was the invasion by the European. The slave trade had a devastating effect on some African kingdoms and was largely responsible for the collapse of ancient West African kingdoms. The official abolition of the slave trade and the attempts by European powers to establish areas of influence was a more direct cause of the collapse of the kingdoms. The industrial revolution which resulted in the production of more goods in Europe led to a situation in which Europeans wanted areas of influence where they could collect raw materials and sell their finished products. At first, the Europeans were content to stay at the coast, and they relied on the African middlemen to bring them the raw materials from the interior. But the middlemen took advantage of the stiff competition among the Europeans to maximise their profit, particularly during the period of the scramble for Africa.

The Berlin West Africa Conference of 1884, during which African states were assigned to European nations, specifically conferred on some European nations the right to penetrate and establish their rule on the African territories. European traders realized how much of the profit margin they lost as a result of the activities of the African middlemen. They therefore sought ways of trading directly with the interior where the raw materials existed. But the African kingdoms, with their well established authority and effective machinery for the conduct of trade, were seen as obstacles to the realization of the goal of the Europeans whose officials, such as consuls and governors, either took advantage of rivalry among rival local groups, as in the case of Asante and Fante, or the Yoruba civil wars in 1888. Sometimes, they directly attacked the kingdoms, as in the case of Benin in 1897, thus bringing an end to the kingdoms. The collapse of the kingdoms was accompanied by the establishment of colonial administration.

Two European powers, the British and French, established their presence in West Africa. The French policy of association and assimilation did not leave much room for the continuation of the African traditional system of government. But the British policy of indirect rule was essentially a continuation of the traditional system, with the imposition of an agent of the British government at the apex of the administration. At independence the essentials of the traditional system still remained and were recognized by the African governments. They were made the basis of the local government administration in the African nations.

Economic factors

The trans-Saharan trade enabled Africans of West Africa to make contact with North Africa and the Middle East. It was made possible by the camel, an animal with a unique capacity for carrying heavy loads over lengthy waterless tracts. The exact date of the beginning of the trans-Saharan trade remains a matter of much dispute. Evidence from records and Arabic accounts [Trimingham 1962] suggests that major trade in precious metal may have begun as early as the 8th century AD. The exchange of goods and services has been an important feature of economic activity in West Africa since time immemorial. There were three distinct markets in West Africa during the era of the slave trade. These were:

    a) the domestic market

    b) the trans-Saharan market, and

    c) the Atlantic market.

The domestic market provided Africans in the various areas of West Africa with an opportunity to exchange their surplus produce and obtain those goods that were in short supply. In order to facilitate trade, regular market days were instituted on which traders gathered to buy and sell goods. The commodities traded varied in accordance with the regions concerned. In the case of foodstuff, for example, in the forest zone areas such as Niger Delta and parts of Yoruba land yams, palm oil, gari (cassava flour), dried fish and fresh fruits and vegetables would have been the major items of trade, in the sixteenth century. However, a clear record of the trade emerges from around the mid-eighteenth century.

Prior to the discovery of the New World, gold was the most important item in the trans-Saharan trade. In fact, the Sudan was the major source of gold, both for Europe and the Muslim world. Although the quantity traded across the Sahara diminished, following the advent of Europeans to the West African coast, gold never disappeared entirely from the trans-Saharan trade. Next to gold, slaves were the most important export across the Sahara. During the period 1600-1800, demand appears to have fallen away in places such as Egypt, Tunisia and the Fertile Crescent. However, this was offset somewhat by increases in demand in Morocco and in the Ottoman regions of the north-eastern Mediterranean. After 1800, the demand for slaves in the Islamic areas again increased, especially after supplies from the competing Caucasus regions were cut off by Russian expansion.

Apart from gold and slaves, the forest and Sudanic zones exported leather goods, gum arabic, wax, ivory and ostrich plumes to regions across the Sahara. The goods imported into West Africa from North Africa and the Middle East were for the most part, luxury and military items. These included fine cloths, horses, armour and weapons (sword blades and scabbards). The trans-Saharan trade was dominated by Muslim merchants.

Caravans for crossing the Sahara usually assembled at towns founded by Muslims along the northern frontiers of the desert. These included a) Sijilmasa, near Morocco; and b) Wangla in south-eastern Algeria and Ghadames in Tunisia. The Sudanic merchants operating on the West African side of the Sahara supplied the Muslim merchants with items to be traded in the north and distributed the imported goods in the forest and Sudanic zones.

The Atlantic market was opened up following the advent of the Europeans in the fifteenth century. During the period 1600-1800, slaves were the most important item of trade. Although estimates vary, 10-15 million slaves were traded to the New World while the trade was in progress. Apart from slaves, the other commodities traded include bees wax, indigo, ivory, cotton and palm oil. However, these items were never as important as the trade in slaves. During this period, West Africa's imports from Europe comprised mainly iron goods, weapons, cloth, silks and glass beads.

The development of the Atlantic market marked the beginning of an era which ended with the European conquest of West African states in the nineteenth and early twentieth centuries. The trade in slaves was controlled by European merchants (who operated from forts which were built along the West African coast) and African rulers and middlemen who secured the slaves to be exported from the interior. When the English arrived on the coast of the then Gold Coast, the Portuguese and the Dutch had set up bases from where they operated their trading activities with the local people. Kromantse,[5] a small settlement of the Fante-speaking people of the then Gold Coast, became the first location from which the English commenced their operation while settling in.

It was from Koromantse that the English began in 1631 to ship out their very first consignment of slaves from the Gold Coast, now Ghana. Consequently, all slaves coming from that point of embarkation were referred to as "Coromantin" slaves. The town called "Kromantse" by its modern inhabitants was and still is a small fishing village on the coast very close to Cape Coast and Elmina, the latter being the largest slave trading locations on the coast of the Gold Coast.

Controlling that whole area of Cape Coast and Elmina was the traditional kingdom of Efutu, whose kings were the first to have been involved in trading activities with the Europeans. However short the slave's stay at the coast may have been before being shipped out, life in the Efutu kingdom was clearly the last one that they experienced before being forced into the journey across the Atlantic to various destinations in the Caribbean.

Historians and archaeologists have now agreed that the slaves often referred to as "Kromantee" did not all come from Kromantse. The memory of the last experience of life before leaving the West African coast is one that did not seem to have been passed down well by the slaves, and the colonial records that attempted to describe some of them have failed to present the information that would lead to a meaningful reconstruction of the cultural formation and transformation of Maroon societies, which the contributors to this volume will in various ways attempt to address.

Continuities

Rarely do human societies transfer, intact, social systems from one locale to another, especially under circumstances that brought African people to the West Indies and also as the people involved came from diverse cultural groups [Price and Mintz 1992]. Nevertheless, it has been recognized by scholars that Africans from the West African coast brought with them knowledge and information unique to their individual cultural traditions and that later, in their new areas, they developed groupings and institutions that met their needs. There are some specific characteristics of the West African social system that can be cited as examples to demonstrate this cultural carry-over or retention.

Many scholars claim that Africans brought to the West Indies used their experiences of ethnic affiliations to organize themselves, and have identified groups of people as Yoruba or Nago, Mandingo, Ardra and Congo. In many areas, the runaway slave populations are known to have formed bands that were often grouped along ethnic lines. In Jamaica, for example, a Maroon society exists with names of leaders such as Cudjoe, Accompong, Quaku, Kishee and Quao—names that are strictly derived from the West Africa coast. Quite clearly, although derived from diverse ethnic backgrounds, Africans who were brought to the Caribbean employed similar elements, as they formed strong and viable communities [Alleyne 1988; Price and Mintz 1992].

Religious ideas and practices have also persisted. Elements of Yoruba religious practices around cults such as Orisha and African magic, known in the West Indies as obeah and its connection with witchcraft (*bayie*) or witch (*bayifo*) of the Akan of Ghana are quite well known. Elements of music and dancing characterized by a rhythmic complexity involving several distinctly different signatures are also discernible in African-derived West Indian cultural traditions. Warner-Lewis and Whylie examine this aspect in their chapter. The survival of the talking drum as means of communication and entertainment is a well known example. How often have we not heard of master drummers from Africa in the Caribbean? West African traditional art and symbolism have not yet been demonstrated in the cultural milieu of the West Indies, although one suspects that some ideas related to these have been carried over. Customs related to birth, death and marriage seem to have been revived, though not in their entirety.

Another area of social continuity is the African tradition of folklore and oratory, which often featured animal trickster (Ananse) and Rabbit. The nature of folklore, the mode of presentation as well as the use of formal speech patterns, have left their impact. Some of these folklore traditions have forms similar to biblical storytelling or are evident in libatio (prayers) and in proverbs.

Most importantly, although the family systems developed in the West Indies were derived from different backgrounds, social organizations such as the family survived despite the unfavourable conditions of slavery. Evidence for this exists among slave societies, particularly those in Jamaica and Haiti. Above all, is the fact that West African-derived societies have not, on the whole, become fully part of the societies into which they were introduced.

Notes

1 The term "maroon" has been defined in various ways. Richard Price in *Maroon Societies* (1969) has this to say: "The English word 'maroon' like the French 'marron' derives from Spanish 'cimarron'". As used in the New World, "cimarron" originally referred to domestic cattle that had taken to the hills in Hispaniola [Parry & Sherlock 1956: 14] and soon after, to Indian slaves who had escaped from the Spanish as well[(Franco 1968: 92]. By the end of the 1530s, it was already beginning to refer to Afro-American runaways [Franco 1968: 93]; see also Guillot [1961: 38], and had strong connotations of "fierceness" of being "wild" and "unbroken". According to Pereira (ed), *Caribbean Literature in Comparison* [1990] the term "maroon" has different social connotations in different areas. It is noted that "in Jamaica 'maroon' is applied generally to members of those free communities. The equivalent in Cuba is *apalencado*, or inhabitant of a *palenque*; while the term 'runaway' in Jamaica or 'cimarron' in Cuba applies more specifically to individuals not organized in a community". Bilby and N'Diaye [1992] spell "Maroon" in the lower case when its used in its original descriptive sense, synonymous with "escaped slave" and

capitalize only when used generically to refer to contemporary peoples or ethnic groups. Evidence available on the Maroons indicates that the term does not apply only to individuals, communities or groups of people of African descent.

2   A much more detailed discussion of the issue of a chronological scheme for the archaeology and history of the Caribbean may be found in Agorsah [1993]. Chronological schemes in archaeology always aim at providing frameworks for reconstructing the trend of cultural development. They possess two crucial features: the time dimension and the various stages or events of transformation within the development. The result has often been the listing of sequences of events or chronological charts as depicted by the material evidence, or attempting to determine the relative ages of different groups of artifacts. One such attempt and probably one of the earliest, was made by an American geologist working in the Dominican Republic in 1869. From a cave near Samana Bay in that country, the geologist William Gabb [1872] observed what has been referred to as pre-ceramic layer beneath a ceramic layer indicating that there had been in the area a cultural tradition that pre-dated the use of ceramic equipment. Similarly, in 1919 the historian Adolfo de Hostos, observed from the site of Ostiones in Puerto Rico that within the ceramic tradition, similar to what Gabb noticed in the Dominican Republic, there were differences. For example, he distinguished between red slip and incised decorated pottery and noted an increase in the quantity of pottery with those types of decorations from the lower stratigraphic levels [Adolfo de Hostos 1919]. The implication was that the ceramic tradition observed at the site of Ostiones became much more complex in decoration during later periods.

It was Gudmund Hatt, a Danish anthropologist, who first attempted to use similarities in ceramic styles to build, not only a sequence, but also posit cultural diffusion within the Caribbean. Hatt, using material excavated from various sites in the Virgin Islands in the early twenties, proposed a two stage-sequence:

1. Pre-ceramic (Krum Bay)

2. Ceramic: a) Coral-Longford b) Magens Bay – Salt River

The earliest cultural tradition known from the Krum Bay site was referred to as prehistoric because it lacked pottery, while the ceramic phase was divided into two stages of development on the basis of decorative motifs. Ceramics from the Coral Bay and Longford sites were painted white on red, while those from Salt River and Magen's Bay were incised. The latter was considered to be a more complex tradition and, therefore, later. Hatt [1924] drew comparison between ceramics from the Lesser Antilles to the South and the Greater Antilles to the west and suggested that the two groups of pottery were derived one from the south and the other from the west. However, in 1933-1934, further excavations in Puerto Rico by Froelich Rainey indicated deposits of white-on-red painted pottery like that of Hatt's, beneath incised pottery similar to pottery observed in the Dominican Republic by de Hostos. Rainey [1940] on that basis, then proposed two successive cultural traditions he referred to as Crab and Shell on the basis of associated remains and postulated migration of cultural traditions from South America. Later, Rouse's study, beginning 1936, detected flaws in Rainey's sequence. Rouse observed a continuous sequence in the data from Puerto Rico, although that feature was not clear from evidence from the Virgin Islands and the Dominican Republic [Rouse 1939, 1941]. He therefore proposed a scheme which, although based on localised pottery styles and "cultures", did not effectively depart from Hatt's sequence [Rouse 1948] as follows:

Period I – Pre-ceramic

Period II – Ceramic (White-on-red painted)

Period III – Ceramic (Largely plain pottery)

Period IV – Ceramic (modeled incised)

Later, George Howard, then a student using evidence from sites in Venezuela referred to Rouse's Periods II, III and IV as Early, Middle and Late Ceramic [Howard 1943, 1947]. Terms such as "cultures", "aspects", "phases" or "periods" were ignored. About the same time, Alfred Kidder [1948] was also proposing a stratigraphic sequence for Venezuela, using material from the sites of La Cabrera and Valencia, a sequence that was complemented by that of Howard as Early and Late Ronquin cultural traditions from the site of that name located in the Orinoco basin of Venezuela.

The dependence on ceramic styles as a crucial factor in the analysis of the archaeological record is quite clear from schemes proposed so far. This is not an unexpected situation because in those periods in the development of archaeological research, the appearance of pottery was considered to be one simple significant sign of the development of human culture. The idea of the beginning of food preparation, permanent settlement and urbanism, were related concepts.

Emphasis on pre-ceramic and ceramic traditions also featured in Guyana where Clifford Evans and Betty Meggers of the U.S. National Museum, have identified a "pre-ceramic lithic horizon", "a largely pre-ceramic phase" and three "ceramic" phases [Evans & Meggers 1960]. In the Lesser Antilles in St Lucia, Marshall McKussick, a student working under the supervision of Rouse, also identified four ceramic "styles" the first two of which were fitted into Period II and the other two into Period IV of Rouse's scheme [McKussick 1960]. A similar sequence of six periods was proposed for Grenada by R.P. Bullen [1964]. Rouse's Period V was an additional period that was proposed by him to take the historical period into consideration.

Although radioactive dating methods and techniques became available at the beginning of the 1950s, many of the chronological schemes were still referred to in vague terms. For example, Rouse and Cruxent in their revision, used the term "complexes" to describe cultural traditions if they were pre-ceramic, and "styles" for ceramic tradition, a purely arbitrary and subjective approach. Similarly, the use of such terms as "series" and "units", and the addition of such suffixes as "-oid" to differentiate those "complexes" or "series", assumes not only stylistic homogeneity, but also common origins and uni-directional development of those "complexes" and "series". Such an approach does not constitute an objective framework for understanding the individual or local cultural traditions. Further, it lacks a basis for cross-cultural or comparative analysis. The result has been that chronological charts which have been drawn do not exactly provide the objectivity required in the interpretation of the data they represent. The main cause of this problem has been the continuedattempt to relate the archaeological material to already existing schemes based on evidence from North American archaeology [Willey & Phillips 1966]. In a scheme later proposed by Rouse, the Palaeo-Indian, Meso-Indian and Indo-Hispanic periods of North America are used as standard measures for cultural traditions of the Caribbean [Rouse & Cruxent 1963]. The stages of cultural development in North America were defined as follows:

1. Palaeo-Indian – presence of chipped stones big game hunting.

2. Neo-Indian – ground stone and shell artifacts; emphasis on gathering and fishing.

3. Neo-Indian – appearance of pottery and agriculture.

4. Indo-Hispanic – European artifacts and foods.

Considerable reliance has been placed on the use of pottery as a main feature for the scheme which also uses the term "series" to describe groupings within his classification and gives the impression that stylistic homogeneity or similarities of certain attributes or types and forms should be considered to show common origins or movement of populations.

Kozlowski [1974] in an attempt to revise Rouse's chronological scheme, used his knowledge of Venezuela, and Cuba and other areas of the Caribbean to propose a scheme that was not effectively different. Although he professed to use economic and social transformations as bases for his scheme, his descriptions employed the same technological factors used by Rouse and other scholars. He identified the following:

1. Palaeo-Indian I : – Development of stone implements (blade, flake and leaf-shaped points); hunting of big land animals.

2. Palaeo-Indian II : – Chipped stone tools, leaf-shaped points and ground and pecked stone tools; marks transition from hunting of big game to gathering and incidental agriculture.

3. Meso-Indian – Characterized by shell bone and wooden tools; decline in big game hunting; and fishing.

4. Formative : – Appearance of pottery; more intensive food production; beginning of urbanism.

5. Neo-Indian: – Formation of classic Meso-American cultures.

Kozlowski's scheme, although not specifically indicated, more or less follows that of Gordon Willey, whose scheme has formed the basis for the chronological framework used in North America [Willey 1956]. Kozlowski [1978] seems to have, however, placed emphasis on the socioeconomic development somehow "pretending" to have de-emphasized chronology and refers to the first of these stages of human movements as prehistoric.

Recently, Rouse and Allaire [1978] have proposed a four-period sequence which has been quite popularly used. He refers to the first of the three stages, the Lithic Age, which is said to be the time between the beginning of stonework and the appearance of ground stone, shell and bone artifacts. This period covers Kozlowski's Palaeo-Indian I and II. The Archaic, the second stage, is the time from the appearance of ground stone artifacts to the appearance of pottery (Kozlowski's Meso-Indian). The third stage is the Ceramic Age which starts from the time of the advent of pottery making (Kozlowski's Formative and Neo-Indian stages). The final stage, according to Rouse and Allaire, is the Historical period starting with European contact. With the advent of radiometric dates since the early fifties, chronological schemes gained a more meaningful dimension and much more accurate and reliable local sequences. The result, however, is the arrangement of sites according to dates, while little attention was being given to explaining the cultural context within conceptual frameworks that were devoid of diffusionist principles. For example, Rouse and Allaire [1978: 437] stated that:

> The time has come to drop Cruxent and Rouse's distinction between pre-ceramic complexes and ceramic styles. Not only is this cumbersome but also it clashes with the trend among some workers to define ceramic units in terms of pottery styles rather than elements of style therefore, we shall drop the term style and call all the local chronological units complexes, regardless of whether they are pre-ceramic, or ceramic. Whenever possible, the complexes will be grouped into series, as in previous formulations.

However, the decision to drop the use of styles was reversed soon after, when it was realized that it was only by stylistic classification that comparisons could be drawn between cultural traditions [Rouse 1986].

Another impact of the advent of radiometric dates was that inconsistencies began to be sorted out in some of the sequences. For example, dates from sites such as LaGruta, Ronquin Sombra and Corozal in the Orinoco region of Venezuela, raised questions of doubt in the local sequence of the area. While they were *considered too young* [Rouse & Allaire 1978], the main reason may have been that they did not fit into the sequence already established on the basis of the ceramic stylistic classification.

Sanoja and Vargas [1983] have criticized Rouse and Roosevelt [1976] that by the use of their chronological ordering for the site of La Gruta, several long gaps have been created. Rouse and Roosevelt are further criticised for assuming great ceramic stability in the sequence. The development of archaeological approaches, particularly in the New World [Patterson 1990] require that archaeologists working in the Caribbean must adopt a logical, objective approach in interpretation of cultural events as well as using single factors, such as ceramics, to generalize on issues. Clearly, therefore, there is the need for a review of the chronological framework(s) applied to the Caribbean in order to render them more effective and meaningful.

The schemes developed for the Caribbean identify at least two major periods: prehistoric and historical. Within these broad periods local sequences have been worked out, some going back several thousand years. The earliest dates come from Venezuela. In fact, Kozlowski [1978] speculates that early prehistoric industries in Venezuela could date to about 17,000 years before present (BP), although the earliest dates confirmed so far centre around 7,000 years ago. Because earlier dates have been obtained for cultural traditions in the areas outside the Greater and Lesser Antilles, scholars have always felt strongly that areas with cultural evidence dating later than others are receivers of cultural influence coming from outside.

For a proposed new scheme, see Agorsah "An objective chronological scheme for Caribbean archaeology and history", *Social and Economic Studies* 42, no. 1 (1993): 119-48.

3 See R.S. Price and S.W. Mintz, *The Birth of African-American Culture: An Anthropological Perspective* (Boston: Beacon Press, 1992); K.E. Kiple, *The Caribbean Slave: A Biological History* (Cambridge University Press, 1984); M. Craton, *Testing the Chains: Resistance to Slavery in the British West Indies* (Ithaca: Cornell University Press, 1982).

4 In recent times, the identification of connections covers several areas such as social, economic, artistic and artistic expressions, as well as technological which has been a major areas of research in the West Indies. See Goucher [1991].

5 Kromantse was a small fishing village on the coast of the former Gold Coast, now Ghana, which was the first port established by the English to facilitate their trade in slaves and commodities obtained in parts of the West African region. Many of the slaves coming through this port have always been referred to as "Kromanti" although they may have been derived from areas outside the traditional area of the village.

two

The True Traditions of my Ancestors
Colonel C.L.G. Harris

Introduction

If a prize should be offered to any section of the Jamaican population that has been able to establish the longest and most colourful association with the island as its undeniable accomplishment, the winner would be my ancestors, the Maroons, and by a wide margin. Only the aborigines—the Arawak Indians—surpass the Maroons in terms of duration of occupancy. The story is a short and simple one, but to tell it in a meaningful way means a long and winding chain of explanations of various aspects of the story.

The majority of Maroons, as my ancestors came to be referred to, originally came from West Africa. Oral tradition claims that the majority of those who came were mainly of the Ashanti ethnic group, who were forcibly brought to Jamaica as slaves by the Spaniards who, as history has it, were later defeated by the English. Consequently, some of the slaves fled to Cuba. Others who did not flee swore never to be slaves again. They stood by their word, escaped from bondage and fought to maintain their freedom for over eighty years of bitter warfare against the British. The victory of the Maroons had far-reaching implications for world history.

Firstly, for black people throughout the world it established the fact that slavery was not an acceptable condition of life. Secondly, compliance might have eased the conscience of those devout men in England who argued for the abolition of the system, and allowed their tacit support. Unequivocal repudiation by the Maroons created an atmosphere charged with life-giving oxygen for the lungs of sanity. Today, it is not immediately obvious to people from outside Jamaica, and even to many insiders, how different the Maroons were or are from other communities. This is so because of the long period of association, access to common resources as well as experiences shared over the centuries. Some of the outstanding features that are more characteristic of the Maroons than other group of Jamaicans constitute the discussion of this chapter. The focus is on the Maroons in eastern Jamaica, popularly referred to as "Moore Town Maroons".

Maroon Lands

Thousands of acres of land are involved and no one has any legal document for the individual portions owned. This fact, taken in conjunction with the population explosion, would seem to suggest an exceedingly fertile area for disputes among Maroons. However, the contrary is true and the few cases that arise are mostly concerned with boundaries.

The early Maroons controlled large portions of the island in the days of the struggle. No deliberate effort was made to cordon off areas because of the nature of the wars they had to fight. However, whether on the move or stationary, the specific location of each Maroon settlement was very well defined and controlled, making it extremely difficult for colonial forces to penetrate. My ancestors devised several ways to secure each victory, such as using certain types of landmarks to guide their military movements. Knowledge of the terrain, plant and animal life were crucial for the control of land by our Maroon ancestors. It was after the peace treaties that land occupied by Maroons came to be surveyed and mapped. Many of the sites occupied by Maroons in ancient times are now being identified and studied. For us, the Moore Town Maroons, sites such as Nanny Town, Watch Hill, Killdead, Gun Barrel, Marshall's Hall, Pumpkin Hill and Mammee Hill are but a few of those ancient towns.

The order for the first land allotment was made by Governor Sir Edward Trelawny on 12 December 1740. This order was carried out by Thomas Newland, a surveyor, on 22 December 1740, and his signed declaration to this effect was witnessed and sealed by the three commissioners, John Smith, Richard Farril and John Ashworth. The patent contained five hundred acres and was at first named Nanny Town. Soon after, however, certain historical and geographical considerations combined and resulted in the change of the name to New Nanny Town.

Years later, the Grand Chieftainess after whom the original Nanny Town was named, requested more land because of the increased Maroon population. The governor, General Archibald Campbell, was greatly impressed, and on 28 December 1781 he signed an order granting her request. This order was carried out by the surveyor, Dugall Macpherson, on 31 July 1782. He was told by the Maroons that the name of their community was changed to Moretown, but it is evident that he did not understand that this new name was in anticipation of *more land* being received. He spelt it *Muretown* and some of his contemporaries even spelt it *Muirtown*. His declaration was sworn to before Commissioner Thomas Gray on 6

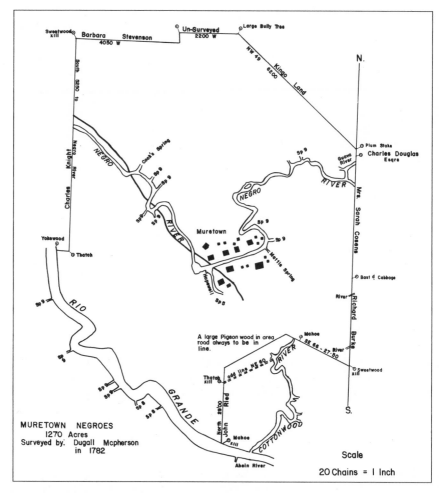

Fig. 2.1 Moore Town in 1782

December 1782. When the mistake was pointed out and eliminated, another mistake, in the form of an extra "o" resulted and so instead of "More Town" we have "Moore Town" (Fig. 2.1). This small point is of critical importance to any effort aimed at determining the period in which the great Grand Lady took her leave of earth. Conjecture regarding the 1750s as the time Nanny died has been given prominence, but this clearly is at least thirty years too early.

In 1884 the Maroons outmanoeuvred the United Fruit Company in the purchasing of an adjoining property to which, for a very special reason, they gave the name "Kent" in honour of the Duke of Kent. The acquisition was made under the agreement for one thousand more acres of land, but in actual fact the acreage was vastly more. The price was sixty pounds. In totality, in this regard they had an extra arrow in their quiver—Colonel James Harrison, whose family they had saved during the

Morant Bay uprising and who had consented to be their Colonel and spokesman. Prior to the purchase of other contiguous lands such as Cornwall Barracks and Ginger House, Mount Cameron had also been acquired and, subsequently, Josiah, Kennedy, Nottingham, Nottingham Pen and Joe Hill were also bought. This briefly provides an idea of the areas of territorial control by the Maroons since the end of wars of freedom against the British.

Sociological Issues

One of the most important sociological issues among the Maroons of Moore Town and Charles Town in Portland was the ancestral language, known as "Kramanti". It was spoken freely up to some six decades ago—in the early 1930s. There were special times and situations in which it was given prominence over vernacular, as at Christmas time, which used to be a decidedly prolonged period of merriment, and during the frequent staging of *Play*, which is an extremely specialized ritual ceremony. "Kramanti", as my ancestors knew it to be called, is regarded as a hybrid having Twi, the Ashanti language of the Gold Coast (now Ghana in West Africa), as the more vigorous of its parents. Throughout that period, however, vernacular was the chief mode of speech, and when spoken by the old people it presented much difficulty to most non-Maroons, since the latter nearly always believed that they were hearing Kramanti in its richest form. A few examples will suffice:

English	Vernacular as spoken by youth	Vernacular as spoken by the old
1. Who is that?	A udda dat deh?	(a) Na umma dareh?
		(b) Na umma da summa?
2. Who will help me across that bad place?	Udda guieh gu help mi ova dat deh bad place deh?	Na umma sa ji mi gudda wakka na dah uggi preh?
3. Your sister came to fight the white man for Moore Town: You told her to go and sit down. All right, all right! Today, today, you will have to kill someone.	Yes! yes! yu sista cuhnh fi faight backra fi Moo Tung; yu tell h'n seh fi gu siddung. Awright! Awright! Tiddeh, Tiddeh, yu wiawfi kill summady.	Yees! yees! hu sissa cuhnh fi fetteh obroni fi Brakka Rubba; hu teyh h'n seh fi gu sroum. Arretteh! Terreh, terreh, hu wiawfi yerrehfu samma.

In the third example above, a woman is being chided for preventing her younger sister from joining the fight against an invader. Although the difference appears overwhelming, once a few key words in the old are understood, all difficulties lose their terrors. Let us consider a few more examples. They are not necessarily in alphabetical order:

(a) *Hunte*: (pronounced hunty) changes its meaning in different situations but generally represents "why", "what", or "for what purpose". The word *na* is often placed before it. Thus, *Na hunte yu cuhnh yeh fi?* means "Why have you come here?"

(b) *Summa*: represents "someone", "somebody", "person", as in *Emba ting seh Chaa Harris no prem ayeh tem na fu-fu summa*, meaning "Anyone who thinks that Charles Harris is not primed at all times is a very foolish person".

(c) *Emba*: represents "anybody" or "anyone".

(d) *Na*: represents "is", "as" or "as to" but is almost unrestricted in its use as mere aural embellishment. However, even in places where it would seem redundant, its removal could militate against desired emphasis or meaning.

(e) *Sa*: represents "able", "is able", "is capable", "willing", "ready", as in *Na umma sa cha di pikibo na di biggi huss?* meaning "Who is able to carry this child to the big house?"

(f) *Umma*: represents "which" or "which of you" as in *Na umma sa fetteh Nyankipon*—that is, "Who is able to fight against God?"

(g) *Uffa*: represents "how" or "whose" and is rendered immortal by a statement once made by an old gentleman who, on hearing that one of his colleagues was preparing to go to the market, shouted to him in these words: *Hai baa, yu deh gu na maakit! Bayh fippance wut a di red mout' grunt—de female one. No kai uffa noh sumeh waice noh nuff.* The speaker almost instantaneously regretted using those words for they were repeated, jocularly, each day by young, old, sick, lame, maimed. This is interpreted to mean: "Hello, brother, you are going to the market! Buy threepence worth of shad (for me). It does not matter how offensive is its odour, provided that it is sold cheaply".

Some very special words common to both the old and the new vernacular, with their meanings are:

Abbehbu proverbs

Brehbrehbeh inclined to gossip

Bubuwahfu physically handicapped

Bussufu known for making statements and otherwise acting with a responsibility beyond one's chronological age

Dappafu known for a tendency to rationalize one's own feelings and philosophize in the case of others

Djijifo to make a mockery of

Karanapo he/she, on being questioned, remained silent

Poo imbussu to do something merely to please someone else with hypocritical pleasure during performance

Sangkuku or *Buttu* to sit on the haunches

Wawatu to make much of someone for accomplishing something worthwhile, for example marriage

Yerfu to kill or destroy

A point that could not possibly escape the attention of anyone who listened as Maroons converse in the old vernacular, was the manner in which many monosyllabic verbs, adjectives and nouns were each given an added syllable by repeating the vowel sound as the final syllable. Thus, *walk* became *wakka*; *good* became *guddu*; *fret* became *fretteh*, and so on.

Consider the question, *Na umma sa ji mi guddu wakka na da uggi preh?* Literally, this means "Who will give me good walk at the ugly place?" But the better (more imaginative) translation is, "Who will help me at that bad (dangerous) place?" Is it strange that even this older vernacular drew far more heavily on English than on Kramanti? No. Theirs was an English-speaking environment and so not only should they (the Maroons) understand, but should also be able to make themselves understood. In order to clear away any lingering doubt in this respect, we may consider a few simple expressions in all three languages.

Vernacular (old)	English	Kramanti
Ba mi sa nyeah summa (idiom)	I am hungry	*Ekom dim*
Pikibo (or *pikkin*) *siddung*	Child sit down	*Akwoda tsina asi*
Ji na hin	Give it to him	*Fa ma nuh*
Wakka guddu or *Guggu wakka*	Goodbye	*Nante yieh* or *Ma dencheh*

It is a sad fact that today Kramanti, for most Maroons, is a dead language. However, greet any Maroon on the streets of Moore Town with the traditional, *Salam aliko* (*Salaam aleikum*) which is interpreted as "Peace be unto you", and you are almost certain to receive the ready response: *Aleiko salam* (*aleikum salaam*) meaning, "And unto you also be peace". This is as far as most would go. However, among themselves the older Maroons have a multiplicity of set greetings and of these the two most used are:

(1) A Maroon meets another whom he has not seen for an appreciable length of time. Both are happy at the meeting and one stretches forth a hand while exclaiming, "*Yengkungkung!*" The other grasps the hand and responds eagerly, "*Yengkungkung srehf srehf!*" The first is saying, "Maroon!" and the second is responding, "Maroon please!" The formal Kramanti expression for "please" is *me sreheh wu*.

(2) Let us suppose person A and person B are greeting each other:

A: "*Breh breh Asante*"

B: "*Asante kotoko*", meaning "Asante the porcupine"

A: "*Wekum apema*", meaning "If they kill a thousand"

B: "*Apem beba*", meaning "A thousand more will come"

Here, reference to the porcupine is significant. As is known, when attacked this rodent rolls itself into a "ball" with its erectile spines sticking out in all directions, and it is claimed that if one of these is broken out another falls into that empty space. It is also said that this special greeting had its roots in the long war with the British. Even if this is not strictly correct, there is no doubt that during that period every Maroon would stoutly declare that if the foe should succeed in killing a thousand of them, then a thousand more would rise up to defend and preserve their freedom which, to them, was the breath of life.

The name for the god *Nyankopong* or *Nyame* and certain objects such as *unsu* (water), *unsa* (rum), *edwiani* (food), *kwedu* (banana), *ekutu* (orange), and *prako* (pig) indicate West African connections, as many of these words are the same in the Akan language of modern Ghana. It is of interest that although the Kramanti word for money is *sika*, at least ninety-five per cent of Maroons use the word *takifa* or *tekofa* to refer to money, which in reality represents only one denomination of currency.

Maroon family and names

Time was when the Maroons found their spouses exclusively from among members of their various communities. Consequently, even up to this day in Moore Town all Maroons are related—very closely in some cases and more remotely in others. It was most remarkable how without written records of lineage, parents would know the exact positions of individuals on the family trees so that their children could be given effective guidance in choosing wives and husbands. It was an unwritten but inviolable law that the young did not enter into formal sexual relationships without the approval of both sides of parentage. The pattern followed was stereotyped: A young man becoming interested in a young lady to the point of marriage would communicate this fact to his parents, who would examine the situation carefully. If the blood-relationship was considered as too close or if there had been a family feud even in the dim and forgotten past, this would be fully examined with him and the matter ended there. If, however, there were no such impediments the parents would communicate with the young lady's parents and a day—almost invariably a Sunday afternoon—would be set for a meeting at the home of the parents of the latter. This was the momentous "asking-for" meeting in which one set of parents, on behalf of their son, sought the daughter of another in marriage. In recent times, things have changed drastically—the formalities are few and anyone is free to take a spouse from outside without going through this process.

One other important tradition which, unfortunately, appears to have almost disappeared except in history books, is name derivations based on the day on which one was born. In the ancient days the tradition was as important to our ancestors, as it is known to have been practised in some parts of Africa from time immemorial. Examples of such names include:

Days	Male	Female
Sunday	Kwasi	Akosia
Monday	Kwadwo (Cudjoe)	Adwoa
Tuesday	Kwabena	Abena
Wednesday	Kwaku	Akua
Thursday	Yaw	Yaa
Friday	Kofi	Afua
Saturday	Kwame	Amma

As late as in the early 1940s, by far the two chief family names were *Harris* and *Osborne*. The true and somewhat amusing story is told of a prominent person who had an important appointment in Kingston. The ease with which he got through the test caused members of staff to regard him as a genius. Later, he was interviewed by the manager who asked where he was from. On being told Moore Town, the interviewer remarked coldly, "You are from Moore Town and your name isn't *Harris* or *Osborne*? Sorry, I don't believe you. We cannot use you."

In the three chief daughter districts of Moore Town (Cornwall Barracks, Ginger House, Comfort Castle) in the modern parish of Portland, a similar predominance of special names occurred.

In the first these were *McKenzie, Fuller*, and *Smith*; in the second, *Fuller, White, Clarke*; in the third, *White, Gray, Anderson*. Today in Moore Town proper, however, although the giants still maintain a significant lead, the numerical disparities have been greatly reduced. Here follows a list of the chief contenders, not necessarily in order of importance:

Anderson	*McFarlane*
Passley	*Patterson*
Phillips	*Pryce*
Roberts	*Robinson*
Sterling	*Bernard*
Brown	*Burke*
Crawford	*Deans*
Douglas	*Downer*
Sutherland	*Thompson*
Valentine	*Ireland*

It may be pointed out that these names are by no means limited to Maroons, although it is certain that they are more prevalent among Maroons than other sectors.

Names and naming

The names discussed so far are family names. In the case of individual or first names, two important factors must be given consideration. The first relates to what is believed to be the reality of incarnation. It should be noted that many persons are often known by the same first name and the reason is that a child is born and it is imperative that the "returnee" be properly identified and his/her name restored.

In this respect dreams play an essential role. On a night close to the time of birth, a member of the family (and here it must be remembered that the Maroon family stretches wide) would be approached in a dream by a relative who was no longer alive. The visitant would send a message to the expectant mother informing her of his/her intention of "coming to stay with her". The message would be delivered and, more often than not, at birth the child would bear some physical signs indicative of the true identity in support of the dream.

As growth takes place, the mannerisms of the "sender" of the message become more and more evident in that person's behaviour. But there are exceptions to the smooth flow of events. Someone could, for various reasons beyond his control, fail to report the message from a dream and so naming of the child would have to be done on the basis of a surmise. Needless to say, this course can lead to mistakes. Here is a case of this latter kind: The baby is named but does not respond physically to the care lavished on it. In fact it becomes frail and feeble. Then a dreamer dreams. In this dream Brother John, who died six months previously sends this message to the worried mother: "I came to stay with you but I am not appreciated and so will be leaving soon." The message is delivered with alacrity. Immediately, Brother John, the new name, is given. Apologies are made for the "foolish error" and as the vibrant image emerges from the dead chrysalis case, so the child arises from the slough of feebleness on to the threshold of warm, pulsating, vigorous life. We are not here discussing some fanciful situation but rather certain hard facts of life. This accounts for the fact that formerly the following note appeared on nearly all birth certificates of Maroon children: *male child* or *female child* instead of actual names. This meant that the "returnee" might not have been satisfactorily identified at the time of registration and the parents took what they considered the safe course—allowing the official naming to await the real blessing. However, there is now a change in this particular practice since nameless certificates have caused too many difficulties when travel and other documents are to be prepared.

Traditional political structure and organization

A cursory examination of the Maroon political structure would seem to indicate a certain lack of sophistication. A closer examination should reveal otherwise. For instance, in Moore Town there is a system of simple codified rules spoken of as the *by-laws* specific to Maroons and which are additional to the laws of the country.

The core of the government comprises the Colonel or Chief, the Major, two Captains, a Secretary, and a Foreman of the Council. All these posts are elective and under normal circumstances are held for the rest of the incumbents' lifetime. A peculiarity of the system is that never has there been a political campaign on the part of those to be elected. However, there is nothing to prevent a supporter of an officer-to-be from very discreetly planting seeds of the latter's pre-eminent qualification in the minds of others. Records of Maroon tradition demonstrate that no one not deemed worthy of a post has ever been known to receive the honour of nomination. It means, therefore, that provided the nominee is agreeable, once nominated he is elected. An election takes place at a general meeting place called safu huss or muster ground.

Two types of meetings are held: township meetings and Council meetings. For the township the *obraafu* (town crier) gives the necessary information in a stentorian voice from a hilltop in the late evening and after this pattern: *"Oooyee! Oooyee! Oooyee! Colonel wants to see all Maroons at safu huss on Wednesday evening."* This is twice repeated and then the message ends with the injunction, *"Oooyee! Udda no yerrie tell tadda!"*—meaning, "Anyone who did not hear is required to tell someone else!". The implication is clear, imperious, irrefragable—that is, everyone under all circumstances, is expected to communicate the information to at least one other person.

Some time before the set hour on the appointed day, the *abeng* or *akikreh* is blown and this means that all adults attending will be free to take full part in the proceedings. As regards Council meetings, the *obraafu* does not shout the information; the abeng is not blown and only members of Council and those summoned to appear may attend. Matters dealt with at these meetings are of various types and are chiefly concerned with the welfare of the community. For example, time was when by virtue of the treaty signed with the British in 1739 every offence except murder would be appropriately dealt with by the Chief and his officers. Even in a murder case, handing over of the accused was dependent on whether he was thought to be guilty by the Chief. However, over the years changes have crept in and there are now only few issues that cannot be transferred to the courts. These are mainly concerned with ownership and administration of Maroon lands, for these are still held in common.

Deeply embedded in Maroon affairs is the essence of cooperative effort which, in the not-too-distant past, was profoundly concerned with the enhancement of individual and collective welfare. It was all-pervading and like the cool, clean, invigorating mountain air of the region, gave zest and meaning to the business of life. When someone, say, John Brown, required community assistance to build a house, the *obraafu* would make the announcement just as in the case of a township meeting, but with the appropriate information, for example: "... John Brown going to carry thatch next week Tuesday morning ..." Thatch, the fronds of a special type of palm that grew in abundance on the mountains, was used almost exclusively as roofing material. On the morning mentioned, members of the community would go into the hills and bring back enough of the material to roof John's house and his kitchen as well. This area of the organization gradually ceased to function as more and more persons turned to shingles and then to zinc sheets for roof covering.

Farming, marriage and death are three of the occasions that produced gems of cooperative effort. On farming, from the cutting down of the bush to the planting of the crop, each person giving assistance worked as though he was the owner and hoping to reap the richest dividends from those operations. In the case of marriage it was similarly everybody's business, but today this all-encompassing character has undergone drastic modifications.

When the death of a Maroon occurs, apart from the long period of mourning and the *table-setting*, nothing has changed and all signs point to a changeless future. Whereas today financial contribution towards funeral expenses is made once, formerly, two separate operations were involved: a fortnight after the funeral the ceremony known as *table-setting* was conducted. An enquirer might have asked a member of the bereaved family, "When are you going to set table?" And the answer could very well be: "Next week Tuesday." Usually a booth of bamboo and fronds of the coconut palm would be constructed immediately before the home of the bereaved and a large table placed in its centre. From about eight o'clock in the morning of the appointed day, people would start arriving in a manner reminiscent of electors about the business of polling their votes. A man with a touch of flamboyance and the voice of an *obraafu* stands at the table. He mentally surveys the scene. At a moment appropriateness of which is determined in his mind alone, he holds onto the sides of the table with both hands, shakes it and thunders, "Walk up, ladies and gentlemen, walk up! Walk up ladies and gentlemen, walk up!" And an orderly procession begins. It moves in single file towards the table on which a shiny silver basin sits. The person at the head of the line reaches it, reverentially places a contribution therein and passes on through to the opposite side. No one takes change from the money thus offered. By mid-afternoon the exercise is over. The money donated is handed to the head of the household and preparations get underway for a lively set of quadrille to last throughout the night.

Military affairs

The war between the Maroons and the British was inevitable, but is only touched on briefly here as it is fully dealt with in later chapters. One of the turning points in Maroon military defence and survival was marked by the appearance at one stage of a supreme leader—a woman of amazing qualities who was popularly known only as Grandy Nanny. To posterity she is the indomitable Grandy Nanny—The Rt. Excellent Nanny, National Heroine of Jamaica. Her four brothers, Kwadwo (Cudjoe), Accompong, Kofi and Johnny were all leaders of high calibre. It was she, however, who was the originator of the camouflage, known among Maroons to this day as *ambush*, that so baffled and deceived the British. Her highly developed extra-physical capabilities were astounding. If to these facts we add the ability to communicate over great distances by means of the *abeng* or *akikreh* and the unerring dexterity with which the *junga*, a heavy spear, was thrown, the unwavering belief that her genius was a result of divine guidance would be appreciated.

Some distance downhill from Nanny Town (spoken of as Stony River by my ancestors) the Magnificent Lady single-handedly defeated a battalion whose members had been forced to peep into the "boiling pot" because of its strategic position on an acute angle along the narrow trail, as she allowed the lone survivor to survey the scene of destruction as the basis of his contemplated report to his superiors.

Calculating that this would spur the foe into making a do-or-die attack on her citadel, Nanny made elaborate plans for such an event. She knew that the attack, when it came, would not be from the north since her sentinels on Watch Hill could never fail to spot any approach. The south, therefore, though vastly more difficult to ascend would be the direction on which to concentrate. The deduction was perfect. It was not long afterwards that the attackers were making their labourious march. This time their array of weapons comprised swivel guns which were bigger than anything ever before against the Maroons. The town was eventually entered and occupied but the inhabitants had fled. The invaders saw the remnants throwing themselves over a precipice to avoid being captured. For the Maroons, the fight for freedom had no end until absolute victory was achieved. That eventually happened.

An era was now rapidly drawing to its close. The governor of Jamaica was Sir Edward Trelawny and the Maroons were asked to become the friends of the government and, in confirmation of this, signed a treaty of peace. Reference has already been made to the treaty. There are in fact two of these documents: one signed by Captain Cudjoe (Kwadwo) on 1 March 1739 and the other by Quao on Grandy Nanny's behalf on 23 June 1739. The time differential resulted from the fact that at the beginning Nanny displayed skepticism regarding the offer. She reasoned that it could be the initial part of a stratagem calculated to do what force of arms had as yet failed to accomplish. But because she was not averse to the idea of genuine peace, she had no objection to Cudjoe's "testing of the waters" provided appropriate security measures were given the necessary attention. It is evident that this time-lag of nearly four months determined the fact of the former, with its fifteen clauses being more favourable than the latter with its fourteen. It is certain that neither Cudjoe nor Quao could read English. It is clear that they signed these treaties in all sincerity. One of the issues addressed was as follows:

> "And whereas peace and friendship among mankind, and preventing the effusion of blood is agreeable to God, consonant to reason, and desired by every good man; and whereas peace and His Majesty George the Second, King of Great Britain, France and Ireland and of Jamaica Lord, Defender of the Faith, Etc., has by letter patent, dated February the twenty-fourth, one thousand seven hundred and thirty-eight, in the twelfth year of his reign, granted full power and authority to John Guthrie and Francis Sadler, Esquire, to negotiate and finally conclude a treaty of peace and friendship with the aforesaid Captain Cudjoe; the rest of his captains, adherents, and others of his men, they mutually, sincerely, and amicably have agreed to the following articles . . . "

— then giving thought to a preceding statement:

> "Whereas upon the late submission of Cudjoe, and all the rebels then under his command, to accept of such terms as the said Cudjoe sued for . . ."

How does one equate splendour with squalor? The Maroon leaders *did not sue* for peace. They were victors who had been approached by the vanquished desirous of negotiating and concluding an honourable peace. They would not have accepted the lie of their begging for peace had they known of its presence in the treaty document. At the end of the last signing ceremony the Wonder Lady for the last time displayed her unusual capability of rendering harmless the bullets fired at her: she asked the British commandant to give the order for a volley to be fired at her. When the request was at last hesitantly granted, she rose from the stooping position she had taken up and handed him all the bullets fired at her, as a memento of the occasion.

Despite the impressive statement declaring the treaty as one of eternal duration war broke out between the government and the Trelawny Maroons in 1795. It became known as the Second Maroon War and the Trelawnys stood alone. There is unchallengeable proof that their counterparts in nearby Accompong Town gave important assistance, even if unwittingly so, to the enemy. There is unquestionable proof that although outnumbered by at least ten to one and at times enduring hardships, their bravery and resourcefulness more than compensated for the superior firepower of the foe who, as they did fifty-six years before, asked for peace. Just before this, the Maroons of Moore Town put together a formidable force in order to hurry to the support of their brethren.

War songs of inspiration roared through the whole of Maroon country, calling for the support of the gods and the spirits of our ancestors. These songs were real songs and were sung in the Kramanti language. Of the two examples given here, one is called "Jawbone Song", sung on the initial uncertainty regarding the fate of our brothers and sisters of Trelawny, and the other a *prapra*, and is related to the decision to become active participants in the conflict. Both songs were spontaneously composed at the time. The first:

> *Wadda hai!*
> *Wabda wha' dem du wid Dumbar!*
> *Maroon! Soldier kill Dumbar?*
> *Du wekkeh du mi nana wanda oh!*
> *Wanda wha' dem du wid Dumbar!*
> *Wanda oh!*

and the second:

> *War dung a Trelawny*
> *War O!*
> *Wi a gu a Trelawny!*
> *Yu nu hear di war?*
> *War O!*

The march had actually begun when news was received that an honourable peace had been proposed by the British. But all was not well. *The Trelawnys had not been defeated in war.* They laid down their arms in a gesture of good faith towards a proposal put forward by General Walpole. Governor Balcarres—that most contemptible of despicable rascals—refused, however, to ratify the agreement drawn up by Walpole, a gentleman. Thus the valiant but deceived Trelawnys were taken to Halifax, Canada, and thence to Sierra Leone. We have since been cut off from our brothers and sisters—relatives who were in that group.

On hearing of the war preparations that had been made by the Moore Town Maroons, Balcarres tried his blandishments and perfidy on them but failed. Enraged, he threatened Charles Town but again Moore Town stood between him and his nefarious designs. If the British government of today—less than a decade from the twenty-first century—could spare just a moment to inform itself of the grievously dishonourable deeds of this man against the intrepid Trelawnys, no restraining force of earth would be capable of preventing it from seeking out the descendants of these people and presenting to them what (even in terms of millions of pounds) could only be a token of the inestimable reparation that is their due.

Maroon religion

Yet there are beliefs and customs whose Christian character would be questioned by some devout servants of Christ. As an example, we shall consider the *Play*. Up to about three decades ago, most of those persons who were seriously ill would be taken to a *Play* to be cured but the practice is not much in evidence today. *Play* is a ritual ceremony held chiefly in a booth made after the pattern of that in which *table-setting* was conducted. The drummers are seated but most of the other participants must stand. The drums (Kramanti drums) are made from hollow portions of tree trunks, covered at one end with tightly drawn goat skin from which the hair has been skilfully removed. They are played by artistes, each of whom is called *ok-remma* and the songs (Kramanti songs) are sung to the music of the drums, and the dance (Kramanti dance) is done by top-rated performers. For the songs the name Kramanti is an umbrella-designation, for under it stand special groups such as Jawbone, Prapra, Sa Leone, Mandinga Country.

As soon as the dancing begins one of the dancers—a dancerman or *fettehman*, becomes possessed by the spirit of a departed member of the clan. In this state, he is called the *grangfarra* or oldman (pronounced owlman). He reveals matters of the past in relation to the illness of the person brought there to be healed and predictions regarding the future are also made. Apologies, if the circumstances warrant, are tendered and after a session of libation, incantations and manipulatory anointment is concluded, the illness disppears dramatically. At other times the healing is of a more gradual nature.

Detecting the petty thief

Various methods of exposing the petty thief were once practised not only by Maroons but by other Jamaican communities as well. What is known today in Maroon tradition appears to have merged with the usual aspects of Christianity. Most of these (such as *the Bible and key, the gold wedding-ring and tumbler of water*) could easily have been manipulated, even if the results turned out to be accurate. One cannot consider this process as completely magical and it varies in procedure from community to community, but with several similarities.

However, there is one process which perhaps is still unknown outside Maroon territory which maintains its mysterious, anti-manipulation character. In the region there is a type of grass known as *mawt grass* because the ladies of those former years would wash their pungent roots and tie them in small bundles which were placed in their tin cases as an insect repellant (all insects that damaged stored clothing were categorized as *mawt* or moths). For the test, a handful of evenly cut grass is held in each hand so that the even end is towards the little finger. A strong person holds both ends of a man's belt at arm's length, one end to a hand, but with one hand lower than the other. Both persons face each other; the first opens his arms wide and utters the words: "By St Peter, by St Paul, by the Living God of all, is Mary Joe tek di pillow-slip!"—and at this moment the bundles are suddenly brought crashing together, end to end, on the side of the belt remote from the speaker. The holder of the belt is now required to pull it through the point of union. If Mary Joe is guiltless the task is easily done. On the other hand, if she is guilty even the aid of Hercules is but a waste of time.

Maroon traditional technology: ancient and modern

Lamp wicks

Years ago cotton grew wide and wild in Moore Town and the down was used for the two main purposes of filling pillows and as material for the manufacture of wicks for the oil-lamps. A stout piece of split bamboo about eighteen inches tall, was whittled smoothly to a circumference of about two inches. A section of about an inch from one end was tapered symmetrically to a point and pushed through a close-fitting hole in the middle of a *kakoon*. This is the lower end. The upper end was carefully split down perhaps for three inches. In this cleft some down was placed and other amounts connected to it until a length sufficient for a start was obtained, and the slack end held by light pressure to the floor. Between the open palms and outstretched fingers the spindle was rubbed in such a manner as to cause it to spin with a whirring sound while at the same time twisting the down into yarn. As the yarn lengthened, it was wound around the lower end of the spindle until the desired amount was obtained. It is from this homespun material that the wick would then be made.

Shot pocket

A Maroon was never without *shot pocket* during the war and even as late as the 1940s. It is made of thick cloth such as fore-bag or denim and, more often than not, measures about fifteen inches in length and ten inches wide. A piece of the same material is sown on the outside across the full width and reaching up to the middle. A vertical double stitching in the centre of this outer portion creates two equal compartments. A V-shaped flap, which is an extension of the back portion, reaches down to the top of this dividing line and a button hole close to its inverted apex fits easily over a button there. The handle is reinforced and attached at both corners where the flap begins. It is long enough to suit the tallest of men and by a series of knots is adjustable for the shortest. It is worn over the shoulder and diagonally across the chest so that the bag itself falls under the left arm of the right-hander and the right arm of the left-hander. If the wearer is engaged in strenuous work on the farm, the string is brought down and tied around the waist so that the bag rests on the buttocks. A *tinder-box*, flint, steel and file are never absent from a *shot pocket* and, as the name implies, it was originally used mainly for carrying shots for the cap guns during the many years of war.

Tinder box

The technological aspects of Maroon life may not at any time bear the stamp of breath-taking intricacy and its utility is often inversely proportional to its simplicity. The *tinder box* (Maroons say tender box) is an example. It consists of a small horn of a cow which is cut off smoothly and properly cleaned. A piece of wood (preferably cedar because of its quality of expansion in water and the ease with which it is fashioned) is used for making a lid which fits closely inside but with an over-hanging rim. A hole is neatly made near the extremity of the small, closed end of the horn, through which a piece of strong cord is passed and the end knotted to prevent it from slipping through again. The other end is connected securely to the lid and the cord's only use here is to ensure the continual safe-keeping of the lid. Some rotten wood is collected in the bushes and dried out in the sun or in the heat and smoke over an open fireplace. When it is thoroughly dried it is cut into small pieces and put in the fire and as soon as these are fully carbonized, they are retrieved and placed in the horn whose lid is replaced quickly to prevent continued burning. A bit of flint and a piece of steel are secured and the tinder box is complete. To make a fire, the horn is held in the left hand in such a way that the thumb and the index finger encircle the rim but are on a slightly higher level. The lid is taken off and allowed to hang freely by its cord and the flint is held firmly between the tips of the thumb and index finger. The steel is then used to strike it an outward, glancing blow, that is, away from the striker. Sparks fly and some of these fall into the horn whereupon the burnt wood is ignited and some of this is placed on a *katta* of dried banana leaf, grass, paper, or any other suitable material. Because of the excessive rains that fall in Maroon territory, the tinder box used to be of paramount importance in the woods at those times when matches would be useless. Access to fire was especially important because all the older male adults were keen pipe-smokers who, when working in the fields, would readily forego the luxury of lunch but never the comforting puffs on their pipes.

Katta

The *katta* is made by winding the material around the hand, removing it while allowing it to retain its circular shape then fastening the loose end by simply pushing it down in the depressed centre. Its primary purpose is to soften the pressure of a weight carried on the head.

Bamboo vessels and containers

In those years there was no piped water in Moore Town and water was carried from the springs in bamboo vessels of from one to three joints in length. The water-carrying process was accomplished mostly by children, each of whom would take along a very thin piece of cloth to cover the hole through which the water entered. After being moistened and put in place, this cloth cover would never fall off even though the journey was rugged and the container turned upside-down. Although these children did not know that a precise scientific law was in operation, they all knew that so long as the containers were absolutely filled, the cloth would remain in place and the container would not leak.

Cowshut

Because of the extreme wetness of Maroon territory the stitches of their farm boots which were almost always wet, could not be expected to last as long as boots worn under less extreme conditions, and so a type of boots known as *Cowshut* was devised. It carries no stitches except at the back and a small right-angled seam bordering the uppermost hole for the lace of the inner side. The name is derived from the fact that these boots are made of specially tanned cowskin (cow's shirt) the smooth part of which is turned inwards. Brass sprigs are used in fastening soles to uppers and so no rot ever sets in around the metal, as would have been the case if steel sprigs were used.

Bangu bige (bag)

This is a container made specially for transporting produce from the field and is made of trumpet tree bark, which is first dried and twisted into a small cord. No one unaccustomed to a *bangu bige* would believe that it is capable of containing the large amount of goods that it really can. The mystery lies in the meshes, not the material, which expand to an almost unbelievable extent. The filled container is transported on the carrier's back while the handle passes across the forehead.

Fishing lances

There are three types of fishing lances. The first is easily made: a long, slender sapling is obtained and at three inches or so from the slightly heavier end, a circumferential incision is made. The whole section is then converted from a circular to an equilaterally rectangular shape. A stout, red-hot piece of metal is used to burn a hole right through the base of this section. Less than an inch above, but on the other side, a similar operation is performed, then a piece of stout wire some eighteen inches long is pushed through the first hole, so that the projections on both sides are of equal length. A slightly shorter length of wire is likewise used in the upper hole and the four ends are now bent upwards neatly so that they touch the pole or are extremely close to it and all four projections beyond the wood are of equal length. The prongs are sharpened and the entire area where wire rests on wood is enclosed in a spiral staircase of fine binding wire or cord. The properly made weapon is called a striker and is used at nights for catching crayfish in the rivers. The other two lances are fashioned by heating and then beating part of a piece of iron to the required thinness. This part is beaten around a slimly conical piece of steel and the resulting hollow is called the *housing*. The other portion is heated, hammered, and drawn out into a four-sided spear. The *housing* is for receiving the slim, strong, wooden shaft. There are also throwing lances and diving lances. The former is shorter but takes a much longer shaft. Standing on a stone in the river or on the bank with lance raised, the hunter waits motionless for a grunt or a hognose or any other fish of suitable size to swim by. The weapon leaves his hand with lightning speed, and on occasions like this a miss is a rarity.

There are times when the conditions favour another line of action. His diving lance held in readiness, the fisherman dives, investigates the large opening under a stone, or chases his quarry there. He impales it and triumphantly rises to the surface. The art reached its highest expression among the men of Ginger House, a subdivision of the Moore Town community, and could be watched in its most thrilling form up to the late 1940s.

Tu'n Rivva

This denotes a manner of very profitable fishing in past years and is described as follows: Assuming a width of river of point A to point C. A wall was raised from point C to another point, B, conveniently located somewhere between the extremes. On the upper side of this wall, that is, the part facing the source of the stream, clay was used for sealing the holes. In a short while water would be flowing heavily between A and B but none, or a mere trickle, between B and C, as far as point D, downstream. A harvest of fish was thus easily gathered after which the embarkment was broken down.

Maroon Economic Issues

Hunting and farming

Hunting and farming have always been prominent areas of activity. The wild hog was always the chief animal hunted and the saga of "John Brownfield"—a unique wild boar of superior size, cunning, strength and dog-destroying capability— played on the imagination of everyone up to as late as the beginning of the twentieth century. The hunters operated chiefly in groups but there were the few who performed as loners. The principal weapons used were the spear (*junga*), the cap-gun and well teamed dogs. The hunters' food in the forest was mainly the *duckun* known also as *kuckunu*, *buoyo*, blue-drawers, or tie-a-leaf. Hunting of the coney, a rodent called *grazie* or *injin cunny* by Moore Town Maroons, takes place only at nights because the animal operates nocturnally. The dogs used are small so that they are able without much difficulty to enter and leave the holes—the habitat which is invariably of a stony character. At times the hunters block the entrances to the holes while the owners are happily feasting in some farmer's field oblivious of the fact that the return journey will end in disaster.

Traps

Animal traps are very common among Maroon hunters. The main types are as follows:

(a) A pit dug in the middle of a hog trail; the earth is removed carefully and the hole covered properly to avoid detection by the animal which now comes and falls in.

(b) A strong but flexible pole is pushed firmly into the earth at a strategic point on one side of the trail and a rope with a noose is attached to the free end. Near the point of attachment a piece of stick of up to two inches in length, depending on the case, is fixed so that one end is longer than the other.

Two short rods on the case are fixed so that one end is longer than the other. The long arms are driven properly into the ground about a foot apart and with the short arms turned toward the trail. The pole, when bent, falls along an imaginary line midway between them and under them is held rigid a piece of stick whose length is slightly greater than the outer distance between the two bifurcations. The pole is bent and a second length of stick, called the pin, set equal and parallel to the first is so placed that one is in front and the other behind the bit of wood. This allows the pole to retain its bent position while two short, bifurcated rods with arms even and turned upwards are placed in direct alignment on the opposite side of the trail with a length of stick laid in the crotches. Using this mechanism and the pin (on the other side) as base, a floor of sticks is laid and covered over very carefully with leaves. The rope, which has been passed through the noose, forms a loop which now opens over the floor or platform and is concealed with more leaves.

The hog steps on the platform, the pin is disengaged and this movement results in the sudden falling of the platform and the release of the bent pole. As the latter flies upwards the rope sucks onto the leg of the animal which is drawn up in such a manner that it cannot escape. This same principle is used in other types of traps. A prime example involves the cutting of a hole in a "bark" or the trunk of a tree. Food is placed in this hole; the loop is set over the opening; no platform is used but the pin is fixed so that it must be disturbed if the food is to be reached by the quarry. At times a stiff, shorter pole called a helper is bent under the first in order to increase the tension on the rope.

A similar principle is employed in the trapping of birds such as partridges and doves. In this case, however, no platform is used and the rod is very thin. A slender, flexible twig is bent in a curve and both ends pushed into the ground as substitute for the bifurcated stakes near the pole. One end of the little piece of wood attached to the cord is hooked behind the wooden curve while the tip of the other end rests on the extremity of the pin which, in this case, is at right angles to the pole with its other end resting against a short stake directly in front. Food is then placed on both sides of the pin which is raised (and the loop of the string placed carefully over it) so that the bird is compelled to make the fatal mistake of stepping on it in an attempt to reach the other side. The whole contraption is called a *springe*.

Other animal traps include the *calaban* and the *benna* or *tambu*. The *calaban* is made by tying four straight twigs at their ends to form a square which is placed flat on the ground. Two pieces of cord, each twice the length of the diagonal, are connected diagonally at the corners of the square of twigs. Sometimes a skilled worker starts with only two twigs. Other pieces of gradually decreasing lengths are now placed on the same plane but on opposite sides alternately, until the pieces of cord are taut and a rough oval is formed, leaving the small hole directly on top to the maker's imagination. Another piece of cord is connected to the corners of one of the two lowest bars in such a way that the apex of the triangle thus formed by bar and cord, barely reaches the middle of the opposite bar. A four or five-inch length of twig, say, quarter-inch in diameter, is given two equally deep horizontal cuts on opposite sides above the middle, and quarter-inch apart. It is broken completely then put back together (it is now called the pin) with the cord—the apex of the triangle—between the jaws and set on the ground so that it keeps the front and two sides of the *calaban* raised, while the back end rests firmly on the ground. The bait is placed under the cord at the back. As soon as it is touched the pin "breaks", causing the calaban to fall and entrap the bird.

To make the average *benne* or *tambu*, a four-foot-long rose apple rod, somewhat less than half an inch thick is obtained and the stouter end bevelled on both sides for two or three inches. Starting an inch from the extremity, whittling is done equally on both narrow sides to result in a sharp median point. Just below the angular section formed by the whittling, a red-hot wire is used to burn a hole through the middle of the flattened part. A small cord with a six-inch noose is made from the bark of the trumpet or mahoe tree and at the end of the noose a small, flat piece of wood about half-an-inch by one-eighth of an inch is attached by passing the cord through the noose and using the wood to prevent the complete action. The cord is passed through the hole until the bit of wood stops further progress then the loose end is tied to the other end of the rod, which is now bent half-way towards the imaginary horizontal passing through the hole. Next, a four-inch-long twig, the "pin", with circumference slightly greater than that of the hole is obtained and a piece of cord is tied to it. The other end of the cord tied to the bent rod which is now the finished article—a *benna* or *tambu*. The noose is drawn almost to its full length from behind, resulting in further bending of the *benna*. The free and properly pared end of the pin is pushed in the hole in such a manner that the noose is kept in position—one part of it on each side—and the tension is not released. The free-hanging portion of the noose is opened carefully over the pin on which the bird must alight to get at the bait. Its aim is never accomplished. The pin falls; the creature is doomed.

The tar stick
The tar stick is an exceedingly tall rod, generally of bamboo. The latex from the jackfruit (that from the fruit is preferred over that from the root) is used to cover the bamboo pole liberally, leaving uncovered three or four inches at one end. When the birds come to feed on the apple blossoms, apples, figs or bassocum, the pole is pushed up at them and they are stuck. At times a cross is affixed at the top and also covered with latex. Left untended it takes care of those unwary, feathered bipeds which, sadly, might have been seeking just a moment's rest.

Chorkie
This may be considered the most primitive of all the traps, for it cannot function unless the trapper is in place. It consists of a long, thin line—generally a vine called hogmeat—one end of which is tied in a slip-knot immediately before the food so high up on the branch that the bird is not scared by the presence of the immobile trapper far below. But when it attempts to eat, the loop is pulled over its neck which is held firmly to the branch. The end of the string is then tied to a branch, a sapling, a stone or any stable object that is conveniently at hand. Once that is accomplished, the trapper then climbs up the tree and gets his quarry down.

The fishpot
For general fish-trapping, a length of bamboo is obtained. Let us refer to the space between two joints as a *span*. Several spans with the joints remaining at both ends are cut and each is split into an odd number of strips to within a short distance of the lower joint which must remain intact. The strips are forced wide apart by pushing a stone down towards the second joint and uncured withes are used to complete a neat wicker work from the top to about four inches down. The stone is removed and we have the finished, funnel-shaped product—the fish-pot. Stones are now used to make a wall across the river and at certain points this wall is broken creating swift, narrow streams. Here the fish gliding down cannot turn back and are trapped in the pots which are placed somewhat below the lower line of the wall. Another type of trap, the *sinking-pot* is also made from bamboo. It is neatly wattled and is shaped like an enormous egg with one end drawn out and the other blunted. Inside the blunt end is a short funnel which prevents the escape of captured sea creatures. The funnel is usually made first and the strips (or *bones*) are then bent over it, tied at the ends, and wattled. Sometimes, however, the funnel is made separately and attached afterwards. The *sinking-pot* is thrown into the deep

and the end of an attached cord is hidden somewhere on the river's bank. The bait generally used is *kakoon* and coconut and the captives are mostly crayfish, mudfish, sandfish and eels.

Cooking

There are diverse ways (some of which may even seem outlandish) of preparing food. For example, boiling done in coco leaves, bamboo, earthen vessels; baking in ashes. In the latter case, a big fire is made and when the coals are mostly burnt to ashes, peeled green bananas, plantains, sweet potatoes or other suitable food are placed on the bed of the fireplace and covered over thickly with ashes. If a large metal vessel (a pot or a bucket)is available it is placed over the heap. A person can turn his attention to something else and not fear that the food will be burnt. These methods were never in general use and were adopted only at the dictates of sharp necessity or just for fun. Yet, much of the traditional cuisine varies from the stand-ard Jamaican fare. Let us examine the following: the *dunkun, duckunu, buoyo,* tie-a-leaf or blue-drawers, is prepared by mixing grated coco or cornmeal with spices, sugar, coconut juice and salt together. The batter is poured onto squares of wild plantain or banana leaves (which had been held for a while over a fire in order to replace its brittleness with greater elasticity) and then folded into neat packets. The packets are then cut into the required sizes. The are shaped like miniature pillows and are tied longitudinally and then across with thin strips of bark from the trum-pet or mahoe tree, or the banana trunk, and boiled in a large pot or tin. There is the baked variation which is prepared by placing the leaves thinly along the sides and bottom of a round-bottomed iron pot. The mixture is poured in and covered care-fully with leaves. A quantity of ash is placed on top of the leaves; the pot is then placed on a fire of coals and a piece of zinc or tin is used to cover it completely so as to form a brim. A fire is made on this piece of metal. When baked, the food is even more delectable than its boiled counterpart, and is eaten hot or cold. It creates a thirst and is therefore very satisfying. It can be kept unspoilt for days.

Kakoon soup
The *kakoon* (cocoon) soup and dish are made from a nut borne on a vine of the same name. This nut after falling naturally from the dried pod is collected, thrown into the fire, taken out after giving off a popping sound, and pounded to extract the ker-nel which kernel is sliced into quarter-inch-wide strips and placed in a bundle made from the fronds of a giant fern known as *ferril macca*; the bundle is placed in the river where it remains for three days. The *kakoon* is then removed and salted. At this stage it can be eaten without being cooked. In combination with *black junga*—a kind of shrimp found in the springs but never in the rivers—it makes both a soup and a stew that are most highly favoured by connoisseurs in the culinary art.

Thatch head is the succulent portion of the thatch palm, which is harvested when the fronds are removed and the outer portion chopped away. It is cut into cubes or strips and made into a soup or crushed and boiled with codfish or janga in coconut milk. A dish called *fufu* was once much loved but is now no longer so. It was made by pounding roasted breadfruit (without the crust) or yellow yam to an even consistency in a mortar, and seasoning and butter added. It would then be served as a whole mould from the vessel in which it had been pounded.

Weaving

Moore Town once produced the finest jipijapa hats to be found anywhere in Jamaica, and perhaps the world. This certainly is a very strong statement but it is supported by a formation of unyielding strength. Two sets of persons excelled in the art. One was the entire family of Crawfords and the other a branch of the Harris family. In 1929 at a show and fair on the property of one Tata Howell, near Manchioneal, Mr J.J. Crawford submitted two *jipijapa* hats. Dozens of hats were submitted but Mr Crawford's won the first and second prizes. The strands were so fine and neatly woven that water poured in failed to find an easy way out. In the late 1950s, two samples were taken to the festival contest in Port Antonio, in the parish of Portland. People were greatly impressed and the festival officer asked leave to take them to the finals in St Ann's Bay. Based on a pledge that the items would be returned, the request was granted. They were never seen again, and Moore Town ceased their participation as a team in the festival. The art is almost dead now, for the only living member of that select band of weavers is Mr Tom Crawford and he no longer plies the trade. Other materials once used in weaving are *mawt grass, coconut leaves* and *curatoe* (sisal). Hats, mats, belts and slippers were woven.

Maroon music and dance

Apart from the general music and dance patterns practised throughout Jamaica and accepted by the Maroons, there were special traditional types which are not found outside of a Maroon community and are described by the word Kramanti. The Kramanti drums, briefly mentioned earlier, are of two kinds—the large and the small. Twine made from the bark of the trumpet or the mahoe tree is used to keep the goatskin in place and wooden wedges regulate its degree of tautness. These drums are played with the fingers and the palms of the hands. At least two drums should be playing simultaneously if a rich, meaningful music is to be produced. The bigger drum is the *long drum* and the smaller one is the *cutter* which repeats the notes and message of the former.

Because of this fact, if there were bad blood between two families and a precocious child of one of the antagonists should be heard making an uncomplimentary remark in respect of the other, an adult standing by would shrug the shoulder and say to another, "Mmm, what little drum seh is what big drum seh". This means that the child was merely repeating the unsavoury remarks of its parents.

The Adowa

This is an equilateral triangle somewhat less than a foot high and mostly made from a steel bar three-eighths of an inch thick, which is sometimes electroplated. At the apex, a circle is formed of the same material (but not added on), and a straight piece of the same material, measuring not less than the length of one side of the triangle is used for tapping to the rhythm of the drums. Most of the songs are almost always in the minor key.

Kramanti dance

Kramanti dance is unique to Maroons in Jamaica. It takes in the synchronized movements of each part of the body as well as those of the body as a whole. The accentuated movements of the pelvic region, which is more or less present in other forms, are absent from Kramanti dance. It is characterized by a sense of seriousness and mission. That is one of the reasons behind the ability of the true Kramanti dancer to glide with such ease, from the purely physical plane on to the metaphysical. Used in certain ways and under special conditions, Maroon songs and dances have been known to become swift and awesome agents of retribution. Such was the case of the deeply wronged woman who, in singing a *jawbone*, simultaneously used a small tumbler half-filled with clear, sparkling water to "throw", not "pour", her libation.

A special type of dance originating in Moore Town which enjoyed phenomenal popularity up to the first quarter of the twentieth century, is that known as *brukins*. The following is an excerpt from a brukins fete: The music was supplied by two flutes, one of wood and the other of bamboo, two drums (a very large bass and a small rattling drum), a pair of bamboo castanets, a grater-and-spoon, a rub-stick and a comb-and-paper. Outside, there were more people than those who were able to find accommodation within the booth and precisely at the first stroke of eight from the large clock at the back of the platform, the tones of the golden-voiced woman rang out in song:

> *Walk een deh, walk een deh,*
> *Walk een deh, walk een daaayh!*

The whole company of singers joined in and the instruments' controlled volume played their part so skilfully that the voices were never drowned out at any time and their messages were always understood. Have you, dear reader, ever had to pass a muddy section of the road while in formal dress? And did some kind person place some small stones on which, if you were brave enough, you could pick your way across? Well, the resultant tentativeness, swaying sideways and backwards and the successful progress, were the motivating force behind the concept of *bruckins*. The dancers were invariably couples because no one danced alone. The entire course of this dance gives the impression of an orderly unfolding of a story, stage by stage, and there is at least one song that is particularly relevant to each stage. It is obvious that the one mentioned above is an invitation for someone to come in, and in this case it is royalty in the form of a magnificently attired queen. As expectancy grows the mood is translated into song such as:

> Wi hear about di noble queen
> Wi want fi si her here tonight
> She's fairer far than e'er was seen
> Her smile of love is sheer delight.

But the wait is long, so something must be wrong! Yes, the road is in poor condition and the song upbraiding some indeterminate person for such dereliction of duty is melodramatically rendered:

> Di queen outa door an' shi want fi come een!
> Oh where an' oh where, an' oh were has she been?
> A wha' mek yu nevva did come buil' di road
> Fi mek di queen come een?

There are only slight pauses in the dancing and as the royal personage makes her way with steps meticulously rehearsed and faultlessly reproduced, another change in song takes place:

> Wi come fi greet mi queen
> To see her lovely face
> The fairest ever seen
> Within this noble place.

And so it goes on until the sparkling climax—the unveiling of the queen. What follows, though anticlimactic, is greatly relished by all because now Her Majesty glories in the common touch—she dances with all who crave the privilege. Then follows one of the crowning songs:

> Mi bruck so, mi bruck so wid mi queen
> Shi bruck so, shi bruck so, shi so sweet
> Shi mek each step so sure an' clean
> I now throw flowers at her feet.

Legal matters

Now we consider one of the infrequent cases of dispute among Maroons. A person complains to an officer (generally the Colonel) of differences between himself and another who, according to his story, has encroached upon his domain. He is told to attend a meeting at a certain hour on a given date. In addition, he is instructed to give information regarding this meeting to the respondent. The time arrives; the Council gathers and each side in the dispute represents its case supported by evidence from others. The matter proves to be simple in nature and is resolved easily then and there.

It could have been otherwise and then a date would be fixed for a visit to the *locus in quo* and in the early morning some members of the Council, in the presence of both contestants and other interested persons, would open the boundary as dictated by the course of justice. Against their decision there is no appeal.

Traditional medicine

As herbalists, the Maroons used to regard themselves as second to none and Maroon territory abounded, and still does, in a multiplicity of herbs with amazing curative value. The common cold could never withstand the might of a potion whose ingredients include cow-tongue, cow-foot, fresh-cut, John-charl, rat-ears, or the juice of the tre-alive (leaf-of-life). The juice from the latter is extracted after the leaf has been warmed over fire. A tablespoonful is considered a dose and it is taken warm after the addition of a small amount of salt. The *anagus* is a tree that grows only on the Long Mountain Range (as far as a study carried out in Maroon territory has shown), and its yellow-coloured bark, when chewed, produces a yellow, slightly bitter liquid. Time was when every member of every family would keep his/her own piece of *anagus bark* at home against an attack of the common cold. It would be chewed, the juice swallowed and relief would be guaranteed within a short while.

The *penguin*, a modified leaf bearing a close resemblance to that of the pineapple, if boiled and drunk reputedly acts as a diuretic. Red *water-grass*, cow-tongue and *cigya-bush* in combination can work wonders against high blood pressure. The water blown from the stem of the *cutting-grass* undoubtedly relieves minor injury to the eyes. The *hog-gum* or *bo-gum*, the resin from the tree of the same name, is used to cure cuts and bad bruises. For more serious wounds, the *nutmeg* is chewed to a smooth paste and placed thereon until healing is effected. It is not too much to say that this cure borders on the miraculous. And here is a cure whose illogicality towers high over Everest; yet it works on almost every occasion: for a headache the older Maroon takes a length of vine known as hog-meat, on which he makes an odd number of tight knots then ties it tightly around his forehead. Within a short while thereafter, the main problem bids him farewell.

For stubborn old sores, there was an infallible cure: certain quantities of snake root, junction root and camomile flowers were boiled together, and when the liquid cooled it was strained and a small and critical amount of potash added. The patient would take this over a two- or three-week period, but immediately before and after his doses, he would also take an obligatory large dose of salt physic (Epsom salts). The patient was forbidden to take table salt during the treatment. However, because of the potential danger in the use of the potash if the patient were careless, in the majority of cases an inert substitute was used and the salt physic would be unnecessary.

The snake-weed, an amazing weed with a remarkable history, was used as the base for many cures. The story goes that among snakes there was one that effected cures to the others and was consequently called the *doctor snake* by the Maroons. Long ago, it is said, two "dancermen" hid themselves and watched as the *doctor* made his way to a *patient*. They killed the *doctor* and took the weed it was carrying in its mouth. This weed they named *snake-weed*.

Cupping

At times, as a result of a hard blow or for other reasons, the knee or some other part of the body may become greatly swollen and painful. When various embrocations fail to relieve the situation a last resort, *cupping* (a procedure that never fails) is employed: A small, round calabash (called *packie* by the Maroons) of about two inches in diameter is obtained, and a hole the size of a ten-cent piece is made at a point regarded as the highest above the imaginary circle enclosing it. It is thoroughly cleaned and has now become a *cup*. Next, a tablespoon of white proof rum is poured in it; a small portion of the affected part of the patient is held between thumb and forefinger, a tiny incision is made on the swelling and the rum is set alight. After a few seconds, the cup is set over the incision. It "holds on" by suction efect, until filled with the extracted putrescent matter and relief is often instantaneous. This describes an actual operation some years ago, and those few persons who were afraid of the operation would resort to vesicants, and in particular one known as *blister*. A portion of the unfolding heart-leaf of a french-plantain was warmed over a fire and *blister* feathered evenly over it. The affected area was then bandaged securely with this heart-leaf which was removed after a few days and the resulting vescicles pricked to release the contents.

Manners in the Maroon community

The standard of good manners and respect for others among the Maroons, particularly elders, was once so high that it is safe to say that it could not have been better in any part of the world. Even a simple, innocuous word such as "damn" would not be used by adults in the presence of their elders, and whistling was similarly frowned upon. Admittedly, it can be argued that there was a touch of severity to the whole matter, for neither a man nor his wife was totally insulated against a thorough spanking by any of their parents. Further, even faultless behaviour could not be regarded as an infallible assurance of immunity, since the parents' perception of excellence or its opposite, in a particular instance, could be at fault. If successive administrations (governments of Jamaica) since the 1970s had coupled this fact with the highly developed sense of unity and cooperation obtaining among the Maroons, and used the amalgam as the standard for an all-Jamaica behavioural pattern, one could be reasonably assured that the entire country would have been enriched culturally, economically, psychologically and spiritually. The citizens of Jamaica would be, for the most part, men and women of goodwill.

The story of my ancestors is a long one and one cannot say everything in so small a space. But it must be concluded that today the Maroons continue to be made of one equal temper of heroic hearts which cherish the achievements of those ancestors who shed blood and laid down their lives that Jamaica may one day have true freedom.

 *three*

The Heritage of Accompong Maroons

Col. Martin-Luther Wright

Introduction

The true traditions of Maroons of Accompong and other areas in western Jamaica trace their ancestry to Arawak Indians, whom Christopher Columbus found in Jamaica on his voyage to the island and Africans, who escaped both Spanish and English domination to establish independent communities. The Arawak Indians have been described as being of brown complexion, short in stature, thick bodied, with flat noses and loose hair. Early estimates indicate that there were approximately 1,000 free men and women living on the island. The Spaniards enslaved them, used them to develop their sugar cane farms and ill-treated them very severely. They rebelled, escaped and took to the hills of Clarendon where they organized themselves and fought fearlessly to maintain their freedom and dignity.

The Maroons of Accompong consider themselves, and very proudly too, as the first real, living freedom fighters in the New World. Some of the famous known and recorded leaders included Kojo, Accompong, Johnnie, Cuffie, Quao and Nanny. On several occasions the entire English regiment suffered serious defeats, and as happened near the Peace Cave on Maroon soil near Old Accompong Town, an entire British regiment was destroyed. In the end, the English asked for peace, the first treaty having been signed in March 1739. The result of these treaties was to make the Maroons of Jamaica a free, independent self-governing group of people. This status we maintain to the present day. Thus the name Maroon means a group or groups of people who resisted European slavery, defeated the colonial forces and gained for themselves everlasting freedom. The true Maroon is the one who is committed to this ancestry and spirit of freedom from any kind of slavery and the preservation of human dignity and self-respect. All Maroons of Accompong and other Maroon communities of Jamaica are proud to be associated with this principle.

The most important thing about the history of the Maroons generally is the fact of their firm stand against slavery, oppression and maltreatment by money-hungry colonialist European countries. Even as late as the nineteenth century when there was a general international outcry against slavery and the slave trade, evidence exists that demonstrated the mentality of Europeans against blacks and particularly my ancestors who openly fought against slavery.[1]

Accompong territory

Accompong is surrounded by Simon Hill on the west (Mahogany Hill behind Simon Hill is also part of Accompong); Manchester Hill to the north-west, Jobo and Copeland Hills in the north. It is said that Simon Hill is the burial place of the head of the wicked Quancoo, who murdered any male born in that area. Owing to his wicked acts, a plot to get rid of him from the society ended in his death. His head was cut off and buried in Simon Hill. The rest of Quancoo's body is said to have been buried with those of other Maroons in the general burial ground on the way to the burial site of Colonel Kojo, who is one of the greatest resistance leaders against the military-plantation governments which followed the arrival of the English in Jamaica. The original Accompong Town grew out of the fortified Maroon outpost established around the end of the seventeenth century, owing to the demands of the major wars between the Maroons and the British. It was established by Accompong at the direction of Kojo.

Today, Accompong consists of several quarters that appear to represent congregations of related family units residing in different quarters of the town. It is not clear whether these units were established at the initial stages of the founding of the town. Information is that these quarters do not follow any predetermined family relationships. These quarters are: Hill Top, Parade, Middle Ground, Over Yonder, Gipson, Guinea Grass, Pondside, Cedar Valley, River Hole, River Pond and Out Yonder.

There are some important sites in and around Accompong Town (Fig. 3.1).[2] The first one is called "Kindah", meaning "We are a family". This site is located just outside Accompong Town to the north-east. It is the place of the annual anniversary celebrations of the peace treaty. It is said to have been the base for consultations for Maroon leaders during their wars against the British forces. Kojo's burial ground, the place where annual offering should be made to the spirits of Kojo and other famous ancestors, is located in a fairly level spot about half a kilometre down a rugged slope north-east from Kindah. That place was the site of Old Accompong

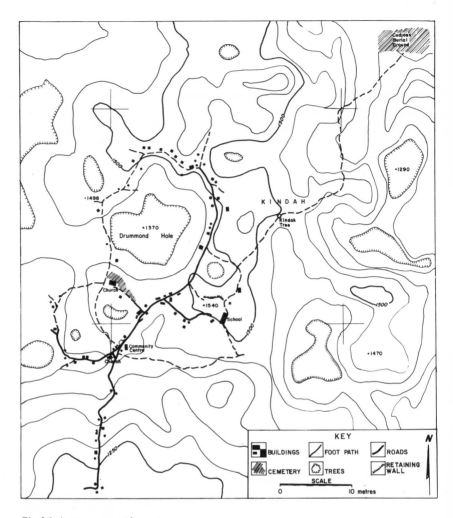

Fig. 3.1 Accompong settlement

Town simply referred to as "Old Town" or more popularly "Amphrey Town" (Humphrey Town). Almost on the eastern border of Accompong Maroon lands is the cave which was used as a spying base by the Maroons as it was the closest convenient location to the opponent's military base situated in the then Aberdeen plantation. This cave is also referred to as "Ambush". It has suffered over the years from environmental damage and appears to have lost its original appearance and features that indicate its importance to the Maroons in the days of struggle. Another location of importance is the Pette River Bottom which featured as the last battleground of the wars between the Maroons and the English forces before the peace treaty. Associated with this location is what has been mentioned in the records as "Guthrie's defile".[3]

The peace treaty

After the peace treaty the population gradually shifted away from Old Accompong Town to its modern location, perched high up in the mountains of St Elizabeth in western Jamaica bordering the parishes of St James and Trelawny. The people of Accompong make up a "nation within a nation" of the island of Jamaica and live on lands granted under the treaty. They continue to practise and enjoy the traditional customs handed down by our Amerindian and, particularly, African guerrilla ancestors.

The people of Accompong are law abiding and trustworthy. The special name we use for ourselves is "Mighty friend", and indeed a Maroon is the best friend one can have. The land of the settlement is communally owned. A deep sense of belonging to a family prevails in this Town. One significant item that identifies Accompong as a free nation is the peace treaty of 1739. Part of it reads:[4]

> "In the name of God, Amen.
>
> Whereas Captain Cudjoe, Accompong, Johnny, Cuffee, Quaco, and several other negroes, their dependents and adherents, have been in war and hostility for several years in the past, King George the second by letters and patent dated twenty-fourth February, One Thousand Seven Hundred and Thirty-Eight granted full powers and authority to John Guthrie, Francis Saddler, Esquires, to negotiate and finally conclude a treaty of peace and friendship with the aforesaid Captain Cudjoe, and the rest of his captains, adherents and others of his men; they mutually, sincerely, and amicably have agreed to the following articles:
>
> Firstly, That all hostilities shall cease on both sides forever.
>
> Secondly, That the said Captain Cudjoe, the rest of his Captains, adherents and men shall be forever hereafter in perfect state of freedom and liberty ...
>
> Thirdly, That they shall enjoy and possess, for themselves and posterity forever, all lands situate and lying between Trelawny Town and the Cockpits, to the amount of fifteen hundred acres, bearing northwest from the said Trelawny Town.
>
> Fourthly, That they shall have liberty to plant the said lands with coffee, cocoa, ginger, tobacco and cotton and to breed cattle, hogs, goats, or any other stock, and dispose of the produce or increase of the said commodities to the inhabitants of this island, provided always, that when they bring the said commodities to market, they shall apply first to the custos, or any other magistrate of the respective parishes where they expose their goods for sale, for licence to vend the same.
>
> Fifthly, That Captain Cudjoe, and all the Captains, adherents, and people now in subjection to him, shall live together within the bounds of Trelawny Town, and that they have liberty to hunt where they shall think fit, except within three miles of any settlement, kraal or pen, provided always, that in case the hunters of Captain Cudjoe and those of other settlements meet, then the hogs to be equally divided between both parties ... "

The Colonel is the chief leader of the town and is elected every five years by a poll of ballots. He administers through a council of thirty-two members of men and women appointed by him. Currently, there are seven female members on the Council. In ancient times, the Chief of Accompong Maroons was elected for life. However, recently, in order to curb disputes that often arose during change-over of the leadership, the term of service has now been fixed at four. The leader at all times commands the respect of each Maroon and receives the support for all authorized activities.

Annual festival

The greatest community event is the festival which is held every January to celebrate Kojo's victory over the British which led to the treaty. This festival is planned to coincide with Kojo's birthday and celebrates Kojo's remarkable leadership and the sacrifice he made fighting for his people in this wild, rugged Cockpit country for so many long, dreary years. The celebrations also remind all Maroons of the hard days of the struggle to maintain their freedom. Maroons reunite in their dedication to stand firm on their traditional values for freedom, liberty and respect for human dignity.

Thousands of people from all walks of life, Jamaicans and foreigners alike, converge on Accompong during the celebrations. The celebrations begin early in the day, but at around mid-morning, with the sound of the *abeng* (the side-blown horn), the Maroon war horn which has been in use in Jamaica for three centuries, the formal start of the festivities is announced. The *abeng* is made from the horns of cattle and at full blast it can be heard clearly over a distance of approximately fifteen kilometres and is one of the traditions that our ancestors brought from Africa where it is also still in use as a means of message communication. This horn was used to communicate messages between Maroon communities. It calls Maroons to assembly and to contribute to Maroon funerals. It played and still plays a major role in many other Maroon celebrations. The *abeng* message is incomprehensible to non-Maroons. On celebration day there is much feasting, selling of various types of goods, the telling of folk tales and oral history sessions are held throughout the day. The highlight of the festivity is the re-enactment of the war dances and treaty songs of the Accompong Maroons. The Colonel of the Town leads the march or procession to the tune of para-military and military songs such as: "Clear road ooo, all the force a como oo, clear the road ooo . . ." as the ancestral spirits are intoned to clear the road so that all the ancient Maroon leader's spirits may be intoned to clear the path of the procession. There are sacred and public ceremonies which build up a colourful fiesta of dances, songs and chants and ends with the celebration day performances at the centre of Accompong town where a monument to Kojo is located.

Ritual on "sacred grounds"

There are usually four major parts to the celebrations. Firstly there is prolonged chanting, singing and dancing in traditional Maroon style in preparation for the visit to the sacred grounds and the grave of Kojo, Accompong and other past Maroon leaders. Secondly, there is the visit to the sacred grounds and at which only full-blooded male Maroons are allowed on the day of the celebration. Next is the return march to the Kindah Tree where the ritual food is prepared by specially selected Maroon men assisted by elderly female Maroons. Finally, there is the march to and along the main roads of Accompong.

It is during the preparation for the visit to the sacred grounds, that the sprinkling of the sacred grounds with rum and the pouring of libation takes place. During that time there is preparation of the food to be carried to feed the spirits of the Maroon heroes. The food includes pork as the meat and boiled yam. At the graves of the heroes, in addition to pouring libation (which among the Accompong Maroons is basically the sprinkling of rum over the sacred grounds) food is thrown around the area. A tense moment comes at the place when the visiting Maroons must have a period of spiritual communication with their ancestors but must be preceded by a long period of silence and meditation — what among them is referred to as a "reasoning session". The return to the Kindah Tree is made by following what is known as the "Old Town path".

Ambush

One of the features of the march is that many of the Maroons are clad in leaves and branches of trees, a reminder that in the olden days of the wars, greenery was prepared and used as camouflage so that on the battlefront each Maroon warrior appeared like nothing more than a clump of bush. Often non-Maroons and especially those who are not conversant with Maroon culture, make the serious error of referring to the dances performed at the celebrations as "ambush dance". There is nothing known as "ambush dance" in Maroon culture. Surprise was the main element in the use of the camouflage and there would have been no reason for the Maroons to have practised a dance in the course of the action they were taking. The term "ambush" refers specifically to the camouflage which was responsible for the dramatic military successes of the Maroons against the British. The Peace Cave is also referred to as "ambush" also, because it was one of the most strategic places for laying ambush to surprise the British forces.

Most of the earlier parts of the celebration, particularly the morning activities such as the slaughter of the sacrificial animals and libations, are centred at the "Kindah Tree" mentioned above. There are strict regulations about the rituals related to the festival. For example, only male Maroons are allowed to enter the Kojo burial spot and the Peace Cave on celebration day. At those places there are certain secret ceremonies that, by tradition, are limited to a certain Maroons of the community. However, other members of the Maroon community, non-Maroon visitors or tourists, are allowed at those two sites on any other day of the year. In the past one hundred years or more, Maroons would only marry to Maroons, but today there is a lot of inter-marriage and once a Maroon marriage ceremony to a non-Maroon is performed that non-Maroon is accepted into the Maroon family. It is during the last part of the celebrations that Accompong people get to meet and know members of their families, beyond those of the Maroon community itself.

Many of the songs of the Accompong Maroons were composed by the ancient Maroons in their struggle for freedom, their victory over the English, their dances and the special plays performed at "nine nights". One of the songs which consists of one line is: "Dis a ya, o, a fi mi yard, oo". Another is: "Walk in de, o, walk in a yard".

The last part of the celebrations take place in the modern Accompong Town at the monument erected in honour of Kojo. That is the part of the celebrations in which Maroon and non-Maroon come in contact and share in the merry-making. Traditional Maroon food, rum, Maroon traditional gumbey drumming, music and dance as well as family re-unions—all against the backdrop of the achievements of the past—are the order of the day. The *abeng* sounds from time to time, sending messages to the Maroons and all who can understand. In recent years, the practice has been to invite a distinguished personality to grace the occasion and thus represent the extension of goodwill to the larger Jamaican and international public.

Past Accompong Chiefs

Since Kojo, the leadership of Accompong has been held by males. The following persons have served as Colonel in Accompong in that order, some serving for two terms: Kojo (Cudjoe), Accompong, Austin, White, T. Crosse, H. D. Rowe, R. J. McLeod, K. T. Wright, H. E. Wright, H. R. Rowe, W. I. Robertson, Isaac Myles, M.L. Wright, T. J. Cawley, W. I. Robertson, Charles Reid, H. Cawley, M. L.Wright, Meredie Rowe (current Chief).

In Accompong, it has been discovered that the surnames Wright, Rowe, Cawley and Crosse are more common to the various sections into which the community is divided. It is also obvious that at least one member of these families, although they were related, was made Chief at some point in time. The fact that they were also related shows that there was a strong tendency towards a kinship-based network or that leadership rested with dominant family groups. In Accompong, women are very active in other aspects of organizations in the settlement. The main political body is the Council, which at the moment consists of thirty-two members, seven of whom are women.

There are five churches in Accompong today (compared to one in 1738), namely, Church of Jamaica and Grand Cayman, Church of God International, Assembly of God, Zion Church (of African origin, otherwise called Pocomanic) and the Seventh Day Baptist Church. All the ministers of these churches live outside of Accompong, but there are local preachers who do the church services in the ministers' absence.

Traditional medicine

Traditional medicine in the form of herbal tonics, mixtures, herbal tea, baths and similar types of medicines are locally available and provided by traditional herbalists as well as some spiritual leaders, particularly women who are either born with those powers or have been specially trained. Roots and barks of trees are used for making drinks of all kinds, some of which are medicinal.

The future

Although local politics have created problems for Maroons of Accompong, there is still that feeling of solidarity and unity. The important thing is one's Maroon identity and a common will to continue to honour the fight for freedom and self-respect. Maroons of Accompong all respect their brothers and sisters of Jamaica and are willing to share their cultural traditions and achievements in all their forms, but in as far as it is not tantamount to being slaves, servants or subjects of any other people. The allegiance of Maroons of Accompong is to the people of Jamaica.[5]

Notes

1 S.A.G. Taylor, "The Diary of Sir Henry de la Beche", *Jamaica Historical Society Bulletin* III, no. 4: 54-56.

2 Map used courtesy of the University of the West Indies Mona Archaeological Research Project [Agorsah 1992, 1993].

3 Alan Eyre, "The Maroon Wars in Jamaica: A Geographical Appraisal", *The Jamaican Historical Review* XII (1980): 5-19.

4 B. Edwards, *The History of the West Indies* (London, 1819).

5 Several publications have been made on the Accompong Maroons: B. Kopytoff, *The Maroons of Jamaica: An Ethnohistorical Study of Incomplete Polities*, 1655-1905 [1973]; C.Robinson, *The Fighting Maroons of Jamaica* [1969]; M.Campbell, *The Maroons of Jamaica* [1990], and Dallas, *The History of the Maroons* [1803]. The interpretations may not represent the true picture of Maroon culture, but these could be used as a guide towards more search and research. Our traditions are rich and we are proud to tell people about them. Unfortunately, some classified details cannot be told without the permission of the entire Council acting and deciding together on the particular issue. Even these details we are glad to share.

four

Maroon Culture as a Distinct Variant of Jamaican Culture

Kenneth Bilby

Introduction

The year 1992 has multiple global significance. For the Americas as a whole, it symbolizes five centuries of transformation and struggle since Columbus' first voyage. For Jamaica, it represents three decades of independent nationhood. And, for those Jamaicans called Maroons, it marks the 150th anniversary of a now-forgotten piece of legislation aimed at their total obliteration, the so-called Maroon Lands Allotment Act of 1842.

If the nineteenth century colonial lawmakers who drafted this Act had their way, the treaties signed by the British and the Maroons slightly more than a century earlier, would have been done away with and erased from memory. In turn, the Maroons' communal lands would have been divided and parceled out. And, as a result, the Maroons themselves would have vanished through a rapid process of social and cultural assimilation into the Jamaican peasantry. But this was not to happen and the Maroons are still with us today.[1]

Most Jamaicans today know the Maroons only as larger-than-life figures in history books. Those who know that communities of Maroons still exist often assume that these surviving descendants of the original rebels have by now become culturally indistinguishable from the rest of the population, even if some of them still claim a separate identity. According to this point of view, the name *Maroon* is today little more than a quaint label to which a few Jamaicans, though they are in fact no longer any different from others, stubbornly and proudly continue to cling. At the opposite extreme are those who imagine the Maroon communities as isolated, "primitive" enclaves where a mythically "pure" African culture yet flourishes. Needless to say, both of these images are far from accurate.

Much of the more serious literature on modern Jamaican Maroons has focused either on the continuing significance of the 1739 treaties, or the unique systems of communal land tenure that persist to this day in Maroon communities.[2] Both the treaties and the treaty lands have undeniably played, and continue to play, an important part in the ethnic self-definition of Maroons. There are also a few surviving items of material culture that are found only in Maroon communities, such as the abeng and certain kinds of drums. These, too, are sometimes treated as markers of identity. But there is another dimension of Maroon identity, one that has received less attention, though it is equally important. I am referring here to that intangible part of culture that exists in the mind.

In this intangible domain, which includes such aspects of culture as worldview, language, music, dance and historical consciousness, substantial numbers of Maroons have retained a clearly distinct intimate culture—a sacred body of cultural knowledge handed down directly from their ancestors. It is precisely this non-material realm that is least accessible to non-Maroons, for Maroons have long, and for good reason, hidden its contents from outsiders. This helps to explain why so little has been written about these intangible aspects of Maroon culture and why some, who otherwise know a good deal about Maroons, still believe that the inhabitants of Moore Town, Charles Town, Scott's Hall and Accompong have been severed from their past and retain nothing more than a few insignificant vestiges of Maroon culture.

In this chapter, a few of the ways in which Maroons have remained culturally distinct are examined, in order to illustrate the validity of the above statements. In doing so, one cannot avoid treading on sensitive ground, for several of the aspects of culture discussed below are not normally discussed in the presence of outsiders. Indeed, there are strong sanctions against speaking about some of these matters to non-Maroons. They are discussed here, only after having acquired permission to do so from the individual Maroon teachers who slowly and guardedly imparted this knowledge to me. Only by probing certain intimate aspects of the Maroons' culture can it be shown that they have a present-day cultural heritage of their own, one which extends beyond colonial treaties, land rights and questions of political autonomy into less visible areas.

The examples which follow are drawn from the three eastern Maroon communities—particularly Moore Town—where I spent more than a year carrying out research in the late 1970s.[3] It should be borne in mind that the western Maroon community of Accompong differs in substantial ways from the eastern ones; therefore some of the statements made below may not apply there.

In the final section of the paper, I will place the material presented below in historical context and briefly discuss the processes of cultural divergence, decreolization and reconvergence, which have produced the layered complexity of present-day Maroon culture. Drawing comparisons with Suriname, where present-day Maroons also remain a minority group within a larger Afro-Caribbean society, I will argue that the distinctive Jamaican Maroon culture that has survived to the present must be seen as a special variant of Jamaican culture.

Historical consciousness and descent

Contemporary Jamaican Maroons remain linked to their past through a large body of oral historical traditions that over the centuries have been kept within their own communities. Even today these traditions are not usually shared with outsiders. Indeed, some of them are not known to the majority of Maroons since they have been passed on by specialists to a select few. Other such traditions, however, are part of general knowledge within the Maroon communities—at least among older people.

The eastern Maroons, in particular, possess an abundance of oral traditions concerning the great Maroon leader, Nanny. Although Maroons are proud that Nanny has been made a Jamaican National Hero, their appreciation of her historical importance does not derive from the government's "canonization" of her in 1977. On the contrary, Nanny has been a powerful, living presence for Maroons for more than two centuries. Grandy Nanny, as she is known to Maroons themselves, is not only their queen, but their "mother", and present-day eastern Maroons are her "children". In a way reminiscent of the founding mothers of clans and lineages among the matrilineal Akan-speaking societies of West Africa, Grandy Nanny is an apical ancestress. It is only because of their ostensible common descent from her that all eastern Maroons, even those who cannot trace any actual blood relationships between one another, are said to belong to a single "family".

Members of this large, clan-like family refer to themselves as *yoyo*, a Maroon word denoting "children", "progeny", or "generation". In the eastern communities, to be a Maroon is to be one of Grandy Nanny's "yoyo". In fact, the word *yoyo* itself has become an in-group term of ethnic identification equivalent in meaning to the word *Maroon*. One Maroon elder recently described the meaning of the word *yoyo* to me as follows: "We is Grandy Nanny 'yoyo', him children; him race of family dem; Grandy Nanny family dem; him seh him 'yoyo' dem, call we him 'yoyo' . . . mean to seh him family dem" [Kent, 4 February 1991].

Another put it this way: ". . . dat 'yoyo' deh now, Grandy Nanny statement now seh, 'a pikibo' . . . A him yoyo him a talk now, you know. . .Grandy Nanny yoyo a we today. You see? . . . Dere is another word fi de 'yoyo'. We now a 'pikibo'. When we seh 'pikibo' dat mean to seh we come like him grandchildren dem . . . we weh left . . . we call weself 'yoyo'" [Comfort Castle, 2 February 1991].

Consciousness of the Maroon past, which forms an important part of the collective identity of present-day Maroons, is intimately bound up with this notion of descent from Nanny.[4] While the exploits of other legendary early Maroons are also commemorated in historical narratives, it is Grandy Nanny who receives the most attention in discussions of the Maroon past. Indeed, the centrality of

Nanny is powerfully illustrated by oral traditions that relate how, during the early days of war with the British, all the Maroon military leaders came together, pooled their spiritual resources and decided to invest their powers in the person of Nanny. While she was still a girl or young woman, the story goes, the most powerful men "groomed" or trained her for the role of queen. Each then transferred a portion of his own powers to her and submitted himself to her authority, making her the central spiritual beacon through whom their collective powers would from then on radiate.

Here are a few examples of this oral tradition, which I have extracted from longer narratives that I recorded on tape. I have left them in the words of the four different Maroons who related them to me:

> "Grandy Nanny never got no man deh . . . A seven brother him got. And de seven of dem deh wid him. De seven a dem a seven obeah man. Learn dat. De seven a dem a seven obeah man. When de white people dem deh fool round dem, dem tek everything off a dem, put pon dem sister" [Comfort Castle, 3 February 1991].

Also:

> "Nanny was a little girl. Dem raise him up as a miss (i.e. as a virgin). A him a de fighter . . . dat mean to seh him no have no dealing wid no man or nothing. Is a girl. And dem train her up. Him put before, as a warrior. You understand. So dat all dem fighting now, whatever dem doing, dem have him before. Dem groom him, and put him before. And dem deh behind" [Moore Town, 30 January 1991].

Another statement was:

> "Grandy Nanny was the queen of the Maroons. All the tribes of the Maroons, they made Grandy Nanny a queen. They crown her queen, and scientifically, they wawatu her . . . In other words, they crowned her. Wawatu is to honour. We honoured her. Wawatu. We honoured her you see? and make her a queen, a queen fi Maroon. So I will impart some of my science to her, you will part some, all these science people part their influence and their knowledge to her. So she's full of wisdom. So she becomes the queen" [Comfort Castle, 3 February, 1991].

Finally:

> ". . . dem put Grandy, trim Grandy, as queen, and put up deh. Dat four man weh min a fight de war, dem trim Grandy and put out dem toe fi dem queen. Truly, truly. Dem put him out deh and show . . . De bakra got a woman sitting fi dem. Dem have a woman who stand fi dem too, as de Maroon" [Moore Town, 25 June 1978].

It is in the context of the ceremony known as Kromanti *Play* that much of what remains distinctively Maroon, in world view, language and music has been fostered and maintained.[5] Only the *yoyo*, descendants, and spiritual heirs of Grandy Nanny can practise the true Kromanti rites and tap the powers of the early Maroons—those who made Nanny their queen. Except on certain rare occasions, outsiders are excluded from serious Kromanti ceremonies—which is to say those dances during which ancestors manifest themselves and communicate through the living.

Although the majority of Maroons no longer participate regularly in Kromanti Play, a few specialists can still be relied upon to summon the ancestral powers in times of need. These ritual specialists, known as *fete-man* or *fete-woman*, keep open the line to Nanny and the other ancestors. As recently as the first few decades of this century, Grandy Nanny was still "visiting" and counselling her *yoyo* on a regular basis through a *fete-woman* in Moore Town who was but the most recent in a long line of communicators for the spirit of this founding ancestress.

Maroon language

Well into this century, some older Maroons still spoke, as their native tongue, a distinctive creole language that differed from the language of other rural Jamaicans, yet was closely related to it. Today, a few Maroon elders retain partial competence in this language and although it is seldom heard in everyday speech, it sometimes surfaces in story-telling contexts or in oral historical narratives. While grammatically very close to the Jamaican creole, or "patois", spoken throughout the island, it differs dramatically in its phonology, and to a lesser extent, its vocabulary.[6] Recent studies [Bilby 1983] point to a direct historical link between this distinct Jamaican Maroon creole and the creole languages of Suriname, including those spoken by contemporary Maroon peoples such as the Saramaka and Ndjuka. The evidence suggests that the influx of slaves from the former British colony of Suriname to Jamaica in the later seventeenth century had a major influence on the development of this unique variant of Jamaican creole. Some linguists have even classified this Jamaican Maroon language as an offshoot of a Suriname proto-creole, rather than assign it to the western Caribbean branch of the English-lexicon Caribbean creoles, to which Jamaican creole belongs.[7] I offer here a few examples of sentences and phrases in this language. For comparison, I follow each example with its equivalent in Ndjuka Tongo, a creole language spoken by Maroons living today in the interior of Suriname and French Guiana:

1. Jamaican Maroon: *Al di sonti wi piik ina wi prandes, yu kya in go de bak a hogi pre. Bot go fring bak a u pre.*

   Ndjuka Maroon: *Ala san wi taki a ini wi paandasi, yu tja en go de baka na ogi pe. Ma go fiingi baka na yu peesi.*

   Meaning: *"Everything we said in our home, you brought it back to a dangerous place. But go and throw it back in your own place".*

2. Jamaican Maroon: *Yu muma se yu sa woko fi bigi moni.*

   Ndjuka Maroon: *Yu mama taki yu sa wooko fu bigi moni.*

   Meaning: *"Your mother said you could work for a lot of money".*

3. Jamaican Maroon: *Ebiba na wan suma. So kaal dem. Akisi dem onti mi e se.*

   Ndjuka Maroon: *Ala na wan sama. So kali den. Akisi den san mi e taki.*

   Meaning: *"All are one. So call them . . . Ask them what I'm saying".*

Hundreds more such examples could be offered. It is also worth noting that aside from the large number of isolated African-derived Kromanti terms that have been integrated into this Maroon creole, there are a number of English-derived vocabulary items that are found nowhere else in Jamaica, but which are very close to equivalent Surinamese forms. The following are but a few of the examples that could be provided:

Jamaican Maroon *arik* or *ariki* versus Ndjuka Maroon *aliki*, both meaning "to listen"; Jamaican Maroon *onti* versus Ndjuka *ondi*, one meaning "what" and the other "which"; Jamaican Maroon *yezi* versus Ndjuka *yesi*, both meaning "ear"; Jamaican Maroon *prandes*, meaning "home" or "yard", which in Sranan, the creole language of coastal Suriname, is *prandasi*; and *suma*, which in both the Jamaican Maroon creole and Sranan means "person".

Jamaican Maroons rarely use this old form in ordinary contexts nowadays and in fact, even among the elders, few can claim even partial command of it. Over the years it has gradually been displaced by the language spoken in neighbouring areas, through a process of decreolization. Today the language of everyday communication among Maroons is a version of Jamaican creole virtually indistinguishable from that spoken in other parts of the country, varying along the same kind of post-creole speech continuum found elsewhere. Yet the old Maroon creole is not dead. The one context in which it comes into its own is the ceremony of Kromanti *Play*. For when the spirits of ancestors manifest themselves on living mediums and communicate through their mouths, this is invariably the language they use. Quite naturally, they express themselves in their native tongue, the language they knew when they were alive.

The other distinct form of language retained by eastern Maroons, one which has received more attention from researchers, is the esoteric language known as Kromanti. Kromanti is different from the old Maroon creole described above. Most of its vocabulary is derived, not from English, but from African languages. The Akan language-group of West Africa appears to be the main source, but several other African languages have contributed as well.[8]

Knowledge of Kromanti varies greatly from one individual to the next. Some Maroons can provide English glosses for a large number of words and expressions and can communicate a wide variety of messages with Kromanti, while others—the majority—know only a few words. To my knowledge, no Maroon alive retains Kromanti as a fully functioning language capable of expressing an unlimited number of ideas. Ritual specialists tend to know more than others. But if the semantic load of certain words and phrases has been lost entirely, their invocational power has not diminished as a result.

In ceremonial contexts, Kromanti functions much like a liturgical language. Many Maroons are still capable of "cutting country", as they call it—that is, reciting lengthy streams of more-or-less standardized, formulaic Kromanti, as a means of drawing on ancestral powers. Here is an example, excerpted from a tape recording of a man from Moore Town "cutting country". Such recitations can go on for several minutes without interruption: "O fantan du, o werewu nanti, o pikibo dinkamadi . . . o kikye ka kikye kandi kofi kofi antemesunga . . . oko bi noko noko bisani hoko bi noko noko bisani . . . hoko bi noko noko bisani, o prati mati mati baimba dinto . . . o seru mandi o bosu mandi o fantan du koro o do bidi . . . o, kikye nangka nangka nangka kome bisho o fantan do mati mati baimba dinto!" [Rivers-view, 4 September 1978].

This esoteric language is unique to Maroon communities. If investigators hoping to find traces of an African language in the eastern Maroon communities have had a hard time collecting more than a few fragments of Kromanti, it is not because it has already died out, as some have assumed, but because there are spiritual sanctions against improperly revealing it to outsiders.

Maroon music and dance

Jamaica is world famous for its rich musical culture, but the distinctive musical traditions of the Maroons remain virtually unknown outside of Maroon communities. Outsiders may continue to refer to well-known neo-African styles such as kumina as "Maroon music", but any Maroon brought up in the tradition knows otherwise. The second a Maroon drummer hears the rhythms of kumina, he identifies this music with an outside tradition.

The true music of the Maroons is that associated with Kromanti *Play*. Like the abeng language, Kromanti music is not known or played outside of Maroon areas. Each Maroon community possesses its own repertoire of Kromanti songs belonging to discrete stylistic categories, with names that can be traced to specific ethnic groups or regions in Africa, such as *Papa* (or *Prapa*), *Mandinga*, *Ibo* and Mongala.9 The drumming, songs, language and dance movements that go with these categories are not found in non-Maroon areas. A knowledgeable Maroon who hears a Kromanti song being sung off in the distance can tell not only to which stylistic category the song belongs, but which specific Maroon community the unseen singer is from; to a non-Maroon listener the same song remains indecipherable.

Maroon songs that are not found outside of the Windward Maroon communities probably number in the hundreds. Here are the words of one such song, as sung by Charles Town Maroons:

> *o jo fara liba, o jo a de*
> *o jo fara liba, o jo a de*
> *o wiri angkoma, o jo a de*
> *o jo fara liba, o jo a de*
> [Charles Town, 21 September 1978]

Slightly different versions of this same song are known in Moore Town (Portland) and Scott's Hall (St Mary) as well. Like many such songs, this one contains an emotionally potent reminder of the Maroon past. It refers to the days when British troops employed hounds to track down Maroons in the forest. The Maroons, the song recalls, adopted the survival strategy of moving along rivers, jumping from stone to stone in mid-stream causing the hounds to lose the scent.

The foregoing illustrations of Maroon distinctiveness of course represent but a tiny portion of the unique cultural heritage that has survived in Maroon communities. Although many, if not most, younger Maroons have lost touch with this heritage, it remains a living force among those elders who have patiently absorbed the lessons of the past.

Maroon culture as Jamaican culture

How does the distinct culture of Maroons fit into the larger picture of Jamaican cultural history? This complex question can be given only the briefest consideration here. A few observations might help to suggest directions for further historical research.

One basic fact can be stated at the outset: if one goes back far enough in time, the histories of Maroons and other Jamaicans of African descent converge. Not only were their ancestors brought from the same regions of Africa, but they underwent the same or similar processes of enslavement, forced adaptation to a new land and cultural creolization. Except for the few individuals who escaped into the interior immediately upon arrival and those remaining from the Spanish period, they shared the common experience of plantation slavery in a British colony and at least some exposure to the new, mixed forms of Afro-Jamaican culture emerging on the plantations. Indeed, there is evidence that before the 1739 treaties, which created a clear political and legal division between Maroons and slaves, the two communities could not really be considered separate. The boundary between Maroons and slaves remained fluid, for new escapees flowed steadily from the plantations into the rebel communities. During this period, Maroons and slaves maintained close social and economic ties and some were linked by blood ties as well.[10]

It was after the treaties of 1739 that the process of cultural divergence advanced most significantly, although it had probably begun earlier. In some cases, Maroons were able to maintain ties with slaves even after 1739, but the flow of new recruits into the interior was stemmed by the treaties and the boundaries between the Maroon communities and the plantations became much more rigid than before. Only on rare occasions could new escapees be smuggled past the watchful eyes of the colonial superintendents and successfully incorporated into the Maroon populations. The Maroon settlements became closed communities and the inhabitants acquired a separate identity based on the principle of exclusion. The boundaries of this identity were protected by a defensive rule of secrecy.

During this period the process of differentiation and dual ethnogenesis that had begun earlier accelerated. Maroons in their mountain settlements and slaves on the coastal plantations—now cut off from one another—developed parallel but distinct creole cultures which continued over the years to diverge from a common base. In both areas, African cultural forms and concepts exerted a powerful influence in the creolization process, but there was variation in the ways in which specific elements were combined, recombined and emphasized.

Geographic and demographic differences further complicated the picture and produced differing outcomes. For instance, after the treaties, Maroons remained more isolated from European cultural influences than did the slaves on the plantations. On the other hand, whereas very few if any African-born individuals were still alive among the Maroons by 1800, the slave community continued to be augmented by fresh shipments of Africans well into the nineteenth century.[11] Thus the creolization processes in the interior and on the coast were shaped by different balances of African and European cultural elements—balances which continued to shift over time.

In any event, by the latter part of the eighteenth century Maroons had developed a distinct cultural identity that clearly set them apart from slaves on the coastal plantations. This separate identity was based not only on the treaty privileges won by the Maroons and their special status as free British subjects in a slave colony, but on objective and easily discernible differences in speech, music, dance and other cultural domains.

With the finalization of emancipation in 1838, the main legal distinction between Maroons and slaves suddenly vanished. All were now free and the external barriers that had once separated the two fell away. Maroons still held on tenaciously to their treaty lands and certain private cultural institutions and traditions. But as they moved out into the wider society and mingled with the former slaves and their descendants, they were exposed, with increasing frequency, to the creole culture of the plantation, from which their own had begun to diverge more than a century before.

Over the next century the Jamaican peasantry rapidly expanded into the areas bordering the Maroon settlements. Surrounded and greatly outnumbered by their non-Maroon countrymen, the Maroons gradually became acculturated to the Afro-Jamaican mainstream. As a consequence, Maroon culture underwent a process of re-convergence; the branches of the tree that had long before separated at the trunk grew back together and merged to form a new trunk.[12] Along with the mainstream culture, Maroon culture also underwent a process of decreolization. Under the surface, however, Maroons retained much of their distinctive culture in private contexts, even after the last fully competent native speakers of Kromanti and the Maroon creole language had died out. Indeed, as we have seen, much of this distinctive cultural heritage survives to this day, as part of the Maroons' intimate culture.

Today it is difficult to tease out and trace the individual historical strands that have become intertwined in modern Maroon culture. It is clear that some cultural items shared by Maroons and other Jamaicans, such as jerk pork, were borrowed from the former by the latter. Many other instances, however, are not so clear. For example, as far back as can be remembered, Maroons, like other Jamaicans, have had a tradition of dancing Jonkonu during the Christmas season. Has this always been the case, or was this tradition borrowed from outside after emancipation? Both Maroons and Jamaicans of African descent know how to prepare the dishes known as *dokunu* and *konkonte*, which owe their names to the Twi language. Have these African-derived culinary traditions always been shared by Maroons and non-Maroons?

Both Maroons and their neighbours in the parishes of Portland and St Thomas have wake traditions known as *bangga*, as well as anansi stories displaying the same themes and characters. How long have they had these in common? A great many other cultural parallels could be cited to give an idea of the extent to which Maroon culture and the larger Jamaican culture overlap.

The point I wish to stress here, however, is that even many of those aspects of culture peculiar to Maroons belong to the same tree earlier mentioned. They stem from the same trunk, but represent branches that remained concealed and never reconverged. Maroon culture and the larger Jamaican culture must therefore be viewed as cognate, springing as they do from common roots that extend back to the early plantation experience and, ultimately, to Africa.

Today's Kromanti tradition provides a good example of this. Though uniquely Maroon, this tradition is clearly related to the myal cults that flourished on Jamaican plantations during the eighteenth century. Not only was the myal religion closely associated with slave rebellions, but it contributed to nearly every indigenous form of Jamaican religious expression existing today, including Revivalism, Convince, Kumina and others.[13] In this sense, these religious traditions and Maroon Kromanti are cousins. Likewise, Maroon music is full of references and stylistic features that with some work, I believe, can be shown to be historically related to musical traditions that were once practised by slaves on plantations islandwide. Versions of these old pan-Jamaican music and dance traditions have survived, relatively unchanged, in a few isolated pockets of the islands, and a trained ear can single out unmistakable similarities between these varieties and certain Maroon styles.

The same point can be made with regard to language. The distinctive creole once spoken by Maroons as their native language, and which is still spoken by the spirit medium in the eastern communities, is a close relative of Jamaican creole. Although the two are not entirely mutually intelligible, they are descended from a common Jamaican ancestor. In fact, the Maroon creole might actually be seen as a variety or dialect of Jamaican creole, though an especially conservative one. It is close enough so that over the years it has been assimilated to the basilectal end of the post-creole speech continuum in Maroon communities. Some older speakers are capable of subtly sliding between it and the ordinary Jamaican basilect, when wishing to emphasize their cultural distinctiveness. Indeed, nowadays the Maroon creole is heard in its older form only in the speech of a possessed medium. Even in this form it is partially intelligible to non-Maroons.

Similarly, the Maroon Kromanti language of today, though not known by other Jamaicans, is not entirely foreign to them, for its history overlaps with that of their own language. In fact, a large number of isolated Maroon Kromanti words also occur in Jamaican creole, with the same or similar meanings. More than half of the words in the vocabulary of Jamaican creole that are derived from African languages have been traced to Twi (or closely related neighbouring languages—also the main source of Maroon Kromanti.[14]

Even when emphasizing their distinctiveness as Grandy Nanny's *yoyo*—her descendants—Maroons point out that they are part of a larger family tree that also includes other Jamaicans of African descent. For according to a well-known Maroon oral tradition, Nanny had a sister who remained on a plantation and raised her children there. From these children issued the generations that remained in slavery until emancipation in the nineteenth century. Because of this, today Maroons and other Jamaicans are sometimes characterized as "two sister pikni", two first cousins. This tradition helps to explain how the culture of Maroons and that of their neighbours can be so similar in some ways, yet so different in others.[15]

The case described here is not unique to Jamaica. In the Dutch colony of Suriname, a similar process of dual ethnogenesis occurred during the seventeenth and eighteenth centuries, leaving that country with a variety of social and cultural divisions comparable to, though much more conspicuous than, that which still exists in Jamaica. Suriname was one of the few plantation colonies in the Americas where maronage and resistance to slavery were even more common and dramatic than in Jamaica. The vast inland rain forests of the Guianas, which lay beyond the reach of the coastal society, afforded the hundreds of escaped slaves who banded together in the interior and formed new societies, a degree of isolation and independence that the Jamaican Maroons never enjoyed. Even after the Dutch made peace treaties with the Ndjuka in 1760 and the Saramaka in 1762, new communities of rebels continued to spring up in remote, uninhabited areas. As a result, Suriname today is home to more than 50,000 Maroons, who belong to six separate "tribes" or ethnic groups: the Saramaka, Ndjuka, Matawai, Paramaka, Aluku and Kwinti.

Today no one in Suriname questions whether these Maroon peoples possess distinct cultural traditions. For one thing, they speak their own creole languages, Saramaccan and Ndjuka; while the former language is not intelligible to speakers of Sranan, the coastal Afro-Surinamese creole, the latter is only barely so. Not only in language, but in a great many other respects, including dress and other external aspects of their culture, the Maroons remain immediately and easily distinguishable from coast-dwelling Surinamers of African descent. In fact, the Maroon populations constitute distinct societies with separate social and political structures. In the 1970s one could still speak of the "cultural autonomy" of Maroons in Suriname. The same largely holds true today.16

At the same time, there is no doubt that Maroon cultural history is an integral part of Suriname cultural history. The process of culture-building that occurred among Surinamese Maroons owed a great deal to an earlier layer of creole culture developed on the plantations, which had itself already incorporated cultural influences from many different parts of Africa. As a result, present-day Maroon tribes all speak closely related creole languages with lexicons derived in large part from

English, and possess cultures that are very similar in their broad outlines. All tribes, for instance, are divided into structurally similar matrilineages and/or matriclans known, respectively, as *bee* and *lo*. Most of them display their own versions of the same basic variety of African-derived religious cults (which, moreover, are also found among Afro-Surinamers in certain parts of coastal Suriname).[17] One can cite, for example, the *kumanti* or *komanti* traditions of Maroons versus the non-Maroon coastal *kromanti* cult; or the *papa* and *ampuku* (or *apuku*) cults found both among Maroons and certain communities of Afro-Surinamers whose ancestors remained on coastal plantations until emancipation.

The basic affinity which can be seen to underlie the many surface differences between the cultures of Maroons and coastal Afro-Surinamers stems from their common historical origins. They are cognate cultures, branches of a single tree. In Suriname, however, unlike the case in Jamaica, these branches have not reconverged, although there is some evidence that they are beginning to grow closer together as Maroons are increasingly exposed to the Creole society and culture of the coast.[18] In a sense, the current cultural landscape of Suriname, with its culturally discrete yet related Maroon and non-Maroon populations, helps us to imagine in a general way what Jamaica itself must have looked like in past centuries.

Some general observations

That Jamaican Maroons—at least some of the—differ culturally from other Jamaicans in certain significant ways is beyond doubt. Maroon culture is multi-levelled, consisting of a number of different historical layers. As we have seen, Maroons today still possess, in addition to the larger creole culture they hold in common with other Jamaicans, their own distinct and private variant of Jamaican culture, the remnant of an older layer which diverged from the creole plantation culture long ago. The historical relationship between this old Maroon layer and the larger Afro-Jamaican culture resembles that between the cultures of Maroons and coastal Creoles in Suriname today.

It would be easy for Jamaicans, from whom this older layer of Maroon culture has remained hidden, to come to the conclusion that it no longer exists. But such a conclusion would be wrong. Maroons today do remain culturally distinct, though in a way that is thoroughly Jamaican. Like their beloved ancestress, Nanny, and the traditions surrounding her, this distinct variant of Jamaican culture belongs first and foremost to the Maroons themselves, but it also forms part of the national cultural heritage—the memory of which deserves to be preserved for posterity.

Notes

1 The Maroons Lands Allotment Act is discussed in detail in Barbara Kopytoff, "The Maroons of Jamaica: An Ethnohistorical Study of Incomplete Polities, 1655-1905" (Ph.D. diss., University of Pennsylvania, 1973), 270-83.

2 See, for instance, Barbara Kopytoff, "Colonial Treaty as Sacred Charter of the Jamaican Maroons", *Ethnohistory* 26 (1979): 45-64; Leann Thomas Martin, "Maroon Identity: Processes of Persistence in Moore Town" (Ph.D. diss., University of California, 1973); David Barker and Balfour Spence, "Afro-Caribbean Agriculture: A Jamaican Maroon Community in Transition", *The Geographical Journal* 154 (1988): 198-208.

3 The results of this research may be found in Kenneth M. Bilby's "Partisan Spirits: Ritual Interaction and Maroon Identity in Eastern Jamaica" (M.A. thesis, Wesleyan University, 1979) and a number of subsequent publications.

4 Further discussion of the tradition of descent from Nanny can be found in Kenneth Bilby and Filomina Chioma Steady, "Black Women and Survival: A Maroon Case", in *The Black Woman Cross-Culturally*, edited by Filomina Chioma Steady (Cambridge, MA: Schenkman, 1981), 451-67; Kenneth Bilby, "'Two Sister Pikni': A Historical Tradition of Dual Ethnogenesis in Eastern Jamaica", *Caribbean Quarterly* 30, nos. 3 & 4 (1984): 10-25. A sensitive treatment of Nanny's importance to present-day Maroons, making some use of oral traditions, is to be found in Kamau Brathwaite's *Wars of Respect* (Kingston: Agency for Public Information, 1977).

5 For further background on Kromanti *Play*, see Kenneth Bilby, "The Kromanti Dance of the Windward Maroons of Jamaica", *Nieuwe West-Indische Gids* 55 (1981): 52-100.

6 Kenneth Bilby, "How the 'Older Heads' Talk: A Jamaican Maroon Spirit Possession Language and Its Relationship to the Creoles of Suriname and Sierra Leone", *New West Indian Guide* 57 (1983): 49-101.

7 Norval Smith, "The Epithetic Vowel in the Jamaican Maroon Spirit Possession Language Compared with that in the Suriname Creoles", *Amsterdam Creole Studies* 44 (1984): 13-19; Norval Smith, "The Genesis of the Creole Languages of Suriname" (Ph.D diss., University of Amsterdam, 1987); Ian Hancock, "A Preliminary Classification of the Anglophone Atlantic Creoles with Syntactic Data from Thirty-Three Representative Dialects", in *Pidgin and Creole Languages: Essays in Memory of John E. Reinecke*, ed. Glenn G. Gilbert (Honolulu: University of Hawaii Press, 1987), 324-25.

8 David Dalby, "Ashanti Survivals in the Language and Traditions of the Windward Maroons of Jamaica", *African Language Studies* 12 (1971): 31-51; Mervyn Alleyne, *Roots of Jamaican Culture* (London: Pluto Press, 1988), 123-30.

9 Kenneth Bilby, "Music of the Maroons of Jamaica", Pamphlet accompanying LP disc FE 4027 (New York: Folkways Records and Service Corporation, 1981); Bilby, "The Kromanti Dance", op. cit., 74-76.

10 Mavis Campbell, *The Maroons of Jamaica 1655-1796: A History of Resistance, Collaboration and Betrayal* (Granby, MA: Bergin and Garvey, 1988), 57, 80-81.

11 Barbara Kopytoff, "The Development of Jamaican Maroon Ethnicity", *Caribbean Quarterly* 22 (1976): 33-50.

12 Kopytoff, "The Maroons of Jamaica", 260-67.

13 Monica Schuler, "Ethnic Slave Rebellions in the Caribbean and the Guianas", *Journal of Social History* 3 (1970): 374-85; Monica Schuler, "Myalism and the African Religious Tradition in Jamaica", in *Africa and the Caribbean: The Legacies of a Link*, edited by Margaret E. Crahan and Franklin W. Knight (Baltimore: Johns Hopkins University Press, 1979), 65-79.

14 Frederic G. Cassidy, *Jamaica Talk: Three Hundred Years of the English Language in Jamaica* (London: Macmillan, 2d ed., 1971), 397.

15 Bilby, "'Two Sister Pikni'", 11-18.

16 J.D. Lenoir, "Suriname National Development and Maroon Cultural Autonomy", *Social and Economic Studies* 24 (1975): 308-19.

17 Richard Price, *The Guiana Maroons: A Historical and Bibliographical Introduction* (Baltimore: Johns Hopkins University Press, 1976).

18 Kenneth Bilby, "The Remaking of the Aluku: Culture, Politics, and Maroon Ethnicity in French South America" (Ph.D. diss., Johns Hopkins University, 1990).

 *five*

Maroons and Rebels (a Dilemma)

Carey Robinson

Introduction

Not long ago, the concept of freedom as a human right was little understood or accepted. In the Middle Ages "ordinary" people, the majority of whom were slaves or serfs, were ruthlessly ruled by monarchs, princes and aristocrats and kept in line by severe laws. Up to the end of the eighteenth century and on into the nineteenth, discipline and punishments were harshly applied to vagabonds, labourers, apprentices, soldiers, seamen, miners (all the common people). Only the fortunate few, at the top of the social pyramid, could move with self-assurance. Poor men strove desperately to escape from the social trap by seeking fortunes in overseas ventures, so that, if successful, they in turn could "lord" it over others.

Slavery became the spirit of the colonial system. In the early days of British Jamaica, the first settlers converted their less fortunate fellow countrymen into temporary slaves (indentured servants) until the massive influx of Africans made this procedure unnecessary. Africans, brought in to work as slaves, shared the distress of indentured servants; but there were additional dimensions to the plight of the Africans. Their status was meant to be permanent and the colour of their skins made it impossible to hide their identity. A dark skin attracted discrimination and oppression. Consequently, even if black people achieved freedom within the system, they were denied equality of opportunity and treatment.

Their confidence and self-respect were violently assaulted, and they were "educated" to evaluate themselves by criteria which were always to their disadvantage.

Even the texture of their hair and their features, were judged to be undesirable. The laws reinforced these strictures by normally withholding benefits and civil rights from anyone who was less than three degrees removed, in a lineal descent, from the African ancestor (exclusive). An African heritage became a severe disability.

In addition, the world was run by "authority figures" such as monarchs, princes, aristocrats, chiefs, the wealthy large landowners, whose word was law. Order in human affairs was achieved through authority figures, preferably in positions of permanence and armed with the power of life and death. No less a person than the revered apostle, St Paul, asserted that authorities must be obeyed. Slaves must love and obey their masters and serve in fear and trembling. The poor, the weak, the conquered and the oppressed must be content with their condition and obey those placed in authority over them. For authority came from God, and God would be displeased with anyone who resisted those he had placed in positions of authority. Africans were expected to humbly accept the inferior category into which they had been thrust.

In the midst of this kind of social set-up, based on the denial of freedom, and upon servile obedience to authority (a system which was beginning to devalue the humanity of people of African descent), the Maroon movement emerged. It was a phenomenon that exceeded all reasonable bounds at the time; an outrageous threat to God-given authority, and to the practical requirements of society.

Early years

The Jamaican Maroon movement began in earnest in 1655, following the invasion of the island by a British force under Admiral Penn and General Venables. At the time, Jamaica was a neglected Spanish colony with a small population of Spaniards and Africans, and mixtures of both groups. Some also had the blood of Arawaks, the original inhabitants who, as a group, had died out under Spanish rule. Indeed, it was mainly because of the rapid disappearance of the Arawaks that the Spaniards began to build up an African workforce.

The first Africans appeared to be body servants and were brought in between 1513 and 1517. They probably came originally from the Upper Guinea region in West Africa. Because the Spaniards found no gold in Jamaica, the island soon ceased to attract settlers. Many of those who had come as settlers left for places in the region where gold was available and after a while the importation of Africans stopped. But livestock brought by the Spaniards (cattle, sheep, pigs, etc.) multiplied tremendously, and a good export trade in hides and fat developed with neighbouring Spanish territories. Settlers who remained in the island became chiefly occupied with ranching and hunting. One result was that many of the African servitors were released into the freedom of the bush to tend livestock, round-up cattle and hunt, using bow and arrow, lances and firearms. They became in the process very familiar with much of the terrain.

Background of the freedom fighters

Soon the Africans were an indispensable and irreplaceable part of the workforce. Their position was further strengthened by the fact that the island was frequently attacked by pirates (French, English, Dutch). Every able-bodied man was needed for military service and the Africans were soon a mainstay of the defence force. Recognizing their importance, the Spaniards began to treat them "like their own children"; with affection and even respect.

Because of the small size of the colony and its vulnerability, class and racial barriers were weakened. By the time of the English invasion, the society was in a fairly advanced stage of integration. According to one "shocked" British observer, slavery hardly existed.

The real but unofficial status of the Africans at the time of the invasion was exemplified by two of their number, who were specially mentioned in the records. One was a priest from Angola, who acted as a peace envoy between the English and the Spaniards, and was hanged by militant Spaniards who were opposed to peace. The other was Diego Pimienta, a heroic hunter and champion marksman, born in Jamaica. Pimienta fought with great courage and distinction at the battle of Caobana in 1655.

Maroon country

The Caobana (Mahogany) river, known today as the Black River, had strong currents, was lined on either side by wide swamps and abounded in crocodiles. The Caobana had two fords. The British tried to cross one to get at Spanish ranches on the other side. It was at this ford that Diego Pimienta fought, as part of the Spanish guard.

There was also another reported case which shed light on the state of Africans in the Spanish colony. In February 1656, after the British crossed the Caobana and occupied ranches on the western side, an English ship, *The Hunter*, landed one hundred men at Great Pedro Bay (near today's Treasure Beach in St Elizabeth). They camped near a ruined village. The next day a mounted black man rode boldly up to them and said he was living on his own, and would remain there as long as he could find cattle to hunt. This "free spirit" informed the British that he would not fight them unless they interfered with him.

When the British force arrived in 1655, the Spanish governor surrendered almost at once. But a hard core of hunters, ranchers and others, who regarded Jamaica as their home, decided to fight. One of the terms of surrender, drawn up by the British, required "all slaves and negroes" to appear on open ground near the town of Villa de la Vega (Spanish Town) to be informed of "the favours and acts of grace concerning their freedom to be granted to them". The majority of the Africans ignored this command and marched off with the Spanish resistance force.

The Africans fought as if the country belonged to them, and their morale grew, even while the chances of success diminished. Almost from the outset of the five-year struggle, the majority, with a strong show of independence, set up their own camps in the bush. A large number collected in the mountains of Clarendon under Juan Lubolo, who later became known as Juan de Bolas.

It was a time of crisis. A new life was about to begin. The Africans had won a unique position in the Spanish colony and were not prepared to take a backward step by placing themselves in the hands of new masters. Perhaps the time had arrived for them to become masters of their own destiny. Africans were present in every aspect of the struggle. They were outstanding as scouts, hunters and foragers. Without them the Spanish force would have been defeated by hunger alone.

Realizing their importance, the British made strong efforts to get them to desert the Spanish cause and come over to their side. After the major Spanish defeat at Rio Nuevo in 1658, Juan de Bolas and his followers deserted to the British on the promise of freedom, land and status. The rest of the Africans refused to give up their newly found independence. Their foremost leader was Juan de Serras. In 1660, when the Spaniards were finally driven out, de Serras and his community remained in Jamaica, and continued to oppose the British. About three years later, the exasperated British, having failed repeatedly to break the resolve of the Africans, sent Juan de Bolas to destroy them. But de Bolas fell into an ambush. His force was cut to pieces and he was slain.

In a sense this brought the initial Maroon movement, developed by the Spanish Africans, to a point of fulfilment. They had successfully set up their own "state" under their own chosen leader, with their own rules and way of life. The British declared them outlaws, with a price on their heads. But they could not really be regarded as outlaws, for they had never been a part of the British colony.

The word *Maroon* is thought by some to have come from the Spanish word *marrana*, meaning a *sow* or *young hog*. The name was first given to hunters of wild hogs. Others believe that Maroon is a corruption of the Spanish word *cimarrón*, meaning *wild* or *unruly*. The French word for a runaway slave is *marron*. In Jamaica the word *Maroon* was first applied to the Spanish Africans. Later it was given to other Africans who embarked on a struggle for freedom and independence, which resulted in the peace treaties with the British in 1739.

Shortly after the Spaniards were driven from Jamaica, the British discovered that there was a lot of money to be made from sugar. But large-scale sugar production required many workers. Enough Europeans could not be found for such a task and so the British began to import large numbers of Africans to work as slaves. Most came from the West Coast of Africa which, at the time, was divided into petty states or principalities constantly at war with each other. This made it easier for individual chiefs and kings to be persuaded to raid the territories of their rivals and capture people for sale.

Many of the captives came from war-like tribes which were called Coromantins by Europeans. They were described as fierce, bold, proud and courageous; possessing "an elevation of soul which prompts them to enterprises of difficulty and danger, and enables them to meet death, in its most horrid shape, without flinching". Despite their dangerous reputation, British planters preferred Coromantins because of their strength and ability to work hard. However, in an attempt to neutralize the danger, planters began importing very young people, believing that the young could be more easily conditioned into habits of docility and obedience, which were required of "good slaves".

But this device often failed, for it was found that by the age of twelve the Coromantin character was usually well formed. Observers who could attest to this wrote: "the firmness and intrepidity which are distinguished [in Coromantin adults] are visible in their boys at an age, which might be thought too tender to receive any lasting impression, either from precept or example". This observation helps to explain the three African boys who escaped from Sutton's estate during an insurrection in 1690. Their names were Cudjoe, Johnny and Accompong, and they were brothers. They grew up in the hills and forests, along with other rebels, and became leaders in the new rebel movement which developed in the British colony. Cudjoe became the supreme leader in Central and Western Jamaica. A high-ranking British officer later referred to him as a military genius. The British felt that if they could get him to make peace, the rebels in the East (Nanny's people) would follow his example. This was exactly what happened, much to Nanny's displeasure. It appears that Nanny deliberately kept herself away from direct contact with the British. Dr Russell could describe Cudjoe in some detail, and he boasted that he had taken Cudjoe "by the hand". Phillip Thicknesse had long talks with Quao, and slept in Quao's hut. But no account has yet been discovered of any Britisher who got close to Nanny. And there is evidence that she was against any move to come to terms with the British. Intuitively she may have sensed what the end would be.

At first, the British referred to the rebel Africans simply as "slaves in rebellion". But in the 1730s when the war was at its height, the British began to call them Maroons, the name originally applied to the Spanish Africans who by now had been (in all likelihood) absorbed into the ranks of the rebels. Today we tend to think of the Maroons as a separate people; almost as a different ethnic type. But in fact they came from the same root stock, as many, if not most of the Africans in Jamaica. The difference was in the quality of spirit.

The people who came on the slave ships were in various degrees of shock when they arrived. Some never completely recovered. Those who retained sufficient control of their minds and were determined to rid themselves of the condition that had been imposed on them, took the first opportunity to break out. They never accepted the status of slavery.

In fact, the people who came in the ships did not think of themselves as "Negro slaves," but as members of the clans or nations from which they came. Just as Scotsmen thought of themselves as Scots, and Irishmen as Irish, the Africans thought of themselves as Ashantes, Mandingoes, Fantyns, Eboes, etc.

Throughout the years of the war which resulted in the 1739 peace treaties, the Maroon ranks were constantly replenished by new rebels and runaways, sometimes fresh off the slave ships. It appears that the longer new Africans remained in the system, and the longer they were herded, conditioned, fed, clothed and given shelter, the more difficult it became to abandon the "security" of the slave village, for the perils of a free life in the bush. The break-aways had to have a special quality of heart, mind and will. They would be entering a region where the only human help available to them would be what they could give to each other, or what they could receive in secret from relatives and friends who remained in the system.

A return to the African homeland could not be seriously attempted, so they had to create a society of their own, with all the necessary infrastructure: houses, villages, food, water, medicines, strategies for defence, training for the young, division of functions, law and order, government, religious observances, family life, communications, preparations for contingencies, etc. The relationships which emerged in these "free" communities resembled some African social systems. However, there was no hereditary leadership.

Resilience was crucial. When Maroon villages were captured and their crops destroyed, the inhabitants had to move into the bush, and either build new villages or try to recapture the old ones. The whole community was at risk. Sometimes they would burn their houses themselves, as they fled before successful storming parties. The people would suffer from exposure, and often come near to starving.

The British assault forces usually contained contingents of armed African slaves. Often the guides who led these forces to the Maroon villages were black men. These men would themselves be seeking a kind of freedom, within the system, even though it would only allow them to be third-class subjects. So there was no guarantee of solidarity because of common roots or common experiences. People sought to achieve their goals even if it meant aiding the common oppressor against a brother or sister.

Consequently, when the peace treaties of 1739 required the Maroons to suppress rebels and return runaways, the stage had already been set. Nevertheless, there was this great contradiction: the Maroons who had been the chief opponents of the slave society had now become one of its main props. However, the Maroons sometimes hid runaways, and sometimes went on go-slows, or only pretended to attack rebels. But as succeeding generations got further and further away from the original spirit which had motivated the movement, the Maroons became increasingly out of touch with the emerging spirit of freedom in Jamaica.

On the other hand, the Maroons usually enjoyed a vibrant relationship with the British, even though they had many causes for complaint. The British sometimes indulged and flattered them, and the Maroons went so far as to abandon their own names and adopt the names of leading British families. Hence we find Maroons named Montague James, John Palmer, Tharpe, Jarrett, Dunbar, Parkinson, Shirley, White, etc. It was felt by some, however, that this "adoption" process was merely a strategy by the Maroons to pressure influential familes into supporting them. Governor Balcarres, at the time of the second Maroon war, accused some of the leading planters of paying "protection money" to the Maroons in order to safeguard their properties.

In the years that followed the 1739 peace treaties, the runaways and rebellions continued, as the enslaved (particularly the new arrivals) struggled for freedom.

These struggles were made significantly more difficult because of the hostile presence of the expert Maroons, and their detailed knowledge of the hinterland, which the new arrivals, in particular, lacked.

The new rebels could no longer be called Maroons. The word Maroon had become institutionalized. It no longer meant "a slave in rebellion". It had now become the title for a proud, conservative people, who had "won their spurs" in battle and must henceforth be respected. The rebels were just rebels, to be hunted for disturbing the peace, breaking the law and endangering the prosperity of the country. But nothing could stop the drive for freedom.

It is safe to assume that, from the start of the struggle for freedom, even before the appearance of Cudjoe and Nanny, there was no way to account for all the rebels and runaways in the hinterland. The numbers may have been many times greater than the estimates and statistics that were given from time to time. It was reported in 1827 that there were no less than twenty thousand runaways "leading a life of lawless barbarity in the woods and towns of Jamaica". A Captain of the Accompong Maroons admitted that Maroon patrols often accepted bribes to allow runaways to escape, and that only a comparative few were caught and returned to their masters.

We can say therefore, that from the time of the British conquest, there were always free communities of people of African descent, living a life of their own, in the hinterland of Jamaica; creating and maintaining an alternative lifestyle to that which was practised in the plantation slave society. There had always been two Jamaicas, touching at certain points, but with distinct lifestyles. The post-treaties Maroons had a foot in each life-stream, but there was no sensible way in which they could make common cause with the post-treaties rebels.

The future

The Maroons recognized that in the world in which they lived there was no imperative on the part of anyone to preserve the freedom and dignity of a self-liberated, self-rescued group of black people like themselves. More than thirty-five years after the treaties were signed, the Americans in declaring their independence from Britain and their commitment to freedom and equality, were unable to include Indians and Blacks in their declaration of man's inalienable rights.

If the Maroons broke their commitments to the British, what did they stand to gain? A doubtful linkage with some rebel group, perhaps fresh off a ship, in a movement that would probably not be able to sustain itself? And a movement under whose leadership? How could the veteran Maroons surrender leadership in a break-away venture to anyone—whether the name was Tacky, Sam Sharpe or Paul Bogle? Tacky, Bogle and many others had asked for Maroon assistance, and instead, found Maroons arrayed against them. The basis for mere sentimental solidarity had been destroyed. The best the Maroons could offer was to go easy now and then in their conflicts with rebels, and to hide the odd runaway.

The broad mass of the population, prior to universal adult suffrage, had little to offer the Maroons. The Maroons were better off than the broad mass; better off than Tacky, Blackwall and Three-Finger Jack; better off than Sam Sharpe and his people, and Bogle and his people; better off than than all those struggling for recognition, identity, justice, land, respectability, equality, unity, civil rights and responsible government within the system.

The Maroons governed themselves up to a point; their territory could not be touched as long as they maintained their commitments. They chose their own leaders. They were courted by the powerful in the interest of the security of the colony. They could appeal directly to the highest authority. They had a strong sense of who they were and what they belonged to; they had nothing to gain and much to lose by making common cause with the confused, disorganized and disinherited, who had even become tainted with the poisonous philosophy of racial inferiority.

Even now, should the Maroons be expected to give up their special heritage, and be absorbed into a society which the broad mass seems unable to control? Should they abandon their clear identity for a general one which is little understood or appreciated? Should they surrender their sense of community for full membership in a larger state, where unity is confined to a motto and the social framework seems in danger of disintegrating?

Yet, how can the Maroons continue in a separate existence within an environment that is in the grip of rapid and severe changes, and in which the terms of their treaties are no longer practical or valid?

six

Maroon Heritage in Mexico*

Joe Pereira

Introduction

The African presence in Mexico has, until fairly recently, been ignored or swept under the carpet of the Indian-Spanish weave. And yet, for almost the entire colonial
period, there were more Africans in Mexico than Europeans.[1] When to this is
added, under the entire colonial period, the increasing number of Mestizos—
whether Afro-European or Afro-Indian—the African presence in Mexico has had a
significant impact demographically.

Ironically, even more recent studies[2] open up a massive panorama of an African
presence and influence centuries before Cortes arrived in Mexico. It was mainly
centred on the Olmec culture in the Gulf coast region until its subsequent expansion and influence through areas of present-day Veracruz, Puebla and Guerrero
states—coincidentally, some of the very states in which post-conquest Africans
were to be located (Fig. 6.1). Virtually all the Africans arriving in Mexico in the colonial period were brought as slaves to work, not only on the sugar estates being
established in Veracruz, but also in other branches of agriculture, in domestic
work, in the gold and silver mines and in various aspects of urban industry. As a
result, in addition to the regions mentioned above, Africans became located in
most of the central highlands around Mexico City, stretching as far north as the
mines of Guanajuato and Zacatecas, west to Taxco and Acapulco and south to
Chiapas.

In the sixteenth century, the majority of Africans came from the Cape Verde
area and West Africa in general, but by the seventeenth century, the main areas

*This study was made possible by a research grant under the Government of Mexico-UWI protocol.

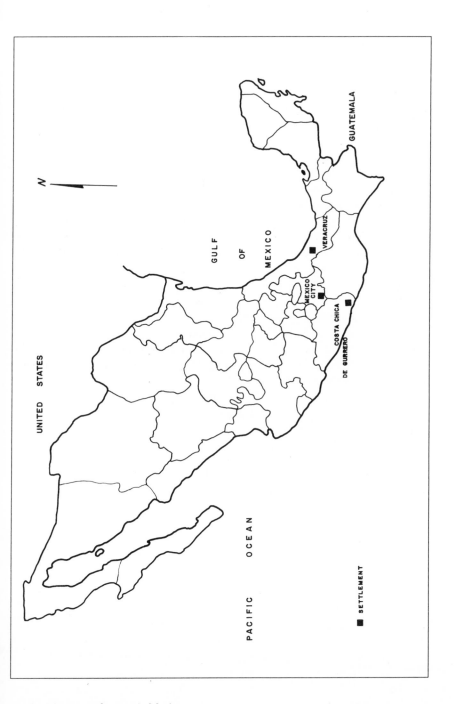

Fig. 6.1 Maroon settlements in Mexico

of provenance had shifted to the Congo and Angola.[3] Because of the shortage of African women, relationships soon developed with Indians. Similarly, Spaniards developed relationships with African slaves and the whole process of this racial mixing expanded inexorably. Five hundred years have produced a decidedly, if not always admittedly, mixed population in much of the areas mentioned above.

Maronage in Mexico

As happened throughout the Americas, the slaves did not take passively to their enslavement. A variety of forms of resistance rapidly developed, including rebellion and maronage. In an exceptional reference to the Maroons' own historical sources, archival documents of 1767 quoted one Maroon leader thus, concerning the existence of palenques: "According to what the old folks tell us, they have always been there since the conquest of this country".[4]

Within three years of the fall of the Aztec empire, reference was being made to African slaves who had fled to live among the Zapotec Indians.[5] For generations, there were complaints of Maroons attacking and robbing travellers on the Veracruz-Mexico highway. In 1576, blacks and mulattoes who had established themselves in a place called Cañada de Negros, carried out numerous attacks against the Spaniards of the newly-established town of Leon. Some even seized land there, among other "insolences". When the Spaniards tried to capture or control them, they simply fled beyond the jurisdictional limits of Leon.[6] It was established that by 1570, fully one-tenth of the black population (which then totalled about 20,000) had fled.[7]

It was calculated, also, that in 1609 there were some 500 runaways in the Orizaba area between Puebla and Veracruz.[8] Data for the sugar estate near Cuernavaca belonging to the Marquis del Valle, indicate that the incidence of maronage in the area increased in the eighteenth century, one cause being that there were now more mulatto slaves who could more easily disappear amidst the now sizeable free mulatto/Mestizo population.[9]

Lifestyle of Maroons in Mexico

If the circumstances and location of runaways were varied, so too were the lifestyles resulting from maronage. There were isolated runaways, many of whom sought to lose themselves in towns or areas of free coloureds or Indians. There were many others, who joined together (or with other racial groups) in gangs of vagabonds and bandits, living off the proceeds of robbery and general pillage, while operating mainly along main roadways.[10]

There were others who set up their palenques or communities, especially, though not always, in the mountains, such as the Sierra de Zongolica, Veracruz, or the Sierras de Guerrero. While many of these communities developed an agricultural lifestyle, others supplemented their farming activities with proceeds from robbing the colonists.

Equally varied was the relationship between Maroons and other social groups. From very early, partly because of the paucity of women in their groups and partly because the child of an Indian was born free, Africans took Indian women as their mates. There were repeated instances of Maroons seizing Indian women, as for example, in 1609 when the Maroons of Yanga raided a ranch and took off with six Indian women.[11] Speaking of the townships of Colatlan set up with Tlaxcalan Indians, colonial documents explain how mulattoes arrived in search of freedom, and the Indians themselves sheltered them. After a few years they either married Indian women or claimed frontier militia rights.[12] Indeed, in general terms, complaints were made to Phillip II in 1574 that it was impossible to enforce the prohibition of black/Indian unions since "the Indian women are slack and very taken by blacks, so they prefer to marry them rather than Indian men, and just so the black men marry them rather than black women, so as to have free children".[13]

The frequency of male African Maroons having Indian women is an important determinant of the subsequent racial, ethnic and cultural assimilation of the Maroons and their post-abolition descendants.

Such relationships with Indian communities as a whole were not always so congenial. In fact, the above feature would indicate a certain amount of hostility towards blacks on the part of Indian males. Some Maroon communities did get on fairly well with neighbouring Indians, usually for economic reasons,[14] but the majority had contradictory and sometimes hostile relationships. In the remote areas of the Costa Chica de Guerrero, hostility towards Indians was general among the mixed Maroon/free Afro-mestizos, who usurped their lands and livelihood, and abused them constantly.[15] While the majority of Spanish colonists were antagonistic to and fearful of the Maroons, some found them a useful source of paid manpower or traded profitably with them. Indeed, one of the leading petitioners for the establishment of the free Maroon village of Amapa in the 1760, was the chief magistrate of Teutila. He used the Maroons as agents in the vanilla trade and provided them with supplies—even weapons.[16]

Among fellow blacks and mulattoes, Maroons were usually well received.[17] It would seem, also, that some even made regular visits to their women still in slavery, since one of the conditions sought by the planters in the establishment of Amapa was that such women should be sold to their now free men, rather than have the latter visit them on the plantations.[18] However, there were also cases of betrayal of Maroons to the Spaniards by fellow Maroons or slaves—usually with the bribe of freedom—with disastrous results for the palenques in some cases. A law of 1574 granted freedom to runaways who handed in other runaways.[19] Additionally, mulattoes and Afro-Indians were used in campaigns against Maroons.

Reaction of Spanish colonists

In trying to curb the phenomenon of maronage, the Spaniards used a variety of measures, chief among which were punitive ones. Severe punishments were legislated against runaways, including castration and, particularly for leaders, death. At times, the authorities were reluctant to return runaways to their "owners", and preferred to keep them imprisoned. In most cases, a runaway was valued at much lower than normal fees because of the economic risk of their repeating the act. In some areas, runaways were sent to work in the mines.

And yet, throughout the entire period of slavery, the most virulently punitive measures proved incapable of stopping the process of maronage. Other measures were equally ineffective. For example, the establishing of the Spanish town of Córdoba in 1617 as a sort of garrison town along the Puebla-Veracruz highway, to control maronage and slaves in the area, did not prevent them from running away and damaging colonial property.[20]

Armed expeditions against the palenques met with some success in the Veracruz area, but failed in the more remote and difficult terrain of Guerrero. But these military campaigns proved to be very expensive and also diverted the militia members from productive work on their farms. The Catholic Church was trying to convince the Maroons that Christianity and pacifism were the correct paths to follow, teachings which seemed to have had some subversive effect on members of some palenques.

Where the path of violence was inconclusive in controlling the Maroons, and partly because it was a costly and debilitating strategy, the colonial authorities in two exceptional cases almost one hundred and fifty years apart but within the same general region, agreed to a negotiated settlement with Maroons although with some reluctance. This in the face of opposition from the planters, who feared the effect these examples of freedom from slavery would have on their slaves.

The two cases, Yanga/San Lorenzo and Amapa, have been the focus of much study and comment, partly because since their creation impinged on the state structure, documentation exists. Unfortunately, precisely because they represent communities of some assimilation into the dominant state, they reflect fewer African retentions than would have been the case in the more remote and "rebel" palenques which have had scant documentation.

The Maroon town of Yanga

Some confusion exists as to whether the establishment of San Lorenzo in 1630 was a distinct development separate from the recognition of the palenqueros, headed by the most famous African in post-Cortes Mexico: Yanga (or Nanga). A Jesuit priest of the day writes: "Yanga was a fine-bodied black, from the Bran nation and of whom it was said that were he not captured, he would have been king in his country; with those lofty ideas he had been leader of the rebellion from some thirty years, in which his authority and fine style towards those of his colour had considerably increased his followings".[21]

By 1608, Yanga's palenques located in the Zongolica range near Orizaba were the most threatening to the colonists. The data indicate that by then, because of his age, Yanga kept the civil and political authority for himself, but entrusted the military leadership to an Angolan, Francisco de la Matosa.[22] Most of the historians base their views of this period on the testimony of the above-mentioned Jesuit priest, Laurencio, to the effect that in 1609 a force of some 600 men comprising Spaniards, Indians, mulattoes and Mestizos was sent against Yanga.

Yanga is said to have captured a Spaniard and sent him to the leader of this expedition, Gonzalez de Herrera, with a letter to the effect that the Maroons

> had withdrawn to that area to free themselves from the cruelty and the perfidy of the Spaniards, who without any right sought to be masters of their liberty; that in attacking the Spaniards' places and plantations, they were doing nought but compensating themselves by force of arms for what was unjustly denied them and that they [the Spaniards] should not think of peace but should come and test forces with them. And, so that he [Gonzalez] could not in cowardice claim ignorance of the path, he was sending him a bearer whom he had chosen not to kill so that he could serve as a guide and save the job of seeking them out.[23]

This message was clear and indicated the determination of the Maroons to maintain their freedom by any means available to them.

Occupations

In the face of such defiance, the Spaniards attacked and managed to defeat the Maroons, who withdrew from that palenque into others situated in more difficult terrain to continue in freedom. Laurencio's description of what the Spaniards found in the palenque gives a glimpse of the sedentary agricultural life that the Maroons sought to establish even as they were on a constant war-footing. "Provision grounds of corn, tobacco, pumpkin, banana and other fruit trees, . . . beans, sweet potato, vegetables . . . an abundance of chickens and a large number of cattle . . . as well as about sixty huts that sheltered approximately eighty adult males, twenty-four black and Indian women and an indeterminate number of children".[24]

Consequences

The historians all agree that Maroon activity and resistance persisted in the area until the Viceroy agreed in 1630, to the establishment of a free town of Maroons. Some historians, perhaps with insufficient archival data,[25] ascribe to Yanga after the defeat described above, a proposal for a peace treaty. However, Aguirre Beltrán has quoted documents of 1608 (corroborated by García Bustamante) that set out

Yanga's peace proposals, the most fundamental being that Yanga be governor and after him his children and their descendants. Another condition was that Franciscan friars and no others were to administer the area.[26]

Naveda lists other demands: that all slaves who had fled before 1608 remain free, that no Spaniard live in their community and that they have their own cabildo. They also offered to pay tribute and to hand over any slave who ran away.[27] Aguirre Beltrán regards 1608 as the year in which the Crown effectively negotiated a settlement with Yanga, which was legalized and recognized finally in 1630.[28] Israel also interprets the data as a separate settlement with Yanga at the end of the first decade of the century.[29] Aguirre, in support of his claim, refers to a document of 1608 in which a Franciscan friar, Benavides, testifies to his activities over the preceding four to five months amidst Yanga's community, and this is seen as fulfilling Yanga's demand that only Franciscan clergymen deal with his people.

The Franciscan's report gives us another first-hand glimpse of social life within the palenque. Benavides reports that he wanted to solemnize the marriage of a mulatta, but Francisco Angola (the same de la Matosa that Yanga had made military commander) objected, since the girl's mother and the man who had carried her off to the hills both opposed the marriage. For Francisco Angola felt the validity of the marriage required the consent of those parties.

Benavides quotes another Maroon as explaining that "marriage in the hills is not like that in the town". One can extrapolate from this Maroon norms of consent concerning marriage. Benavides also indicates the problems he had with Catholic religious observations among the Maroons: on days of abstinence, i.e. when they should not eat meat, the Maroons, nonetheless, persisted in eating meat, even though the friar points out that they had ample recourse to fish and vegetarian foods that would have allowed them to adhere to the Catholic rules for abstinence.

On another occasion, while the priest was encouraging the Maroons to attend mass, he met with angry, scornful opposition from one of them who answered that he didn't want his mass and that he, the friar, was a deceiver.[30] Aguirre implies that Laurencio was either totally wrong or at least had his dates and one or two other details mixed up. However, Aguirre does not elaborate on the subsequent fate of Yanga. Herrera cites tradition as holding that he died "in a strange and violent way at the church door of San Lorenzo".[31] However, García Bustamante infers from documents of January 1619—which refer to the capture of 36 Maroon rebels including their leader who "for fifty years had been active in those hills"—that this must have been Yanga, and that he was executed at that time.[32] Israel refers to a new Maroon rebellion between 1617 and 1618, and the arrest of its leader and thirty-five of his men, but he makes no link whatsover between this leader and Yanga.[33]

Viceregal recognition in 1630 of the town of San Lorenzo as a community of free blacks is seen as a significant breakthrough, since it is the first documented legal recognition of the freedom of the Maroons and their right to land ownership—a right denied even free blacks. Pardoned of all crimes, they were also granted the right to form their own local government, and indeed, documents of 1641 refer to Gaspar Yanga "son of the same" Yanga as their Captain,[34] vindicating Yanga's original demand that he and his descendants be recognized as governors of the community.[35]

However, in such situations of bilateral compromise, the Maroons also had to make concessions: they were to be vassals of the Crown, pay tribute and be available for special militia needs, as well as have a priest assigned to them and a church built.[36] This last aspect is a significant feature of Spanish treaties with the Maroons that distinguishes them from the British, and would contribute significantly to the process of assimilation of the African communities into a Catholic culture.

But the most important clause in this settlement, as far as the Spaniards were concerned, was that the Maroons should seek out all slaves who had run away and hand them over to the Spaniards.[37] The same type of clause is to be found in the British treaties with the Jamaican Maroons, and for the same obvious reasons that both colonial powers hoped would compensate them for the humiliation of a pact with the erstwhile slaves: that instead of being a model which the other slaves could imitate in the hope of achieving their freedom, the Maroons would contain the freedom of others in order to assure their own.

Taken at face value, this was a blow to, if not a betrayal of, general freedom for the slaves. Indeed, Israel laments that it is very sad that between 1630 and 1650 the blacks of San Lorenzo "earned their bread chiefly from the rewards given to them by the Spaniards for the fugitive slaves that they returned".[38]

While it is true that in the ensuing years after the establishment of San Lorenzo Cerralva (better known as San Lorenzo de los Negros) there were many cases of runaway slaves being returned, the Maroons, as happened in Jamaica, also sheltered others. This sometimes led to legal complaints against the community for harbouring runaways in breach of the treaty.[39] All sorts of contradictory motives would have gone into the acceptance of this clause. Similarly, adherence to it would have varied according to varying circumstances, depending on the individuals involved.

Another feature of this Maroon free town was that its inhabitants soon became dissatisfied with their geographic surroundings for being "very hilly with poisonous animals and insects, lacking in land and pasturage for their livestock".[40] They therefore sought to move not only to better agricultural lands but to land that was closer to the main road and indeed, to the colonial settlements. Despite the objections of some of the colonists of the area, this was eventually permitted in 1655, when the community was relocated to its present site about twenty kilometers from Córdoba. This is an important aspect in the absorption of this Maroon community into mainstream Mexican society, turning away from the essentially isolationist palenque culture.

An Italian traveller in 1697 testifies to the mainstream tendency of San Lorenzo by the fact that he had stopped there to eat on the way to Veracruz. His version of the village is concisely revealing: "Since it is inhabited only by blacks, it appears as if one is in Guinea. They are of attractive features and dedicated to agriculture. They have their origin in some fugitive slaves who were permitted to live freely there as long as they didn't receive other runaway blacks but instead returned them to their masters, which they observe faithfully".[41]

However, the apparent docility of the inhabitants of San Lorenzo was not sufficient to gain peaceful coexistence with the surrounding colonists, who both pressured them from the point of view of trying to get labour for their tobacco and cane enterprise, and carried out a range of petty assaults on the rights of the community of San Lorenzo, including seizure of land and even of citizens, under the protection of the authorities in Córdoba, even though the Viceroy instructed otherwise. Thus by 1768, the colonists were affirming that the majority of blacks had abandoned San Lorenzo and gone off to other wretched districts.[42] It is certainly true that today there are very few blacks in the town.

The Maroon town of Amapa

But the establishment of San Lorenzo did not end the phenomenon of runaways and maronage. During the century which followed, there are incessant reports of runaways, rebellions and Maroon attacks on colonists in the region around Córdoba. An interesting development took place in 1748, when the mayor of Teutila, Andrés Fernandez, himself the beneficiary of Maroon labour in his enterprises, proposed the formation of a free village in the style of San Lorenzo.[43]

While Fernandez put forward as motive the facilitating "of the salvation of their souls with the teaching of Christian doctrine, which sustenance they pitifully lack", it would seem that economic motives underpinned his proposals, since the anti-Maroon campaigns were costly not only in relation to the expenses of the armed force, but also in the disruption of agricultural commerce. However, the Viceroy did not respond to these initial proposals and it was not until several years later, when Fernandez once again became mayor, that the proposal was adopted by the authorities.

If the Crown was hesitant for some time, the Maroons were not. Reflective of the contradictory forces within the Maroon communities, a young mulatto underling, Fernando Manuel, supported the proposal of a pact with the Spaniards, while the old Maroon Captain, Macute, opposed the idea. This division led to an armed internal power struggle in which Fernando Manuel won, his defeated opponents were returned to their master and Macute was handed over to the Spaniards for execution.[44]

Such was the depth of ideological division among the Maroons. Macute represents those forces that saw independence as requiring an isolation from the alien, dominating culture. It is a reflection of the cultural penetration of Catholicism that Fernando Manuel prayed to the Virgin of Guadalupe that should he win against Macute, he would dedicate the new town to her. A further reflection of the subordination of Fernando to Spanish colonialism is to be seen in his sending his forces to Veracruz in 1762, to offer their services to the Spanish Crown to fight the English who were threatening to attack—and this occurred while they were still criminal renegades in the eyes of the colonial law.[45]

Such behaviour convinced the Viceroy of the "loyalty" of this particular Maroon group whose leader, Fernando, in 1767, petitioned the Viceroy for recognition of their freedom in exchange for handing over any future runaways[46] and by 1768, the foundation of the town of Amapa was authorized and dedicated to Our Lady of Guadalupe. However, as in the case of San Lorenzo, the colonists of Córdoba opposed the location, which they wished to have sited in more difficult terrain. But their case was dismissed and Amapa established with its church and thirty-three houses, and a Catholic service held to mark its foundation.[47]

That the land was in fact taken away from the native Indian population much to their resentment, did not bother either the Viceroy or the Maroons, even if it was another instance of Indo-African friction. The terms of the authorizing document followed somewhat those of San Lorenzo, particularly in the clauses which stipulated that they should harbour no runaways but should return them forthwith and assist in hunting down runaways in the region.

Little documentation exists as to whether there were breaches of these clauses, but it seems unlikely that Fernando Manuel would have posed problems in this regard. Indeed, within the first two years, they had captured forty-four runaways and were tracking eight more.[48] This eighteenth century case of a "treaty" has a far less conflictive context in cultural terms than the seventeenth century treaty with Yanga, since the Catholic Church and the formal colonial agricultural economy had very much penetrated the lifestyle of these Maroons of Amapa.

But there were other Maroons besides those of Amapa who continued to be involved in subsequent revolts in the Zongolica-Orizaba mountains. This continued right up to the Independence Movement, when many slaves ran off or openly revolted in support of the independentistas, who in 1810 had proclaimed abolition, and whose eventual victory led to the decree of the independent Mexican government in 1829 which abolished slavery and, as a consequence, ended the phenomenon of maronage.

Pacific-Coast Maroons

If the history of the Gulf coast (i.e., Veracruz) Maroons is relatively documented, the experiences of the Maroons elsewhere, especially on the Pacific coast, are not so easily gleaned from documentation. This is partly because the area was relatively out of the mainstream of communication and colonial authority. The area stretching from Acapulco south along Costa Chica through the province of Guerrero and into Oaxaca was largely left by the Spaniards to a few large cattle ranchers with huge ranches. The ranchers in turn used overseers, many times black slaves, to look after things on spot.

Such remoteness from the mainstream colonial society was ideal for maronage and so it transpired that from the hill regions closer to Mexico City and Oaxaca, or from the port area of Guatulco, slaves fled further and further into Costa Chica, where they joined the relatively unrestricted cowboy slaves or grew corn and cotton, and kept livestock on small ranches.

At the end of the sixteenth century, the Viceroy was complaining that for some thirty years, Maroons had had their houses and provision grounds "living as if they were actually in Guinea and a rifle-shot away from the provision grounds of the natives of the area".[49] So, as in the Veracruz area, the Viceroy ordered an armed campaign against them, but as in the Gulf coast, so was there little success with this anti-Maroon effort on the Pacific side. The Maroons retreated further into the inaccessible coastal lands, where, over the next two centuries, they and their slave counterparts would live and let live. It was not easy to separate the two groups.

For the cattle-ranchers, this state of affairs was not a problem, since the Maroons sometimes provided manpower especially at round-up time, just as in Veracruz where some Spaniards had found it profitable to use the paid labour of Maroons. For the authorities of the Viceroyalty it was, however, a source of distress that there were these "daring, bellicose and disobedient" blacks. But there was little that they could do about them. Indeed, the general black population, free, slave or Maroon, enjoyed a relatively anarchic existence, and a document of 1801 complains of their anti-social nature including their disrespect for payment of tribute due for the Church and for the merchants they owed.[50]

Maroons here merged with other blacks to develop a reputation of being a law unto themselves and a culture of aggressiveness, seen as continuing into the contemporary period. This aggressiveness was, if anything, encouraged by the big cattle-ranchers who had used their black workforce to drive the corn and cotton-based Indian communities out of the territory for their cattle. The black community, including the Maroons, used the Indians as a sort of beating stick and generally terrorized them, although there were cases in which they inter-married with their women out of necessity.

Today, there exist some one hundred "pueblos de morenos" along the Costa Chica, who have remained less racially mixed with the rest of the national population than anywhere else in Mexico. However, with the development of Acapulco, modern communications including radio, television (and satellite dishes) and the building of a paved coastal road from Acapulco south, these communities have been brought much closer to "mainstream Mexico" and there have been population drifts to the new income-generating tourist centres. Nonetheless, they still exhibit the greatest retentions of an African cultural heritage, although in much diluted form, where the influence of Catholicism and Indian cultural patterns of the region have whittled away much of the African substrata or forced an acculturation and accommodation.

The Maroon heritage

While it is generally true that Afro-Mexicans have been marginalized and socially discriminated up to the present, the history of Maroon resistance to the dominant power has created an attractive political symbolism. In the last decade of the nineteenth century the historian Enrique Herrera Morena, became Mayor of Córdoba and named the newly built city hospital in honour of Yanga, against whose descendants the Córdoban colonists had battled for over a century. In 1933, in the anti-religious wave of the then Mexican government, the Catholic name of San Lorenzo township was changed to Yanga. More recently, various literary works have taken Yanga as their central character and symbol of liberty.

Even though the Maroon/African population of the town has dwindled severely over the years, it was at Yanga in the mid-1970s that a group of Afro-Mexicans formed the Yang Bara Club, and with the assistance of the Embassy of the Ivory Coast, initiated in 1976, an annual carnival held on San Lorenzo Day, in celebration of "the First Free Town of the Americas". In 1986, the Municipal Council took over the organization of the carnival and although the Yang Bara Club is now defunct, it triggered off a consciousness of a heritage and the expression of a form of negritude however mestizized.[51]

On 6 July 1991, in Pinotepa Nacional on the Pacific side, the Catholic Church sponsored the first "Encounter of Black People" in an effort to "look at our history, talk about our life today, plan to move forward".[52] The tensions symbolized by Captain Macute and Fernando Manuel are still being played out in the descendants of the Maroons, as well as the wider Afro-Mexican society: absolute absorption? Or a conscious and distinct "Third Strand" in the Mexican national fabric, recognized and respected?

Peculiarities of maronage in Mexico

It may be proper to close the discussion of this chapter by examining some factors that have influenced the different development of Mexican Maroon culture, compared with that of Jamaican Maroons. The resistance to slavery in both countries led Maroons to the hill country because the difficulty of access and unsuitability for military campaigns favoured them against the colonists. Maroon communities in both countries created such threats to colonial security and wore down the colonists so much that the two colonial powers eventually found it best to come to peaceful settlements through treaties. In both countries, however, these treaties led to further undermining of the Maroon communities as in Yanga in Mexico or the "exiling" of Maroons to Nova Scotia, Canada, and then to Sierra Leone, in the case of Jamaica.

Beyond these overall similarities, the Mexican Maroon societies have not maintained the strong African influences that one finds in Jamaican Maroon communities. Much of the explanation for this is to be found in the different conditions under which both groups of Maroons existed as follows:

In the first instance, the presence in Mexico of a major, developed civilization and firmly established native Indian communities and cultures meant that the Mexican Maroons had to relate not only to the European enslavers, but to the Amerindian peoples who shared a good deal of the same problems of subordination and exploitation by the Spaniards that were experienced by the Africans. Inter-marriage and some cultural similarities between these two ethnic groups created a creole culture that showed much of the numerically dominant Indian influences. In Jamaica, the indigenous population of Indians was not very developed and was almost wiped out by the colonizers, so the Africans related only to one other race, the European, where the relationships between the two races were not as fluid.[53]

Secondly, within this numerically overwhelming Mexican-Indian population, the African presence was a very small minority and so tended to get submerged and absorbed over several generations. In Jamaica, it was the opposite situation. The African population was the overwhelming majority.

Thirdly, the Roman Catholic religion of the Spanish enslavers was far more pervasive and hegemonic than the Protestant denominations of their British counterparts. There was a militant catholicizing of the Indians and Africans in Mexico, with vigorous scrutiny of their dictated religious practices. The Inquisition (painful religious "cleansing") was very active in enforcing ideological and theological orthodoxy and there was a strong relationship between planters and priests. All this created an intense presence undermining, by religious conversion, African cultural retentions in a numerically small ethnic population.

In addition to these, the extended period in Mexico of a single colonial power dominating the society from the start of the sixteenth century, meant a longer period of exposure to the two other cultural pressures coming from Hispanics and Amerindians, compared with the situation in Jamaica.

Also, the closeness of some Maroon communities to the main routes of communication and commerce of the dominating culture, helped to determine the extent to which, over time, the African/Maroon population became absorbed into this mainstream. In Jamaica, the Maroon communities were distanced from these routes and so suffered less exposure and pressure.

Finally, the relatively lengthy period of 170 years since Mexico's independence in 1821, compared with Jamaica's short period of 29 years, meant that many generations of Afro-Mexican Maroons have been involved in the formation and development of a national Mexican identity, even if this might be expressed at the level of a regional identity, and where the minority group of Afro-Mexicans have been largely ignored or marginalized by the dominating elements of Mexican society.

In Jamaica, independence has increased at the national level, the self-esteem of an African oriented identity, elevating Maroon heroes, heroines and African cultural traditions. How far this identity in either country is to be maintained accepted or appreciated will, however, depend on the extent to which the general national consciousness of the importance of the history of our Maroon heritage is effectively developed.

Notes

1 Gonzalo Aguirre Beltrán, *La población negra de México* (México: Fondo de Cultural Económica, 1984), 234.

2 Notably van Sertima (1976) and José Luis Melgarejo Vivanco, *Breve historia de Veracruz* (Xalapa: Edta del Gobierno de Veracruz, 1975).

3 Aguirre Beltrán, op. cit., 240-41.

4 Adriana Naveda, *Esclavos negros en las haciendas azucareras de Córdoba, Veracruz, 1690-1830* (Xalapa: Universidad Vercruzana, 1987), 129.

5 Norman Martin, *Los vagabundos en la Nueva España: Siglo XVI* (México: Edit Jus, 1957), 120.

6 Ibid., 123

7 Ibid., 130.

8 Melgarejo Vivanco, op. cit., 124.

9 Ward Barrett, *La hacienda azucarera de los Marqueses del Valle (1535-1910)* (México: Siglo XXI, 1977), 195.

10 Martin, *Los vagabundos*, 95.

11 Adriana Naveda, "La lucha de los negros esclavos en las haciendas azucareras de Córdoba en el siglo XVIII", *Anuario II*, Centro de Estudios Históricos, Universidad Veracruzana (1980): 80.

12 María del Cármen Velazquez, *Colotlan: Doble frontera contra los bárbaros* (México: UNAM, 1961), 17-18.

13 Martin, op. cit., 99.

14 Gonzalo Aguirre Beltrán, *Los pobladores del Papaloapan* (México: Instituto Nacional Indigenista, pre-edición mimeo #19, 1956), 65.

15 Gonzalo Aguirre Beltrán, *Cuijla: esbozo etnográfico de un pueblo negro* (México: Fondo de Cultura Económica, 1958), 87.

16 Adriana Naveda, *Esclavos negros*, 143.

17 Fernando Winfield Capitaine, "La vida de los cimarrones en Veracruz", in *Jornadas de homenaje a Gonzalo Aguirre Beltrán* (Veracruz: Instituto Veracruzano de Cultura, 1988), 87.

18 Adriana Naveda, *Esclavos negros*, 147.

19 Jose Rogelio Alvares (Dir.) *Enciclopedia de México. Vol. IX* (México: Enciclopedia de México, 1975), 370.

20 See Enrique Herrera Moreno, *El cantón de Córdoba. Vol. 1* (México: Ed Citlaltepetl, 1959).

21 Miguel García Bustamante, "Dos aspectos de la esclavitud negra en Veracruz", in *Jornadas de homenaje*, 221.

22 Herrera, *El cantón*, 90.

23 Ibid., 92-93.

24 García Bustamante, op. cit., 222.

25 Naveda, *Esclavos negros*, 126; Herrera, *El cantón*, 96-97.

26 Aguirre Beltrán, "Nyanga y la controversia en torno a su reducción a pueblo", in *Jornada de homenaje*, 133-34.

27 Naveda, *Esclavos negros*, 126.

28 Aguirre Beltrán, "Nyanga", 132-33.

29 Jonathan Israel, *Razas, clases sociales y vida política en el México colonial, 1610-1670* (México: Fondo de Cultura Económica, 1980), 77.

30 Aguirre Beltrán, "Nyanga", 132-33.

31 Herrera, *El cantón de Córdoba*, Vol. 2, 246.

32 García Bustamante, op. cit. , 220-21.

33 Israel, *Razas*, 79.

34 Bustamante, 230.

35 Beltrán, "Nyanga", 133.

36 Bustamante, 230.

37 Ibid., 227.

38 Israel, op. cit., 79.

39 Naveda, *Esclavos negros*, 128; Bustamante, "Dos aspectos", 226-27.

40 Bustamante (translated), 231.

41 Giovanni F. Gemelli Careri, *Viaje a la Nueva España* (México: UNAM, 1983), 151.

42 Naveda, *Esclavos negros*, 131.

43 Octaviano Corro, *Los cimarrones en Veracruz y la fundación de Amapa* (Xalapa: Veracruz Comercial, 1951), 22.

44 Ibid., 23.

45 Ibid.

46 Naveda, *Esclavos negros*, 145.

47 Ibid., 33-34.

48 Naveda, *Esclavos negros*, 147. Of the twenty-nine clauses of the legalizing document one-third relate to prison and punishments, three relate to maintaining the relative isolation of Amapa including specifically from San Lorenzo, and six relate to the constitution and operation of the local authorities, plus clauses on obedience to the Church, to the State and to providing militia as required. Corro, *Los cimarrones*, 36-40.

49 Beltrán, *Cuijla*, 60.

50 Ibid., 62.

51 The First Meeting of the Analysis and Study of Negritude and Freedom in America which was scheduled for the 1991 Carnival celebrations had to be cancelled along with the Carnival after six persons were shot dead in Yanga the night before the start of festivities, apparently victims of a vendetta.

52 Promotional leaflet for *Encounter*.

53 Archaeological evidence becoming available from recent studies appears to indicate that at a point in time, perhaps in the early years of maronage, slaves of African and indigenous Amerindian origin shared settlements from which they fought against colonial forces. See Agorsah [1993(a), 1993(b)].

seven

"Resistance Science": Afrocentric Ideology in Vic Reid's Nanny Town

Carolyn Cooper

Introduction

The African presence in the Americas predates the European. This fact defines a pan-Africanist context within which Maroon ideology throughout the Americas may be reconceptualized. Resistance science, as elaborated by Vic Reid in his Maroon novels *Nanny Town* and *The Jamaicans*, denotes a tradition of sustained subversion of European hegemony in this hemisphere.

This ideology and praxis of resistance manifests itself as a geopolitical continuity in societies such as the Palmares of Brazil, the Palenqueros of Colombia, the Djukas of Suriname, the Cimarrones of Mexico and Cuba and the Maroons of Jamaica.

The starting point of our history of Africans in the diaspora is not slavery and conquest, but the common human heritage of freedom and exploration: discovery that was a trial of skills and a mastery of self, not the automatic proprietorship of the "other" that is at the heart of imperial European enterprise. A naturalized consequence of the European appropriation of land was the assertion of the right to rewrite history. Those peripatetic Italians, Amerigo Vespucci and Christopher Columbus, in the authoritarian act of naming the lands they "discovered", became revisors of our history.

Naming is a constant reminder of that narcissistic imperial acquisitiveness that imprints the colonizer's image on captured land—squatters' rights. The very designation, "the Americas", is thus problematic, signifying as it does genocide—the effacing of the indigenous landscape and the erosion of the cultural autonomy of its original inhabitants.

Given the self-aggrandizing, revisionist instinct of European imperialism, it is not surprising that many Africans in the Americas do not know that their ancestors came to this region before Columbus. Some Jamaicans know that at least one crew member of Columbus' entourage was African, but we have not been taught a history of the region that makes sense of that fact, or, by extension, of the Maroons.

If you have been taught that Africans are savages—certainly no explorers—who were redeemed from primordial darkness by Europeans, then the evidence of sustained African resistance of slavery and enforced europeanization, becomes an aberration—a unique adaptive strategy of a specialized group. Maronage is not seen as the natural response of free people to dehumanizing attempts to restrict and restructure them—if slavery can be defined in such mild terms.

Caribbean historiography

Caribbean historiography needs to place the resistance science of the Maroons along a broad ideological continuum of cultural autonomy that manifested itself, however guardedly, even within the very belly of the plantation. Indeed, the well documented conflicts of interest between the Jamaican Maroons and the slaves "marooned" on the plantations clearly resulted from a too-narrow definition of who constituted the community of essential political affiliation.

For example, in Vic Reid's 1983 novel, *Nanny Town*, Gato (the Sun Cat), the hot-headed warrior who has taken two young Maroon boys into town for the first time on an exploratory "walk-bout", is angered when they appear attracted to the clothes and manners of the coast people: "Old cast-off clothes from a Red-Ants slave owner! That is what they wear! Our pigskin and lace-bark shirts we got by our own hands! Not ashamed of mud on our feet either, boy. Mud on the feet is a sign that we broke away! Mud on the feet and burr in the hair—signs of freedom, boy!"[1]

It is Kishee with "the Griot's gift of standing at the cross-roads and seeing all ways at once" [p.39] who provides a more complex reading of the coast people's clothes, carefully cautioning the young boys about the dangers of too readily dismissing the town people as being essentially alien:

> *'All of us on the mountains came from out of the coastie people. The Bell-People down there have never ceased to fight and to make their own lives, no matter that they wear the same clothing like the Red-Ants. When, after your Learning, you grow up to be a Griot, you must look hard into the matter of the flatland people and sing a song for them. That clothing Gato speaks of was bought by the money they make from their marketing. And many of them save their money and buy*

themselves free. Not everyone was born to be a Break-away. Some do a buy-away and live a good life, tiki. Those on the sugar plantation, they are our own blood, boy. Our brothers and sisters. It is true they are walking on anothe[r] road. But all roads lead to St Jago if you travel for the king!['] His one eye brightened. *'When you travel for the King, all roads lead to Spanish Town'. A saying of Queen-Mother Nanny. He liked to speak the proverbs of Nanny and sometimes added to her meanings* [pp.38-39].

Mechanisms of resistance

This use of clothing as a metonym for the surfaces of things, raises the complex issue of cunning, masking and role-play as mechanisms of resistance science—as powerful as overt confrontation. A wolf in sheep's clothing is a much more dangerous enemy than a bare-faced wolf. The boys Kwame Oduduwa and Kobi, on their first "walk-bout", are cautioned by Gato about not answering to their Maroon names; to preserve their identity they must assume an alien cover: "The English had a law which removed the thunderous Old Country names from the Bell-People, and punished them with such names as Prudence and Patience, and Toby and Jody, and left them no family names. So for safety on the coast, we left our real names in the stronghold. We were slave piknis. Jump and turn if a planter bellowed: 'Hey!' That was your name. 'Hey'"! [p.22].

The African-American slave narrative tradition, like our own, provides numerous examples of slaves assuming disguise, both literal and metaphoric, as a protective device. Feigning stupidity—"playing fool fi catch wise"—often proved to be a particularly effective strategy for survival. One of my favourite gems from an African-American slave narrative is reproduced in Gilbert Osofsky's edition of three slave narratives, entitled, *Puttin' On Ole Massa*.

The very use of the imagery of "puttin' on" to signify deception and cover-up, illustrates the linguistic cunning of the African-American tradition of covert resistance. In his "Introduction" to the slave narratives, Osofsky recounts a wicked instance of naming in which the slave, Pompey, ascribes to the master his true, true name, in a mock catechism:

> *"Pompey, how do I look?"*[2]
> *"O, massa, mighty"*
> *"What do you mean 'mighty' ,Pompey?"*
> *"Why, massa, you look noble."*
> *"What do you mean by 'noble'?"*
> *"Why, sar, you just look like one lion."*
> *"Why, Pompey, where have you ever seen a lion?"*
> *"I see one down yonder field the other day, massa."*
> *"Pompey, you foolish fellow, that was a jackass."*
> *"Was it, massa? Well you look just like him."*

A Jamaican slave narrative, the *Narrative of the Cruel Treatment of James Williams, a Negro Apprentice in Jamaica from 1st August 1834 Till the Purchase of his Freedom in 1837 by Joseph Sturge, Esq., of Birmingham, by Whom he was Brought to England*, includes a little detail about the possible uses to which a stone is to be put and which cunningly allows for at least two conflicting interpretations:

> I am about eighteen years old. I was a slave belonging to Mr. Senior and his sister, and was brought up at the place where they live, called Penshurst, in Saint Ann's parish in Jamaica. I have been very ill treated by Mr. Senior and the magistrates since the new law came in. Apprentices get a great deal more punishment now than they did when they was slaves; the master take spite, and do all he can to hurt them before the free come;—I have heard my master say, "Those English devils say we to be free, but if we is to free, he will be pretty well weaken we, before the six and the four years done; we shall be no use to ourselves afterwards . . .
>
> When I was a slave, I never flogged,—I sometimes was switched, but not badly; but since the new law begin, I have been flogged seven times, and put in the house of correction four times. Soon after 1st August, massa tried to get me and many others punished; he brought us up before Dr. Palmer, but none of us been doing nothing wrong, and the magistrate give we right . . . [here comes the stone]. When them try me, massa said, that one Friday, I was going all round the house with big stone in my hand, looking for him and his sister, to knock them down. I was mending stone wall round the house by massa's order.[3]

These instances of insidious slave revolt on the plantation clearly reinforce Vic Reid's representation of the common heritage of resistance science that is shared by both the break-aways and the bell-People. The Maroon griot describes the relationship between both groups thus:

> 'The Bell-People are those brothers and sisters whom the English stole from Africa, from the Old Country and enslaved on their plantations. There [sic] were forced to live out their lives answering the bell which told them when to wake, eat, sleep and when to appear for punishment. But many broke away and became famous Maroon men and women. They were known on the flatlands as the Break-aways' [p.8].

The break-away was often psychological, the enforced physical presence on the plantation concealing acts of sabotage and covert rebellion, such as poisoning. The science of resistance required the cultivation of the conspiratorial arts of secrecy.

Whatever the facts of Maroon treachery to runaway slaves after the peace treaty with the British, Maroon complicity with the European power élite and the potentially alienating Maroon assertion of cultural and political autonomy within Jamaica, the myth of the Maroon as the embodiment of essentially *Jamaican* aspirations to individual freedom is firmly embedded in contemporary popular culture.

Grandy Nanny

Thus the Right Honourable Nanny of the Maroons has been installed as a national heroine. Louise Bennett, Lorna Goodison and Adugo Onuora have written and performed poems in which Nanny is celebrated as the quintessential Jamaican female.

In "Jamaica Oman", Bennett establishes in the opening two verses of the poem the cunning of the Jamaican woman and then proceeds, in the third verse, to summon Nanny, wittily suggesting the unexpected complementarity of the militant, magico-religious powers of the ancestor figure and the verbal skill of the modern schoolgirl. Both verbal expansiveness and physical prowess seem to come naturally to women, though one is often used to cunningly mask the other:

> Jamaica oman cunny, sah!
> Is how dem jinnal so?
> Look how long dem liberated
> An de man dem never know!
>
> Look how long Jamaica oman
> —Modder, sister, wife, sweetheart—
> Outa road an eena yard deh pon
> A dominate her part!
>
> From Maroon Nanny teck her body
> Bounce bullet back pon man,
> To when nowadays gal-pickney tun
> Spellin-Bee champion.[4]

In Lorna Goodison's "Nanny" the poet assumes the mask of roots woman, presenting Nanny as the forerunner of all the nurturing mother figures of Jamaican balm-yard folklore. This Nanny, schooled in the art of herbal warfare, is specially sent to nurture the Jamaican people in secret ways that preclude biological mothering. Nanny is thus the prototype of a host of Jamaican women such as Aunt Alice of Erna Brodber's *Jane and Louisa Will Soon Come Home*, and Miss Gatha of Brodber's *Myal*, to name two fictional examples, who, though presented as childless, in fact mother the whole community through their knowledge of herbal medicine and the related arts of the arcane, obeah and myal.

Such women fulfil the promise of the final couplet of Goodison's poem, which I quote in its entirety:

> My womb was sealed
> with molten wax
> of killer bees
> for nothing should enter
> nothing should leave
> the state of perpetual siege
> the condition of the warrior.

From then my whole body would quicken
at the birth of everyone of my people's children.
I was schooled in the green-giving ways
of the roots and vines
made accomplice to the healing acts
of chainey root, fever grass and vervain.

My breasts flattened
settled unmoving against my chest
my movements ran equal
to the rhythms of the forest.
I could sense and sift
The footfall of men
from the animals
and smell danger
death's odour
in the wind's shift

When my eyes rendered
light from the dark
my battle song opened
into a solitaire's moan
I became most knowing
and forever alone.

And when my training was over
they circled my waist with pumpkin seeds
and dried okra, a traveller's jigida
and sold me to the traders
all my weapons within me.
I was sent, tell that to history.
When your sorrow obscures the skies
other women like me will rise.[5]

The wryly defiant line, "tell that to history", reminds us of the complicity of personified (eurocentric) history in the distorted representation of African diasporic culture. The sending of Nanny implies that conscious strategies of warfare were employed by Africans on the continent to succour Africans in the diaspora. This sending reconstructs one of the common distortions of history: that all Africans willingly sold inferiors into slavery.

In this guilt-ridden rewriting of European expansionism, the slave trade now becomes an absolutely joint enterprise! It therefore becomes difficult to ascribe blame and/or disentangle loyalties from treachery. Indeed, the divide-and-rule concept of class as a significant variable in indigenous slavery in Africa, pre-figures the Maroon/slave ethnic divisions in Jamaica.

Nanny – Jamaica's great warrior woman.

In Goodison's re-reading of political alignments, Nanny's waistbeads, her "traveller's jigida" is a band of history, a shared heritage of resistance science, reconnecting Africans at home with Africans abroad—to summon the spirit of Marcus Garvey.

In Vic Reid's novel, *Nanny Town*, it is this town named for Nanny, and its ethos of resistance, that are the novelist's central preoccupations. The opening lines of the novel establish several points of reference for the ensuing narrative:

> *Kishee the Griot of Nanny Town stood by the Learning Rock and told us of the Grande. 'She is the mother of many rivers. She was born in the Cuna Cuna hills and comes flowing down the Sierras de Bastidas, holding the hands of her many children.' He used the old name, Sierras de Bastidas; the name by which our ancestors called it, before the coming of the English who named it the Blue Mountains. 'The Mountain and the River, the father and mother of the Forest People. Our provider and protector'* [Reid: 1].

In this ecologically correct celebration of the land as nurturer that must itself be protected, is an image of organically conceived socio-political relationships that should not be violated. As ancestor figures, the personified male mountain and female river are not objects for exploitation but subjects of veneration. Like the land, the griot-"remembrancer" must himself be honoured, because he holds the key to not only the past but the future.

But the line of ancestry can be complicated. The renaming of the Sierras de Bastidas by the English is a rewriting of the name itself imposed by the Spanish on the indigenous landscape. Over time, the Spanish name has been naturalized, becoming for Kishee, the griot, the preferred name of his ancestors. This process of constant revising has resonances of an archaeology of cultural sedimentation. Maroon/Spanish antagonism becomes Maroon/Spanish collaboration in the face of a new joint enemy—the late imperialism of the English.

The novel documents the battles fought between the Maroons and the English. Resistance science becomes, in these physical battles, quite specific techniques of military precision. But cunning and disguise remain essential constituents of this literal resistance science. The venerated landscape actively participates in warfare, providing a natural cover for covert military manoeuvres: "The Mountain People have no great-guns. No grand-cannons or other ordnance. The ambush is the great-gun of the mountain people. It is the ambush that makes us come out even with the cannon-people. 'They were too many for us, so we turned the forest trees into soldiers'. We armed and drilled the rocks and gullies and waterfalls and made them fight for us" [p. 147].

The combolo/machete, the preferred implement of Maroon warfare, is celebrated by Vic Reid for its two-sidedness, its duplicitous nature. In an extended praise-poem to the combolo, Reid elaborates on both the domestic and military functions of this dangerous weapon:

It is the great tool of the Jamaican people, men and women. To plant their food, reap their fruits and fight their battles. It is greater than spear or sword, greater than the musket. Some fine machete-men can make it sing as it works its trade. It is not ugly as a gun, nor nasty as a knife. It is serene, friendly and hardworking in peace time; and, even in anger, it is resolute but not vengeful. You must study the care and use of it. You have seen your mothers and fathers, as the first matter of the morning, reach for it before they open the house door. And the last thing at night, after they have cleaned and polished the blade, put it away carefully as a baby in its cradle [pp.155-56].

Reid, a good griot, proceeds to give the history of the word:

The English have one close to ours which they call a cutlass, but cannot act as our combolo. The word is from our Spanish ancestry. It means companion and knife. Friend and protector. Combolo. It is also known as wamperer. In the Old Country, it bears the fine names of afana and afini. But by whatever name, our machete feeds us and fights for us. And is always a peacemaker; for who will pick a quarrel with a man who has his combolo to hand [p.156].

The ambiguous image of domesticity and militancy that the combolo embodies is replicated in Reid's presentation of the function of women in Maroon culture. Nanny is the prototype of all less celebrated, unnamed Maroon women who excelled at both the domestic arts of nurturance and the military arts of survival. Maroon women, as much as men, were warriors actively defending their communities.

If slavery was the first equal opportunity employers of black men and women—to cite Johnnetta Cole—the free societies of Jamaican Maroons also provided equal opportunities for men and women to engage fully in the double-sided life of the community.[6] The need to establish settled communities also had to be balanced against the need to be able to move quickly at the threat of invasion.

There is a powerful incident in the novel that illustrates this duality of function of Maroon women—both nurturers and fighters. A boa constrictor attacks one of the young women who is part of a group of men and women on an exploratory mission from Nanny Town to the land of war-chief Kojo. Let the griot speak:

I have been in many battles in my long life, but I tell you, pikni-Learners, never have I seen such violence as that morning when the daughters fell on the outsider who had broken in upon their duties of wives and mothers. Duties they had taken so as to accompany us on this hard journey. The foolish boa had made them appear weak and easy to assail; and this was a matter about them which was not true at all. Not true of our Maroon warrior-daughters. The boa had put himself in jeopardy. 'Howsoever, what can a poor bungo-man say of daughters? You know, no sooner had they cleaned up after they were finished with Bro' Boa those daughters were back at their tasks, soft as kittens, sweet as cane molasses, melting as coconut custard on the tongue, just as if they had never mashed an ant. Only when you looked closely in their eyes did you see the anger still lurking there.' When we laid out the boa and paced its length, none of us had ever seen longer [p.215].

That final sentence, proclaiming the extraordinary length of the boa, also affirms in good oral narrative style the authority of this essentially archetypal tale of female power. Vic Reid, the novelist, puts on the mask of griot to tell the tale within a tale of the making of a griot. Reid's first-person narrator is a "prentice griot" learning his trade which he defines thus: "Griot is the name we give to our *Remembrancers*, the men [and women][7] whose gift and duty it is to tell us of our past and point us to our future. Kishee ran his eyes over all our faces, the dozen of us sons and daughters at the Learning. Once every week for this year, we will attend at the Learning-Rock to be taught of our past by him" [p.1]. The biblical resonances of Reid's prose suggest yet other layers of sedimentation. The choice of to be taught "of" and not simply "about" is a small instance of Reid's attempt to find an oracular style to convey the gravity of the griot's calling. Like the Old Testament prophets whose "prophesight and prophesay" demanded communal respect, the griot needs words that are weighty with authority. The sonorous English of the King James version of the Bible comes closest, in Jamaica, to bearing the weight of griot gravity.

Reid, who in his 1949 novel, *New Day*, experimented with an artificial, stylized version of the Jamaican language as a way of voicing an indigenous sensibility, is himself a griot struggling to find the right idiom for his literary version of resistance science. Nanny Town is a celebration of our distinctive Maroon heritage. But it is, as well, an affirmation of our common heritage as Jamaicans, struggling to claim as our own this island which we were forced to embrace as home. In the words of Kojo: "We, all of us who call ourselves Maroons, form a chain. A chain of freedom all along this great backbone of mountains. If any link in that chain is weakened, all of us will become weakened. Somewhere, we will break" [p.239]. Men and women, Break-away and Bell-people, together must transform the chains of slavery into an empowering link. That, ultimately, is the embodiment of resistance science.

Notes

1 Vic Reid, *Nanny Town* (Kingston: Jamaica Publishing House, 1983), 38. Subsequent references cited in text.

2 Gilbert Osofsky (ed.), *Puttin' On Ole Massa* (N.Y.: Harper, 1962), 22.

3 Extract reprinted in Jean D'Costa and Barbara Lalla (eds.), *Voices In Exile: Jamaican Tests of the 18th and 19th Centuries* (Tuscaloosa: University of Alabama Press, 1989), 75-76.

4 Louise Bennett, *Selected Poems*, edited by Mervyn Morris (Kingston: Sangster's, 1982. Reprinted 1983), 21-22.

5 Lorna Goodison, *I am Becoming My Mother* (London: New Beacon Books, 1986), 44-45.

6 Johnnetta Cole, unpublished lecture (The UWI Lecture Series: "Facing 2000").

7 I must admit to a revisionist instinct to include the women here.

eight

Nanny, Palmares & the Caribbean Maroon Connexion

Kamau Brathwaite

Introduciton

I have six sounds to say here this morning, not knowing that it would be in this format [I had assumed that each of us would be a lecture or full presentation of about 60/90 minutes or so & prepared accordingly. I did not know that we would be involved not only in a panel arrangement with some six xciting others, but that because of constraints of time, we had no more than 10 minutes each!] So I am happy to let you know what the six sounds would have been. And I shall speak on as many of them as I can & in as much detail as I can as time permits

[What follows is a revised, built-up and edited version of the transcript of Prof Brathwaite's talk. The six 'sounds' (or soundings) have become nine]

I maronage: definition and overview

First of all I wanted to speak about Nanny & give an account of the research which went into the declaring of her as a National Hero. That was in 1975-76.[1] I say this because even though that research has been done & has been published in this book, *Wars of Respect*,[2] we still go on seeing in the newspapers and elsewhere, even in fact in other academic works, the notion that *no one knows anything about Nanny* & the myths about her seem to be as abstruse and unclear (or clear!) as ever

Second thing I wanted to speak about was Nanny as a(n) historical person and as a symbol – which I will come back to

Then I was going to look at Nanny within the context of Jamaican maronage in general because one tends to isolate her these days & see her as a (very precious) icon without realizing that she was first & foremust a *Maroon/person* & that therefore the culture & cultural skills that went into maronage were very much part of her personality & achievement

Fourthly we should have looked at Jamaican maronage within the context of African culture & its adaptations in the Americas – & this is another big debate & problem within our historiography – that people look at the achievements of Maroons & of slaves & slave rebels but they do not see this achievement as an aspect of the *culture* from which the people come. In other words we are invited to see maronage & slave revolt & African people survival as a kind of miracle & therefore quite inexplicable, when in fact the culture informs the achievement

Fifthly, therefore, I wanted to look – & will look a little – at maronage within the context of the plantation system of the Caribbean Americas. And there is some on-going research which I want to share with you just briefly

And **finally** as a result of all this, there should have been a redefinition of maronage – the term itself – & a widening of the notion of it to include things like *psychological maronage* which we in the present day & kind of world [Third, Developing, underDeveloping, neoColonial/ suppressed/downpressed Cannibal & Calibanistic etc] are very much part of & certainly very much involved with/in one way or the other

But I am going to confine what I say this morning mainly to Nanny as a(n) historical person & symbol & to Jamaican maronage within the context of the Plantation though other aspects of my overview will be touched on if & as necessary

2 grandeenanny & the african-jamaican culture of maronage

With Nanny the big thing really is her buttocks. I think that is really where the whole thing rests. Wherever you turn you get this image of the woman with the buttocks who turns towards the enemy, catches their bullets into these buttocks and farts them back out – successfully – at the enemy. I mean this is something scholars are asked to accept And the mere fact that we seem to accept it suggests that we have been trapped into this ideology of buttocks. In other words, we are in danger – no – we are losing sight of the person for the sake of a part – a very distinguished part unquestionably – but still only a part. And this has been the problem of the research & everything else. Why is it that Nanny is only a part of the whole?

As a matter of fact, the tale & image of Nanny's buttocks does not arise from the contemporary (early 18th century) record, but appears for the first time, much later, in the late 19th century, as far as I know, in H T Thomas' *Untrodden Jamaica* (1890)[3]

'The notorious Nanny was a woman

[Thomas had to say that because at that time the rumour was that she was really a pot, a bird, a witch, or at best a cat & one of the reasons why it was felt necessary to research her 'suitability' for the nation's highest award in 1976 was to ascertain *if in fact she existed at all,* since (again) the almost universally accepted rumour was that she was a 'myth' or 'legend' – old wives' 'Nancytory']

'and the wife of the leader Cudjoe – or I presume, one of his wives

[There has always been a suggestion that Nanny, leader of the Windward & Cudjoe, leader of the Central or North Coast or Accompong Maroons, were related – Maroon tradition suggesting that they were siblings. But contemporary reports indicate that she had a Windward husband, Adou who for some reason or other 'never went into their battles'[4]

Thomas is however correct on the subject of Maroon polygamy – one more aspect of their African tradition, & necessary under the crisis of Maroon conditions for the certain generational continuation of the group (marginal food producing land, a minimum survival quotient in this ecology with an xcess of warrior males)]

'and like all unsexed women who have had a freebooter's life

[I don't know how Thomas got to know the 'unsexed' aspect of Nanny or if he means what I think he means -- he probably meant something else, using the rumour that she was a witch – described by the only English writer who probably saw her (the English officer, Philip Thicknesse), as an 'old Hagg']'[5]

'ten times more ferocious and blood-thirsty than any man among the Maroons

She was possessed of super-natural powers, and spirited away the best and finest of the slaves from the outlying estates. She never went into battle armed like the rest, but received the bullets of the enemy that were aimed at her, and returned them with fatal effect, in a manner which decency forbids a nearer description [of]' (Thomas 1890 p.36/my emphasis)

This story, as I say, has been repeated – uncritically repeated – by nearly every if not every writer since Thomas – INC MAROON LEADERS AND WRITERS THEMSELVES INVOKING ORAL TRADITION – and has continued, as I say, as if I had not written *Wars of Respect*[6]

It is Craton who perhaps puts it most confidently & positively, even providing (uncited) 'xplanations' and 'parallels' in Africa: 'the story that during **attacks she was able to catch cannon balls** [WOW! cannonballs/not even bullets now] **between her buttocks and to fart them back with deadly effect HAS MANY AFRICAN PARALLELS during the long period of resistance to the Europeans** (my emphasis)'[7]

Beverley Carey, a Maroon & holding a position in the hierarchy & one of the finest indigenous reconstructors of Ja Maroon history known to me, in her still unpublished *A history of the Maroon peoples of Jamaica* (1975ts/p29), shifts the myth from bare buttocks to bare hands: 'Nanny was not above using some of her great powers of auto-suggestion on the [Br] troops. She created metaphysical manifestations to frighten them and according to Maroon oral tradition, she actively participated in battle'*[could she not 'participate' in any other way?]*

I would say that these distortions have come about because in the first place it must be clear that Nanny could not be 'real' to the historians (both 'then' & now) who were (are) dealing with this kind of *serious* icon. She could not be 'real' because she was a visible woman living at the end of the 17th century – a period when 'visible' women – apart from a few White Queens – were almost impossible to conceive of & therefore to perceive in PUBLIC FUNCTION AND PERSONA. She was also *buttockicized* (& that the word is awkWEIRD & ungainly is no accident) because she was black & therefore a slave no matter what & therefore how could she possibly be a leader, far less a *black* leader - far less a black *woman* leader – & physically & metaphysically so successful that by 1720 the Br (certainly some key planters in the Port Antonio area – on the GrandeeNanny firing line, as it were) were contemplating abandoning their Plantation Xperiment in Jamaica since as long as the Maroons occupied the space at the height & centre of the island – as long by militantly & successfully occupying the mountains & by cutting off easy & dependable communication between the North & South coasts where the major plantations were located & by their 'Zionism' were creating a kind of NewAfrican heaven & haven & kingdom at the visible heart of the island (in those always visible & (to them) viable Blue & John Crow Mountains) which would increasingly be an attraction to hundreds perhaps thousands of the enslaved & therefore a threat or cut-throat to the whole xpensive & would-be xpansive Plantation System from Port Antonio through MoBay right around to Morant Bay – there could be no guarantee that the Plantation would continue to be a profitable investment under such conditions (& indeed the Maroons held up the manifest destiny of Br Plantation in Ja for 85 years)[8]

In fact Nanny was far far more than 'simply' a political & military leader of her people (though that, Nyame knows, was already a great deal). She was also a prophet & healer and religious leader – an *ngunza*, to use the term that the Congolese anthropologist, Fu-Kiau K Kia Bunseki-Lumaniza used of Miss Queenie of Jamaican kumina.[9] But she was far far more even than that; being abov(e) all, Queen Mother & 'Keeper of the Tribe'; what the Asante of Ghana would have called (would call) *ohemmaa* – like Nzinga Nzinga of Angola & the long line of Ashanti Queen Mothers recorded as having accompanied armies into war: among them Juaben Sewa of Juaben, Ata Birago of Kokofu, Akyia of Asansu & Yaa Asantewa of Ejeisu, who was xiled with Prempeh after the 1895/96 war with the British. All these women 'were old and had *passed the menopause*'[10] hence I suppose, Mr Thomas' 'unsexed'[11] (above) – though I have never seen any of this recognized &/or taken up in any of the work on maronage since 1976/77[12]

In other words, we do not seem to assert/affirm this particular but essential aspect of the woman Which again can only make & leave her 'smaller' than she is; for I think – I mean I know – that without recognizing her full **stature** -

& there is not yet – as far as I know – even a **statue** of her – a public official ceremonial representation or icon of her[12] – in National Heroes Park (or anywhere else for that matter – not even I suspect on our postage stamps) – even though she 'became' National Hero in 1977[13]

So that until we can recognize Nanny's stature (& statue) – the *true-true meaning of her nature/culture* – not the mere stone or 'story' or Bump Grave – we will never comprehend the fullness of what this Woman – this *Ohemmaa* – awe & all – *represents* & therefore we will never properly & respectfully be able to 'account' for her success – & through her, account for the success (if you can call it that) of maronage in Plantation America

She comes as I say from a long line of *ohemmaa* like Yaa Asantewa & Nzinga Nzinga & many many others like them throughout Africa as well as within the Caribbean/Americas. But because she was this kind of special person, capable of transporting or receiving the transmission of ancient ancestral cultural resources in ways that we can't yet overstand/xplain & was able to aid in the successful adaptation of these resources to the crisis of the Caribbean/Jamaican/Blue Mt Maroon situation, so that as quickly & as efficiently as possible – that's the point – without too much time spent on apparent practice & apprenticeship & training (certainly no apparent going to formal school etc) – though of course there was a great deal of necessary & intensive apprenticeship & training – the Maroons were able to successfully establish themselves in the inhospitable but defensible ecology of the Americas, adapting themselves to the available food and other supplies, adapting themselves to martial techniques that flowed so naturally out of their environment that they appeared to be like ghosts of the landscape, building & planting in that landscape in ways too that made sense as long as they could keep the situation stable – & developing social & political & religious & military defensive forms that did just that – she had to be invisibilized in the same way & for the same reason(s) that the achievement of Haiti under Toussaint Legba Louverture & his successors had to be invisibilized – because it represents a successful alternative cultural model to the Superior Monopolistic Missile* that Western Europe had developed in their own Middle Passage across the Atlantic & into the Americas

The point I am making – even if I repeat myself – being that the success of Nanny & of maronage in the Caribbean/Americas was in no way accidental or inexplicable – or if 'accidental' the result of 'cultural accident' – of which there is no such thing. Which means that each Maroon leader follower community dreamer had to work as hard as any other leader follower community dreamer to achieve the miracle OUT OF *xtremis* – & that like all 'successes' (even failures) they followed a successful ancestral model – or at anyrate made their model a success. And a vital element of the success of their model was its *difference* to the then-being-promoted European alterRenaissance* model adapted in the Caribbean/Americas as the Plantation with its attendant 'Mentality', 'Economy' & so on

Therefore Nanny had to be shut up & shut down And the buttocks is part of the shutting down/ & the shutting up comes in the archives. Because when I went to London to undertake the research, there were only four references to Nanny that were available And that is perhaps why we have the impression that she did not xist; or if she xists she xists very marginally – although of course 'she lives in the heart of her people . . .'

3 nanny and the problem of archival certification

1733

The first reference is in the Journal of the Assembly of Jamaica,[14] **& it says very clearly that Cuffie, a very good party Negro, claims reward for having killed Nanny**

So she xists – but is dead before she even *begins* – killed by a pawn soldier in 1733. So we can safely say, if we go by the documents, that she no longer xists – ignominiously cut off/cut down before she really achieved anything – since for the Br historian, Prof Posterity, the only significant Maroon 'achievement' will be the Peace Treaties of 1739 & 1740.[15]

1735

The Colonial Office Papers (CO/137) record that **Cupid, an Ibo** (Igbo) **slave escaped from the rebels**, reported that **he saw three white men 'who were taken in some of these parties', carried to the Negro Town 'and there put to death by Nanny'**

She had to be an *ohemmaa*. No 'ordinary' person – man far less 18th century woman – could take a knife like that in the *disciplined* environment of a Maroon settlement

The realization of discipline is **KEY**/ it betokens civilization, something of course denied to Blacks & Maroons; but a Maroon 'camp', like any other civilized community, whether under duress or not, but perhaps especially under duress & under strict military protocol (these people were not brigands or pirates) would have been at very great pains to observe all the necessary legal decorums ('Geneva Convention' etc) especially when faced with (to them) the *legal* xecution of a British army person – an officer & a (white) gentleman – far less **THREE** of them! – to death – unless she had that kind of overarching and constitutional *authority*

That, at least, is what we see in the CO Papers, that is in the *manuscript*. But what do we see in the Calendar of State Papers (CSP) where it comes to be printed? Some genius, perhaps the same man who took the nose of Sphinx & cut if off so that it would not appear to be Nubian, *revises* this manuscript making *one only brilliant slip of the pen* or rather 'eye' to radically alter the appearance of an important document for over 250 years now

three white men who were 'taken in some of those parties', carried to the Negro town & 'there put to death by **hanging'**

That is the printed version, which of course comes down to all historians – *'put to death by hanging'*

I compare the two versions: CO & then CSP. The wording is identical until you come to where, in the manuscript, there was *Nanny* 's name – now, instead, you have *hanging*

& when you look again at the ms, you can see, in a way, that a mistake could have been made since the way *Nanny* is written it could become *hanging*:

N into *h*, *an* = *an* & the *ny* of her last syllable with the long tail of the *y* (we must really acquire a photograph of this) could be/come *ging* especially since there is an *n* in there anyway etc etc

& because the person who was doing the transcription from the manuscript to the printed version **[CK on what year that was if you can]** *assumed that the execution could not have been done by a word he did not recognize* (**Nanny**?/ I mean who/what/Nanny! – just don't make no sense!) *but by a word he <u>did</u> (hanging)*[16]

To *summarize*

Nanny is written in the earliest official document in a way that one could in fact xcusably say that it is *hanging* if you wanted to see it that way – and it is, in fact written as *hanging*. I regard that as deliberate error which was never corrected & of course it conclusively changes 'the course of History' since (first) it allows us to think that the people concerned were put to death by anybody (= **no**/body) when in fact they were put to death by an ohemmaa. And we are 'changing the course of History' certainly Herstory also because the name Nanny begins at this point to *disappear from the records*, permitting by the 19th century a rumour so strong that she did not xist, that even today (October 91) despite academic research & official 'justification' (not that I hold any special brief for either of these as you should have gathered), it is still widely held that *she was never here* although in this same document of 1735 we hear that there are certain people living in a certain area where there is also Nanny & her husband 'who is a greater man than Adou but never went into their battles'. So she is still there in 1735 although the evidence is not as strong as it would have been if both references were present

1740/41

The Land Patent to Nanny of 1740 –

'George 11 by the Grace of God of Great Britain, France and Ireland and King of Jamaica Lord Defender of the Faith . . . have given and granted . . . and do give and grant unto . . . Nanny and the people residing with her and [their] heirs . . . a certain parcel of land containing five hundred acres in the parish of Portland . . .'[17]

This is the one thing [the LAND PATENT TO NANNY] that we hang on to & say that this was really Nanny (of the Meroons/from time to time I use the Ja Maroon pronunciation of their 'name' though they call themselves **********) Xcept that some might come back with/this was a different Nanny[18]

4 buttocks

Finally – we have to confront the business of the **buttocks** & hope that eventually scholars & artists will begin to treat Nanny (& Maroon/maronage) with more respect; and our women & Submerged Mothers with more respect –[19]

I mean, is so easy to invoke the promise & dark sonority of our women's buttocks. What we've got to come to understand is that women *use* their buttocks & that the part is part of the whole & that the whole is part of the culture in a very real way. There is no way that Nanny could have turned her back & done what they say she did. But she could have turned her back, lifted her skirt, & *displayed the derrière* as **a symbol of derision & abuse** which is a very common feature of 'the culture', as you know . . .

But we must remember that the buttocks is also a source and symbol of **power** – what the Kikongo call *mgara* – fulfillment – And in the case of Nanny we see the buttocks, then, not only as a (?negative) symbol of **derision & abuse** but also (more positively) as an xpression of **military power** (she displayed her buttocks during battle) as an xpression of **para-military power** – since she was *guerrilla* too (& you must have noticed what the female chimpanzee/ gorillas do!); a symbolization of her **ritual power**

(the elaborate costumes developed by our people to conceal/reveal the buttocks in kumina, in carnival, and the androgynous effect of the (female) ritual clothing worn by men in cassocks, bubas, konnus, akabuá & the continuation of this into the symbol & xpression of **fertility** most commonly articulate in walk in flirt in dance

And unless we xplore those meanings – *which all-yu know far better than me* – we (the very people of her culture & inheritance) will continue to place her in a dark fatty ghetto of the flesh which only disenables – **disempowers** – you & us & all of her

For when Nanny used/displayed her buttocks to the enemy – or anyone else for that matter – she did it *totally* – & for good (cultural) reasons

5 maroons in the context of the caribbean/americas acculturation & the 'law' of cultural monopoly

Now in the context of the wider Caribbean what I want to say here is this: that in the research that I have been doing I am beginning to recognize that there were (& in some cases still are) six main areas of Maroon activity of tremendous importance & effect And these areas are interconnected In other words what I am inviting you to recognize is that Maroons are not 'people isolated' – *marooned* on a hilltop & trapped (hopefully not *moróned*) into their own communities. Because of their independence they were able to achieve, they were able to xploit, whenever possible, that independence to create connections with other Maroon – & other – communities. And that is one of the ways in which they so successfully, more than 'survived'.

The features of these Maroon power-bases were densely forested x-plantation karsted-type mountain-islands (in the case of the islands/in the case of the mainland: mountains &/or riverain forest) with (in the case of Dominica, the Guyanas, Honduras & Mexico) significant African/Amerindian alliance, consensual intermixture &/or co-operation –

The six main nexuses were ...

(1) Dominica in the Windward Islands where the Carib population, which was not xterminated until 1814, mixed with the slaves of the entire Windward area becoming **the Black Caribs**/see also BELOW (who were not attemptedly xterminated until 1795)

[This may not be quite accurate, but it is my impression that the Plantation, following the 'Law' of Cultural Monopoly & Purity (all five Continental Cultures possess this 'natural' tendency, but it was not of especial consequence until the Cultural Continents began to 'collide' from about 1450 with European Xploration (200 yrs earlier the Chinese had undertaken Xploration but had stopped – in 1350 – no one knows why, at the Straits of Gibraltar – on the edge of the ?fatal Atlantic

But even before that[20] some African & other navigators were probably also edging back the frontiers of the world But none of these cases seems to have resulted in significant – certainly not in catastrophic – cultural collision (which might well involve a major revision in the Law of Cultural Gravity cited above) But after 1450 European xploration, followed quickly by European xploitation (& this, we suspect, is the Significant Variant) began a process of attempted ACCULTURATION in which the xpansionist/aggressive culture developed MISSILIC capability whose objective was to EAT (the 'ac' of 'acculturate') the target culture in order to convert it (the target) to a colonial/dependent/submissive & bastard approximation (but approximation ONLY) of the Man/Boss/Metropole

This period was = a period of considerable VIOLENCE as the would-be Master Culture sought to convert the OTHER to its/his (the Master's) culture (& icons) and of course the targets struggled to RESIST]

(2) Hispaniola – the whole geological island – both Santo Domingo & the Haitian side; where on the crest between the two territories, the Black Mountains became the headquarters for a very large Black Carib/Maroon group founded by CACIQUE HENRI & reinforced by slaves from Diego Colon's estate after their 1522 revolt at a place called Bahoruco (though the Haitian Maroons occupied crucial heights in the NW of the island also & it is this Maroon complex which in the end becomes largely responsible for the success of the Haitian Revolution – a sound that since we do not even *look* at the Haitian Revolution, we hardly ever hear or recognize But the combination of slave revolt & maronage is v much there – as late as May 1785 for xample the Bahoruco Maroons under Santiago were able to negotiate Peace Treaties with the now v Developing Plantation . . .[21] (This Black Mt group (& it is a *complex* not a 'group' as I've been saying & as we tend to say & think) xisted obviously from 'the beginning' – from the Columbian Period right thru to 1804 - the time of Haitian Independence. After that of course the Haitian Maroons (as happens w/ Maroon communities worldwide) begin to 'dissolve' into the general population/tho Haitian psychological maronage & its offshoots (vodoun, paysan, macoute and 'Haitian art' etc) continue their enjambments into today – especially when/whenever there is significant/?xcessive re-emergence/encroachment of Plantation . . .)

(3) **Palmares** (1599-1694) – the 98 year-old Black *kilombo* Republic in Bahia, Brazil – the most dynamic, the most dramatic [perhaps – rather – the one most dramatized/romanticized by Portuguese modernismo & negrismo writers (see also the utterly lovely film on Palmares, A deusa negra by the Nigerian Ola Balogoun/but then there has been nothing even near to comparable written or filmed about Haiti or Dca or the Garifuna or Nanny/Accompong] w/ a lot of connexions w/ trade into Venezuela and, some claim, across the Atlantic into Benin & Yoruba . . .

(4) **The Jamaica Maroons:** from the onset of the Spanish **encomienda** through British slavery right on/to native Independence (1962) to today (October 1991) – a period of almost 500 years. During this time the Ja Maroons, anchored mainly on their four main towns: Maroon, Trelawny, Accompong & Nanny (the last two founded cl700?), like Maroon communities everywhere, maintained close & necessary trade and social relations with the coasts (salt, arm, gunpowder, contraband, selected manufactured goods (axe, machete, pots, buckets, pans, cloth, needles) coins, news, women) & with the island's street corners, markets, estates, farms, Army camps, ware & whorehouses from the very beginning of the colony & we don't begin even to understand its xtent and nature – political military social economic ideological solidarity with Cuba & Hispaniola. Gov Gregory to the Colonial Office[22] admits how the Spaniards in Cuba were 'acquainted with the Action [in Ja Maroon country] before the News of it [reaches] the Govt at Sp Tn'; & there was evidence on several occasions between 1730 & 1737 of alliances between the Windward Maroons & the Spaniards in Cuba[23] & there was, as I say, most probably contact between the Ja & Cuban Maroons who of all the Northern Caribbean groups were perhaps most xtra/territorially active since of all Caribbean territories Cuba (until the emergence of Plantation in the 1820s) was by far the wealthiest & most 'open' societies* with all non-white groups there having more 'leeway' than in most other places*

_____*The Cuban palenques were mainly located in what becomes, in Cuba, a traditional Blk stronghold, the Sierra Maestra Mts of the SE above Santiago de Cuba. The first record of a Maroon community in there comes in the 1730s (Bumba's band). By ?1740, for instance, Gallo's palenque had established links thru White Cuban merchants for trade w/ Hispaniola and Ja. The Cuban Maroons are not 'eradicated' until 1819/ reflecting of course the relatively slow chronological development of the monopolizing Plantation in Cuba

(5) The Suriname/Guiana Maroons: by far the largest (c50,000 in 1980) & second longest-surviving and still largely 'natural'* Maroon (Amerindian/Akan/Kikongo) complex,[24] situated over a huge riverain area xtending up to ?750 miles upriver from the coast (Paramaribo) along the Coppename, Suriname, Saramacca, Commewyne, Cottica, Marowyne, Lawa & Tapanahoni rivers of the NE Amazon, consisting of a 'federation' (in 1980) of some 60,000 people: Njukka, Paramaka, Aluku (aka Boni), Saramacca, Matawai, Kwinti w/ offshoot & 'descendants' throughout the rain forest of the vast interior 'hinterland' (former Br Fr & Dutch Guiana) w/ connexions (hence survival) w/Amerindian communities & cultures throughout the Amazon & the south continent's Atlantic + Pacific coasts & into the Maroon highlands of Venezuela-Honduras-Mexico

(6) The Garifuna (formerly Blk Carib) **of Belize/Honduras**. The 'youngest' of the Caribbean/American Maroon groups, but only if you 'date' them from the time of their xpulsion (1795) from St Vincent. This group, already AfricanAmerindian (Blk Carib) in St Vincent, again interculturated w/ Amerindians along the Honduras coast, developing a basically Amerindian 'cassava' + fishing culture based however on the drum & all that that implies of an African religious choreography & orientation

The adoption of the name Garifuna – for generalized 'Blk Carib' – in the early 70s – was/is a sign of a new consciousness & cultural militance among certain, at least, Maroon groups, especially these 'younger' Garifuna. Note again the sense of connexion: with St Vincent as Ancestral Home & ceremonies of The Arrival (in C America) and with their physical & cultural survival very much a matter of having successfully broken out of the Rattan Is/Mosquito Shore 'prison' intended for them

6 the black carib

I would like finally & very briefly to take a look at the very remarkable but perhaps most neglected of all Windward Is Maroon groups centred on the island of Dominica – its *Morne Nègre* redoubt ('founded' as early as c1500) being regarded in some quarters as the 'Palmares of the Caribbean' & certainly severely limiting in that part of the world, French settlement (1690-1761) & British plantation development after that date

_____*The Suriname Maroons were able to remain 'natural' for far longer than any other in the Americas because of the size & inaccessibility of the terrain in which they lived. The story in Suriname was that xpeditions them had to Climb 40 mountains Cross 60 rivers to 'reach' them. (Need we say therefore that they would be insulted with a cognomen like 'Bush Negroes'?) In the 1960s Modernization decreed a Great Dam on the upper reaches of the Suriname River, resulting (as in so many other places in the Developing World) in a Great Artificial Lake that eventually dispossessed some 6,000 Saramacca & 1/3 of their ancestral land. Since then, in consequence, the interior – as all over Disastrous Amazonia – is being 'opened up' with more & more Maroons being absorbed in to the Labour Force

I have not yet seen any significant account of the origin or 'genesis' of the Black Mountain Dominicans (indeed research/commentary on this important Maroon group is pretty well 'submerged' as you would xpect); but we know that as in all the other (some later) Maroon cases, the 'movement' took advantage of a BREAK-DOWN OF EURO POLITICAL/MILITARY AUTHORITY in this case with the British conquest of the island from France in 1759 & the resulting & continuing 20 years of instability with further conquests & reconquests (1762-1782). It is during this time that the great Dean leaders appear: Congo Roy, Bulla, Zombie (Zambi), Jupiter, Juba, Cicero, Hall, Mabouya, Jacko, Coree (?Gorée), Sandy & Pharcell. And it was only after 1782, when it was clear that it was British mercantilism that was in charge in the area, that the Plantation undertook its war of xtermination > the Morne Nègre Maroons (1795) the Morne Fortune Maroons of St Lucia (1796/using Black troops – the W I Regiment) when + 2000 were killed. The St Lucian Blk Caribs were defeated that same year though the remnant 'Brigands' kept up the struggle until **** & the Deans held out until 1814*w/their leader Quashie placing a reward – DEAD OR ALIVE – on the British Governor's head;* & up to 1793/95 the Morne Nègre & the Windward Maroon(s) were still regarded as a 'crossroads of the Caribbean' with plenty 'traffic' through the area in arms ideas & freedom fighters: Victor Hughes, Fedon, Daaga, the Brigands War of St Lucia, the French Revolution, the effect of Haiti, Civil Rights (for the Free Col) etc etc

Tʰe Black Carib of St Vincent & tʰe Grenadines

It is said that the St Vincent Black Carib came about after a slaveship shipwreck off/on ?Bequia; this core being reinforced over time by Bajan runaways, who must have found the many scattered islets & cays of the Grenadines a ?perfect salvation from their Full Plantation[25] Bajan Hell especially after the abortive slave revolts of 1675 (King Kofi) & 1692 & the resulting Plantation reprisals

Because of the proximity of so many islands & the still xtant Amerindian tradition of movement & trading within these islands, there had developed within their Maroon people (African, Amerindian, AfricanAmerindian/Blk Carib) therefore, not only considerable resistance to the Plantation (as we have already noted/so that in Dominica & to a lesser but significant degree in Grenada St Vincent St Lucia & perhaps Guadeloupe) Plantation development was considerably inhibited – Dominica becoming an Undeveloped Plantation, the rest either Partial or Declining – & because of *maritime maronage* & the continuing co-operation between the islands – a 'cooperation' xtending as far south as Barbados (90 miles away) & north into the Leewards the Virgins Puerto Rico there was enough build-up of people and alterPlantation resources especially in the Headquarters islands of Dominica & St Vincent, for White Settlement & its Programme to feel so threatened/so uncomfortable that they were forced into a final confrontation with Maronage[26]

The final war > Dominica although 'underway' since 1795/96, again with the help of the Black WI Regiment, did not really escalate until 1802 after, in fact, a

mutiny in the Black Regiment (This mutiny – & there were others throughout
the Caribbean wherever detachments of the WIR were stationed – was another
aspect of the new 'Race Problem' initiated by changes in European needs & psychology triggered by the Industrial Revolution(see below)[27]

And one gets the impression that the final destruction of Maroon opposition
not only to Plantation but, it was being perceived, to Br Imperialism & the new
Industrial Mercantilism linked as it now was to a new sense of Race & Culture
'purity' (certainly Superiority) had become (to the Whites) urgently necessary
RIGHT THEN –

*(and don't forget that it was at this same time that Toussaint Legba Louverture & his
family had been kidnapped to France where he was about to die of cold loneliness defeat
apoplexy & a sense of betrayal in White Justice & Culture he had himself 'joined' in an
act of betrayal to his own native Maroon & vodoun connexions & Napoleon-Leclerc-Ro-
chambeau were undertaking their own 35,000 troop-strong War of Xtermination > the
Haitian Revolution and Maroons)*

But these 1795/96 + Windward wars against the Maroons were not 'simply' or
'only' Plantation efforts to remove eradicate or xpell Maroons. 1795/96 was also the
Maroon Wars of the French Revolution & the European Wars of the Haitian Revolution. **But this period marks also a far more significant & far-reaching watershed** (if you can have a 'far-reaching watershed'/but you know what I mean) in
'world' psychology since we are now face to face with the Industrial Crisis of/in
the Plantation System

7 maronage & the industrial revolution

The English (1640), American (1776) & the French (1789) Revolution had all in
their different ways signalled the presence of a new economic procedure &
world-view within European or, if you like, Euro-American mercantilism, in
which mass production, resulting from fuel-consuming locomotive machinery,
was replacing the medieval cottage industries of the past 400 years. In this new
dispensation, labour would have to be used in a different way from the feudal;
& money, markets, trade & investment would now have to be conceived & constructed on a global rather than on a protected national scale with colonies,
which is where Europe had reached when the American(s) xploded in 1776.
The challenge of all the new political revolutions was that they would successfully permit the emergence of a new entrepreneurial class that would be able to
make this new Industrial vision a reality

It so happened that the Plantation System & its accompanying system of
slavery had been all along a precursor of Industrialism but its drawbacks were
that it was welded into the old protected nation-state mercantilism & therefore
could not reach out to world markets & investment; its (slave) labour system
was slow xpensive conservative & sluggish & therefore could in no way meet
the demands of the new science & technology that the use of fuel-dependent
locomotive machinery required. Above all it was being recognized that a

slave/nonindustrial world could not be/come a consumer world since there-was no or little money among the 'teeming populations' of the oppressed – and it was their very teemingness that attracted both those thirsty for new cheap labour but moreso those attracted to the prospect of gullible & captive consum-ers by the *millions* with new fuels & new convertible raw materials under their soils if not under their control

Emancipation (1)

Slavery therefore had to go but even more so *maronage*, since maronage (& the Hai-tian Revolution was making this more than clear) was an intransigent alternative which might be as resistant to the new & still untried Industrial dispensation as it had been to the Plantation. For one thing, maronage was ideologically based on the notions of self-sufficiency & cultural autonomy. The new Industrial Revolution had its mind set on advertising-induced artificial wants, credit dependence, debt slavery & it had to have time & space (but not *too* much) to convince the "teeming populations" (later "the striving masses" etc) of this. All the more reason why physical & with it ideological maronage had *now* to be removed – wherever in the target world it was to be found.

To achieve this, a great new subtle (& sometimes not so subtle) cybernetic cam-paign was set in train under the guise or vehicle or opportunity of **SP colonialism**, the first stage of which, as it had been under the Conquistadores (*how things change & yet as they say remain the same!*) was the brutal frontal destruction of any physical or psycho-physical (i.e. cultural) opposition encountered – as was being encoun-tered in the Caribbean most awesomely in Haiti. Hence the attack on 'Accom-pong', the assault on Dominica, St Vincent, St Lucia & the conversion of what used to be medievally 'courteous' warfare (with parleys Peace Treaties protocols etc/Nanny not just Nobody xecuting the poor Laird of ?Lanceret; the grant of land to Nanny for being a Noble Opponent(?) into race wars – confrontations of physi-cal & cultural xtermination (the North Americans in North America, the British in Australasia & the Pacific & in the Maroon Caribbean, Napoleon in Santo Dom-ingo/his plan to eradicate all the leaders of the Revolution & their families, sup-porters & friends/before Jean-Jacques Dessalines got the measure of him)

8 (?) xtermination (?)

In other words EuroAmerican culture was saying that to realize its new Industrial world-dream, it could no longer tolerate a successful alternative and that this group of people – Carib, Black Carib, Maroon, etc – would have to go. The British sent 17,000 troops into the Windward Is. to do that in 1795. And Le Clerc, Napo-leon's brother-in-law, brought an armada of some 30 ships & at least 30,000 troops into Haiti to do just that. *So was no joke.* They definitely had a plan; and when it did not work – *could not work because of successfullly sustained resistance based, as I main-tain, essentially on community-based cultural resources + mutinies within the European forces* – a policy of xile & xpulsion was then resorted to & you have the movement of St Vincent Maroons into Belize, Honduras & the Mosquito coast; & the movement of the militant ?250 Trinidad & Tobago Maroons into Nova Scotia/hoping to kill them off by cold but their successful counterattack in getting themselves repatriated to Sierra Leone in 1800.[28]

Emancipation (2)

Emancipation, in this context then, would have to be seen as an emancipation of the buttocks in that submerged people were at last given the opportunity to become not their private ?special parts, but them*selves*; an emancipation which had itself come about, in significant part, through an alliance between successful maronage & the principles that the slave populations had absorbed from the Maroons. But after 1814 & the end of the 'wars of xtermination' > the Maroons, the onus, the burden of physical & cultural resistance to the mercantilist Plantation was now placed upon the slaves, rather than on what was now the Maroon remnant. So that after 1814 you have these **wars of liberation** coming out of the Plantation And coming successfully out of the plantation because the slaves were now having – *were willing* – to learn more & more from the Maroon Xperience. They were therefore fighting their wars, not on classical European confrontational patterns, but on a guerrilla choreography suitable to their resources. And they were more & more calling upon their nativeAfrican (creole) resources which were being funnelled to them via the persisting presence of maronage & the memory & xample of successful resistance symbolized in the achievement & reality of QueenMother GrandeeNanny Ohemmaa of the Jamaica Maroons.

9 *veridian*

for GrandeeNanny

high up in this littered world of rock. stone

yucca bush bamboo trash narrow
defiles where there are no sweet painted trees

wind we know always sharp slant sleet howl but warm
as your lips & gentle as a mother with her baby cheek
to cheek misty mornings high noons spectacular sunsets

at the bottom of this high world high above it all we draw
the lion picket our stand and make our testament
boy girl woman warrior elder statesman gunsmith technician food
engineer shamir shama shaman we are all gathered here
guerrilla camouflage flack. jacket

ambuscade thorny stockade. we smell
our cooking & our evening
smoke. the little ones collect
the firewood. i feel

the fire flickering my back. even from five hundred paces
in this hammock
everything looks inwards to this centre
we are not taken lightly in our cups
or in our sleeping bags shocked by surprise
the sentinels along our lifeline ledge of echoes

come down the hill at sunrise w/ eyes that read the dark
m16s that are not
crutches
though we might hold them o so casual against our sides

we have been visited by goddesses & loan sharks from across the
water, from lomé and from abidjan
we make the same blue cloth they make we mix our mortar

similar. our tongues are always rough and bark like theirs
from the same bissi
when children suck their fingers after we have weaned them
from their mother's best breast suppligen
we paint the same green aloes on their slimy biscuit finger
tips & wonder if they ever going to learn there's mullet shrimp
& janga in the rivers & ganja in the harvest valley villages
& gungo peas behind the pissitoires

& yet today the hawks on their warm rising roundabouts
look like dark sorrows. for the portuguese
have beaten us at last at their own game
surrounded us . camped hard all year against us . caius
revved rockets up into the very kidneys of our cooking pots
beguiled the younger female fauns w/ foolish fans & beauty
contestants . have taught them how to shave midden hair & brave
ly bear a bene buonorott' bikini sheer & mare & tender
lion & how i gonna bring you in an early morning breakfast plate a
fruit

tourists let inwards by the sweeper at the marketgate
rush in & shoot us with their latest nikkon liekas & many of our men
are lured away to work at chipping ice in sin

cinnati cutting the canal at christopher
columbus place in panama to scraping braille off battleships'
blind grey green water under
bellies: vieques portobello bahia choc O
black cat nanny nanahemmaa do not desert us now don't let the
harmattan come riding high in here sieve sand through

runagate
runagate
runagate

look how our villages are grown up tall
into this hooting strangled city
tales of another leader
lost
solares . bolivare . palanquin
washed away w/time & frogs & river & the mud & accompong

runagate
runagate
runagate

Notes

1 Carey Robinson (1969) *The Fighting Maroons of Jamaica* (Kingston); Mavis Campbell (1988) *The Maroons of Jamaica 1655-1796* (Trenton: Africa World Press); K. Brathwaite (1977) *Wars of Respect* (Kingston: Jamaica Information Services)

2 Kamau Brathwaite (1977) *Wars of Respect*, a publication by the Jamaica Information Services (JIS) at that time called API/Agency for Public Information, is a record of my research on Nanny and Sam Sharpe, Jamaica Rebell Heroes. It contains all the research on Nanny, xplodes all the myths on her & is out of print & perhaps I can use a few of my minutes to plug the History Department or some other interested agency or organization – perhaps the Maroons themselves? – to see about a reprinting of it . . .

3 H T Thomas (1890) *Untrodden Jamaica* (Kingston). H T Thomas may have been a British policeman. More research needs to be done in this area

4 Ibid

5 Philip Thicknesse (1788) *Memiors & Anecdotes*. 3 vols. (London) Vol 1, 121

6 Brathwaite, op cit. Some random examples of uncritical accounts: J J Williams (1938/ p.389, citing Col Rowe of Accompong); Barbara Kopytoff (1973/p.97 citing, believe it or not, Rattray (1923) and Busia (1951); Col Harris of Moore Town in a BBC broadcast Oct 1975; Michael Craton (1982), Mavis Campbell (1988/p.51) – a Maroon or of Maroon descent and of course herself a woman

7 M Craton, *Testing the Chains: Resistance to Slavery in the British West Indies* (Ithaca: Cornell University Press, 1982), 81

8 'The inhabitants of Titchfield near Port Antonio being by these proceedings deprived of all hope of making the people a farther property and of growing rich by the ruin of their country are now become desperate, and having broke out into flames of sedition, and have without any reason renounced the aid and support of the Government, and by a letter dated the 27th day of September last from that town applied to Sir Chaloner Ogle [the Br Admiral] for his assistance and have offered to put themselves under his protection; and to support their pretended complaints have therein falsely given it to him as a reason, that they had no xpectation of having any assistance from me, and that I had openly declared my intentions of giving up that place, which can have no other con-struction than that I had intended to give up Titchfield to the rebells . . .' [CSP 1734, 345, p250: [Gov] Ayscough to Newcastle, Sp Tn 21 Oct 1734/ref the electors of Titchfield]

9 See E K Brathwaite, "Kumina: the Spirit of African Survival in Jamaica", *Jamaica Journal* 42 (1978): 50

10 See R S Rattray, *Ashanti* (1923, 1955 edition) 81n

11 Thomas, op cit

12 Today (July 1994) though there is no statue – as far as I know – there is now an icon of her no matter that few will see or "hold" it on a Jamaica five hundred dollar note – (ed)

13 As the person responsible for the Research , I was invited early on the morning of ******** when the citation, which I was also asked to write, was to be read at Bump Grave, Moore Tn (we went there, I remember, by JDF smallaircraft. Mrs ************, the then Minister of *************** (who actually read the citation) & myself & perhaps a few others) where we were met by a few Moore Tn Maroon leaders. It was a short, quiet, beautiful & moving ceremony, in a quiet & beautiful & 'historic' setting normally visited by a v few people, but I recall that there seemed to be no persons of the Press or other Recorders present & I don't remember seeing any photos being taken or seeing any afterwards or reading or hearing of any Report on the occasion though of course there must/might (should) have been. All I know, to my everlasting regret & archivalist shame, is that in the hurry to have the Citation ready for the Minister on time, I was not able to make or secure a copy of it, but not to worry, I assumed that a few days – if not before! – the words I had written & she had read would have been on every esp schoolgirls' lip(s) & engraved on every Jamaican (woman)'s heart. But guess what! That moving Bump Grave Ceremony has been as suppressed & submerged as the Research itself, as GrandeeNanny herself – and – by xtension – as the achievement of Africans of the Diaspora in the Caribbean/Americas

14 *JAJ* 3 (1733): 121

15 Maroon peace treaties (list in progress)

    1546 SD/First Bahoruco Treaty

    1599 Palmares Treaty acknowledging the Republic & its Independence

    1684 Suriname

    1739 Jamaican Maroons (Cudjoe)

    1740 Jamaican Maroons (Nanny)

    1750 Suriname (following the ZamZam slave revolt)

    1760s Suriname

    1790s Suriname

    1785 SD/Santiago's Treaty

    1810 Mexico. Treaty with Maroons as part of Emancipation deal

16 Hence the importance of cultural icons [my Hunter College Talk/NY 11 March 92].
I went to the Curator or Supervisor or whoever at the PRO/ then still in the heart of
London (don't think it had yet been transferred to Kew Gardens – at least not yet our
CO/137 section) & he saw with me what/how this would have come about though, as I
say, it could also have been (more) deliberate, especially when we bring our iconography
to bare . . . for xample . . . the Br mode of execution is/was traditionally to '*put to death by
hanging*' (or for v Specials by beheading) The Asante/Maroon mode was to '*put to death
by knifing*' – which is perhaps why Nanny wore all those knives about her like a girdle –
as Thicknesse in fact probably *witnessed* on a different occasion: 'The old hagg, who
passed sentence of death upon [the] unfortunate [Laird of ?Lanceret] had a girdle round
her waste, with (I speak within compas(s) *nine or ten different knives* hanging in sheaths to
it . . . ' (Thicknesse loc cit/p121)

17 The LAND PATENT TO NANNY (PRO/Patents Vol 22. Folio 15B) witnessed & signed 23 Dec
1740 & entered 20th April 1741/reproduced in Brathwaite, Wars of Respect/pp 49-52

18 See the most recent arguments by Mavis Campbell (1988, loc cit) who holds the view that
the Nanny being referred to was 'another Nanny' (I found the same problem with the
other freedom fighter, Sam Sharpe. I 'investigated' at this time. If you take the Records
too 'seriously' you could end up with several Sam Sharpes – all designed of course to
CRIPPLE & OBSCURE THE ACHIEVEMENT) And there were the people in Jamaica & England
around this same time [the period of Nanny's 'elevation' (1977)] who started writing letters to the papers saying that Nanny (& Anancy/Ananse, too) was really a kind of – well
– nanny, whose name might have been Nancy, seen?) So that the whole thing started to
go round & round in little widening circles again: that this parcel of land which we
thought had been granted to GrandeeNanny in recognition of her Honourable Opposi-
tion/her Valiant Warriorship (resulting of course in the PEACE TREATY) could really have
been intended for some faithful Nancyperson who had done oddjobs for the Plantation
. . .

   Some time in the early/mid80s, I rec'd a note from Arnie Sio, Prof of Hist at Colgate
and a Caribbean slave society colleague and friend from way back, saying that he had
come across a ref in I think the **JAJ** of the 1840s, to a (female) descendant of Nanny
living, I think, in Nova Scotia. Prof Soi's invaluable note, like so many other things of
mine, was mired up in the mud and water that Hurricane Gilbert brought to my home
& archives at Irish Tn in 1988 – it has even been difficult to prepare this paper since most
if not all of my research material on maronage has gone the way of so much else up there
– see my unheeded document HELP (1988/89) - & when I got back to Arnie soon after Gilbert, he confessed that he too had probably lost or 'too mislaid' the ref – though of course
is something that any serious or ambitious research asst could track down esp since the
needle is probably in the hay-stack of the JAJ . . .

19 We are only now just beginning to get towards this with the work of Richard and Sally
Price (*Maroon Societies* (1973) & beyond, Hurault (1970), the book on Suriname by those
Black Americans; Fouchard (1972) of course (although his work is one of those clearly &
consciously neglected & submerged) & (of the contemporary a/cs) Stedman's quite remarkable **Narrative and Journal** ('soldier & author' 1744-1797) of his life among **the revolted negroes of Surinam, in Guiana, on the wild coast of South America, from the
year 1772 to 1777 (1796)** See also the novel *Black Albino* (1961) & the art work of Namba
Roy, the Ja Maroon who lived in London ···· ···· & *The View from Coyaba* (1985), the novel
by the brilliant Azanian writer, Peter Abrahams, who has lived in Jamaica since ···· The
celebration & respect for women, well started by some of our (male) novelists, is now
safely in the visionary 'hands' of our female novelists, some singers & songwriters (some
– both male & female here – still 'controversial') & wonderfully perhaps above all, in the
style & power of our actresses. The title of *Wars of Respect* carries a resonance to the song,
'Respect', by Aretha Franklin

20 See for instance van Sertima's *They Came before Columbus* (1990); also Agorsah, this volume (chap. 11)

21 See Fouchard *Les Marrons de la liberté* (1972)

22 CO 137/21 f9

23 Brathwaite, *Wars of Respect*, op cit fn22

24 The formation of the group dates to about 1650; the island Maroon groups probably started earlier

25 The 'story' of *maritime maronage* (numbers involved, transportation, how navigated, the whole management of it) has still to be looked into & 'told', though a start has been made by the Bajan historian Hilary Beckles for the Bajan period of 'high maritime maronage', 1660-1720 – i.e. during the first xperimental years of Barbados' rapidly developing Plantation system

(One suspects that after 1720 w/ their Full Plantation just about fully developed, the Bajan Authorities tightened up effectively on their maroons of all sorts – but this also we'd like to know about)

What has to be assumed, however, is that (the pattern is the same today) after havening in Bequai & the islands for some time, the Bajan and no doubt other island maritimes made their way onto the larger islands of the Windward archipelago (St Vincent, Grenada, Dominica, Martinique & Guadeloupe) where, over time, there 'occurred' the emergence of the Blk Caribs – the details of which would reveal much about cultural action & reaction among different cultures/people faced w/ at least a common predicament

26 The first confrontation in St Vincent against Chatoyer's Maroons at Morne Yarou came in 1765-73 followed by a Peace which lasted for 25 yrs (1770-95/when it was broken by the British beginning their ?final War of Xtermination with/> St Lucia (1700 British troops) - and in St Vincent a progrom which resulted in the xpulsion of the 5000 survivors to Rattan Is & Honduras & the Mosquito Coast where after further 'inter-relationship' with their new 'hosts', they 'emerge' as the Garifuna of the Great Barrier Reef Coast (It is said that the ?few Blk Caribs who had eluded the Plantation &/or remained on as last-ditch guerrillas, were destroyed in the Soufrière volcano eruption of 1812 . . .)

27 I find Black Regiment mutinies in Dominica (1802), Tobago (1805), Trinidad (1805), Suriname (1809), Jamaica (1809), & there may well have been others

28 Mavis Campbell, loc cit, has promised us a study of this little known development which has introduced an African Caribbean creole culture into Sierra Leone . . .

nine

Characteristics of Maroon Music from Jamaica and Suriname

Marjorie Whylie and Maureen Warner-Lewis

Introduction

Between the seventeenth and eighteenth centuries, some of the enslaved Africans managed to escape from the plantations into the forested highlands of Jamaica and the jungles and riversides in the interior of the Dutch South American colony of Suriname. Maroon communities were composed of Africans from a large number of ethnic and linguistic backgrounds, and were people who had been slaves for varying periods of time. Some are referred to as having been taken to the Americas from "Koromantee" in the Gold Coast from where, between 1700-1725, about 17% of the Suriname slaves were derived. This figure rose to 29% by 1735. From the Slave Coast and Dahomey came 64% by 1700, 50% by 1725, 33% within the ten years that followed—this figure dropping off to 1% by the close of the eighteenth century. From the Loango/Angola area came 34% in the 1650s, 33% around 1725-35, and 24% between 1735-95.[1] As regards Jamaica, half of the seventeenth century slaves were drawn from "among the Akan and Ga-Adangme peoples of the coastal strip" of present-day Ghana. 40% were from Angola, 30% were Ewe-Fon from the Slave Coast and Dahomey. However, between "1792 and 1807 approximately 83 per cent . . . came from the Bight of Biafra (Ibo) and Central Africa (Congo), compared to 46% over the entire history of the slave trade to Jamaica."[2]

It is only natural, then, that several generalized features of activity in Maroon life show African connections. These include music, dance, and other art, craft, and artistic expressions. This heterogeneous yet structurally and functionally similar heritage underlying the music of Jamaican and Surinamese Maroons provides clear examples of the life-sustaining element of African cultural traditions in the West Atlantic. The transformations wrought to this heritage were produced by inter-African syntheses and attritrion as well as by the contact of African musical styles with those of Europe and the Americas.

Based on a fairly small sample, this chapter discusses some of the main features of Maroon music of both Jamaica and Suriname, locations at virtually two extremes of the Caribbean archipelago. The musical corpus comprises Kenneth Bilby's *Music of the Maroons of Jamaica* (Ethnic Folkways Records FE 4027, 1981), and a series of tape recordings made by Surinamese musicologist, Terry Agerkop, of mainly Juka music, though occasional reference will be made to a smaller sample of Saramaka songs and drumming. However, for these Suriname examples we have no accompanying notes with regard to instrumentation and function.[3] It should be explained here that the Juka (Djuka) constitute only one of several clans of Maroons in Suriname.[4] But comparison of aspects of the musical culture of Jamaican and Surinamese Maroons provides clear examples of sustained African cultural traditions in the West Atlantic. Furthermore, analysis of the music of these two separate Maroon locations reveals many striking similarities, so much so that it is difficult to distinguish the two traditions in their styles of both singing and drumming.

Singing Style

The melodic structure of both the Juka songs and Jamaican Maroon jawbone (ritual) songs follows the natural minor scale such as shown in *Fig. 1a*. But there is a tendency for the singer to pause on a note which is not the tonal centre of the scale. That gives the impression that the melodic phrase remains in suspension, and the melody is not resolved, or never comes to its rest or natural centre until the very end of the performance.

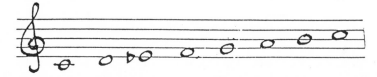

Fig. 1a

Also both traditions exhibit use of both large and small scales. The large scale in this case is the diatonic and carries eight notes comprising heptatones plus the octave as the eighth note. A small scale carrying four tones is called a tetratonic scale; a scale of five tones is pentatonic. It is unusual for one community to utilize both large and small scales in its vocal repertoire, and the fact that both Juka and Jamaican communities do so is evidence of their syncretic nature, that is, that they represent an amalgamation of differing African peoples, with varying musical traditions. The fact that in the Jamaican case some types of rhythms are called *Madinga*, or *Ibo*, and others *Kramanti* and *Prapra (Popo)*, confirms the idea that Maroon communities on the island represented a synthesis of African ethnic groups.

The tetratonic scale in both communities comprises a 1st, 3rd, and 5th in addition to the 8th on the diatonic scale. But the Surinamese songs may also be described as utilizing the pentatonic scale since a 4th tends to occur rather unexpectedly at times, and only when the melodic line is descending. This 4th is not a passing note; rather it occurs on strong beats of the bar. The scale of these songs, therefore, follows the pattern in *Fig. 1b*.

Fig. 1b

While the Jamaican songs in our sample contain both diatonic natural minor scales and pentatonic scales, most are diatonic. This may signal the predominance of an African tradition[5] or an African sub-cultural music which emphasizes the diatonic natural minor scale (*Fig. 1c*). In both, song structure is characterized by a call and response format. In fact, one of the Juka songs presents an interesting interplay between the lead and the chorus, in that the male lead punctuates the song with two staccato calls (*Gi gi*) and then goes on to sing the first of the two lines that form the response, while the choral ensemble of female voices sings both the first and second lines, so that the effect is of overlapping alternation rather than the discrete segmentation found in most antiphonies (*Fig. 2a*).

Fig. 1c

Fig. 2a

Both Maroon traditions use sustained notes at the end of the melodic phrase. In some of the Surinamese songs, the lead singers employ a tremulo on this sustained note.[6] This wavering note produced by glottal constriction is called tɛɛmɛ by the Juka and is a distinctive feature of their singing style, in contrast with that of the Saramaka who do not employ this technique. The samples of Jamaica Maroon singing here similarly lack this feature. Apart from the tremulo, a trill appears to characterize the melodic curve as it begins its descent *(Fig. 2b)*.

Fig. 2b

The singing style among both Jamaican and Surinamese groups is basically open-throated and nasal, with nasality and high pitch being more pronounced in the Jamaican examples of female singing. In Jamaica, female singing is more in evidence among the eastern Maroons, even when a male takes the lead role, whereas male singing typifies both call and choral sections of the Maroon ensemble in western Jamaica. Choral singing in Jamaica and in Suriname is performed, not in harmony, but by means of parallel unison or organum in which the singers find their own pitch level and sing at octaves apart. This type of unison is typical of West African music on account of the tonal contours of languages there.[7]

All the Juka songs in this limited sample are metric, with the pulse being underscored by muted shaka or by loud percussion with a muffled resonance. These may be handclaps of the type which forms the exclusive accompaniment of a Saramaka music called *sekiti*,[8] or it may issue from sticks hit against drum-sides or upon a wood instrument or benches and, in fact, somewhat in the manner of the two-jointed bamboo *kwaat* (anglicized as "quart") used by the Scott's Hall Maroons, though the *kwaat* produces a sharper sound. In Suriname "any two pieces of wood at hand" may be used to produce this sound, but it may also be "a flat board of resounding wood . . . beaten with a hand paddle".[9] But among urban Maroons the "*kwakwa* . . . is a low bench with a hardwood top, beaten with two sticks by a player who squats beside it facing the players".[10] This instrumentation recalls the Jamaican *kata* and Cuban *katá*, two sticks knocked against drum sides by a player positioned in front a drum being played by another. Some of the Juka singing is accompanied by drums, and some by *shakas*, and it is noticeable that the *shaka* in this instance sounds on the beat. When used among the Scott's Hall Maroons, however, it is seldom simply metronomic, but is rhythmically more varied.

The Jamaican collection also offers examples of non-metric chanting *(Fig. 2c)*.

Fig. 2c

This type of music is called *Kramanti,* and is by its form either declamatory or in-vocational. Statements are chanted to the punctuating accompaniment of drum flourishes and rolls which relate more to the verbal phrasing than to regularity of metre. This format accords with the traditional African introit to ritual ceremony—that of an opening declamation which carries instrumental support (*Fig. 3a*).[11]

Fig. 3a

In the selection (*Fig. 3b*) from Scott's Hall, Jamaica, the lead singer maintains a vestige of the tremulo heard in the Juka singing. A comparable invocation (*Fig. 4a*) occurs in the Juka collection, but here the instrumentation is not only muted but also metric.

Fig. 3b

Fig. 4a

Drumming Style

The instruments heard in the limited Jamaican samples are, in the case of Moore Town, two drums called printing, Scott's Hall the grandy and gumbe, and Accompong a bass drum, two side drums and gumbe. In all instances, the drums bear a male-female relationship, the female being the lead instrument or "cutter", imparting to each rhythm complex its recognizable characteristic features.

An in-depth examination of the recorded Jamaican samples shows two distinct functions of drums in the ritual setting:

- non-metric patterns appear as (a) drum language mirroring the tone and rhythm of speech, and (b) "rolls" or vibratory passages inviting or acknowledging the presence of ancestral spirits or deities (*Fig. 4b*):[12]

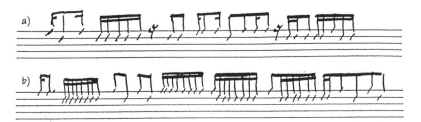

Fig. 4b

- rhythmic phrases are broken into equal numbers of segments within the time span, the pulse structure in the grouping of notes showing regular divisions of differing density (*Fig. 4c*):

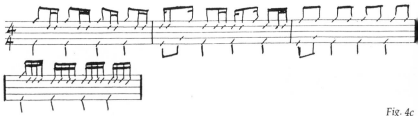

Fig. 4c

It should be noted also that the apparently preferred metre is duple and its divisions into quadruple. In an initial observation of the sample from Suriname and comparison with the example from Jamaica, two clear differences appear. The rhythm structures found in Jamaica's Moore Town, Scott's Hall and Accompong are more densely textured, both in sub-divisions of the beat and in numbers of instruments played. Each group breaks away from regular division, that is, multiples of two, in different ways—syncopation appearing in Jamaica and triplets in Suriname (*Fig. 5a*).

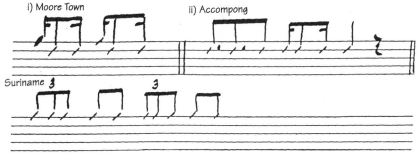

Fig. 5a

Special mention should be made of the instrumentation of Accompong. In the case of the Maroons of eastern Jamaica, the male-female relationship is clear in the cylindrical *printing* of Moore Town, the male as the "roller" and the female the "cutter"; in Charles Town and Scott's Hall, the *grandy*, a cylindrical instrument, maintains the time line—a male function—and the *gumbe* is the "cutter". In Accompong in western Jamaica, however, a military type double-headed bass drum and two side drums to which snares are affixed, produce a density of sound not typical in ostinati patterns, creating an interesting rhythm bass above which the lead instrument—the *gumbe*—cuts (*Fig. 5b*).

Fig. 5b

Although attention has been directed solely at drums in the sample, there was some evidence of body percussion and *shakas* and other percussion of secondary importance. The following up-tempo processional from Accompong, Jamaica, by its language, tempo, and Euro-African drum rhythms *(Fig. 5c)*, points the way toward Jamaican mento and Trinidad calypso. It illustrates how African rhythms and melodic curves transmute into later Caribbean types of music, while at the same time the vocal timbre and unison singing style exemplifies many of the techniques already described.

Fig. 5c

As in many parts of Africa, Maroons identify drums not only by their form but also by the role they play in particular types of performance. For example, the *apinti* is so called when played alone as a talking drum, like the Ewe *vuga* or Akan *atumpan*. But when it takes "a specialized rhythmic role in the drum choirs which accompany women's bandammba dancing and rites to warrior gods and forest spirits", it is called *tumau*.[13]

Though the Yoruba had a type of drum called *apinti*, the word appears cognate with the Jamaican Maroon *printing*, a term in all likelihood derived from Akan drum names like *apentemma* and *aprenteng*.[14] Certainly, some of its Surinamese and Jamaican functions overlap. The Jamaican Moore Town Maroons communicate not only with the side-blown cow horn called by the Twi term *abeng*, but also with the *Kromanti* drums (*printing*). During wars both tonal instruments, the *abeng* and the *printing*, "were used for strategic purposes". However, in the twentieth century drum language is retained for the beginning of religious ceremonies "to invite Maroons from the surrounding area to participate". But drum language is said to have several other applications", among them "invocation and communication with the spirits of ancestors . . . The drum 'language' is kept a strict secret . . . only a few older Maroons understand a significant amount. And the really "deep" knowledge is restricted to a few specialists (*printing-man*)".[15]

In Suriname the *apinti* is a talking drum used at major Maroon council meetings and at certain important rituals. As a kind of town crier at certain community functions, its rhythms officially open proceedings, summoning and greeting gods, ancestors, spirits, and public officials; it is also used to comment on current and past events as with the drum histories of the Volta, Ascend, and northern areas of Ghana, and in many parts of Nigeria, the Ivory Coast, Benin (Dahomey), and Togo. A popular proverb played on the *apinti* translates as: "*smoke has no feet but makes its way to heaven*". The proverb explains the powerful qualities of the ancestral spirits through whom all supplications are made. As in many parts of West Africa, the ability to select proverbs appropriate to particular issues and situations is seen as one of the most important skills of a Suriname *apinti* player.[16]

Among the Juka, the 6 to 8 foot cylindrical *agida* is the bass drum which, "with its low note, dominates the battery with a steady beat. With the *kwakwa* . . . this beat sets the basic rhythm of the more complicated notes played by the drums of higher pitch".[17] The latter are the *nanda* and the small *babula*.[18] However, in comparison with Jamaican Maroon drumming, the pitch relationship between the secondary and lead drums of the Juka is much closer. At Accompong the bass is a two-headed drum beaten with a stick; in Moore Town one of the two *kramanti* drums is tuned quite low, whereas at Scott's Hall the bass is somewhat less resonant because the metronomic beat is kept by the *kwaat*. However, the texture of the two drumming styles is similar, so is the tonal relationship of the notes; and the Juka rhythms, like those at Moore Town in Jamaica, subdivide into duple and quadruple beats with regularly recurring patterns of syncopation.

Another rhythmic pattern in the sample begins, as at Moore Town, with eighth notes (quavers) alternating with two-sixteenth notes (semi-quavers), the accent falling on the eighth note, but then the rhythm diverges into a pattern reminiscent of the Accompong *gumbe* in the way the beat is subdivided. In this case the rhythm breaks into dotted eighth notes with a sixteenth note, then sixteenth notes followed by a rest.

The Juka drumming begins with sequences of tonal invocation, and subsequently the same drum sets the metronomic beat. The lead drum then joins in. *Shakas* later take up a steady straight-line pulse. This streamlined *shaka* rhythm is unusual in Jamaica and it is noteworthy that in the Saramaka sample the *shakas* provide a denser rhythmic pattern than among the Juka.

Conclusion

From the perspective of the "cultural" or "social" historian, features of music help explain the formation, survival strategies, and transformations within a society. They also mirror cultural and aesthetic variations between peoples. So while similarities in musical style unite Maroons within Jamaica and within Suriname, and correspondences unite Maroon music across the two geographical locations, differences do exist—even between the musics of Maroons within the same territorial unit. At the same time, the stylistic elements and changes in Maroon musics provide unique examples of the trajectory along which Caribbean music would have evolved had Maroon communities been the norm rather than the exception in the postColumbian era. In the hostile yet syncretic encounter between Africans, Europeans, and indigenous Americans, the creolizing factor dictated by European political and economic dominance would have been the more recessive gene in the American amalgam.

Notes

1 Sally Price and Richard Price, *Afro-American Arts of the Suriname Rain Foresst* (Berkeley: University of California Press, 1980), 195.

2 Barry Higman, *Slave Population and Economy of Jamaica, 1807-1834* (Cambridge: Cambridge University Press, 1976), 76.

3 We acknowledge the generosity of Terry Agerkop of the Fundación de Etnomusicologia y Folklore (FUNDEF) in Caracas who made copies of Juka music recordings available to Maureen Warner-Lewis.

4 Among such clans are the Saramaka, Paramaka, Juka (Djuka), Boni or Aluku, Matawai and Kwinti. Their populations are as follows: Juka and Saramaka, 15,000 -20,000 each; Aluku, Paramaka and Matawai 1,000 each, and Kwinti 500. The main town, Paramaribo,

continues to attract large numbers of people from each area and this may have implications for the figures. See Richard Price, ed., *Maroon Societies: Rebel Slave Communities in the Americas* (New York: Anchor Press/Doubleday, 1973), 295.

5 On the other hand, Samule Akpabot, *Foundations of Nigerian Traditional Music* (Ibadan: Spectrum Books, 1986), 81, points out that generally Nigerian music uses the pentatonic scale in instrumental music and the heptatonic in song, although the fusion of the two scales does occur in certain cases.

6 This technique, called *gonde* in Trinidad, has traditionally been used in Trinidad's stick-fight or *kalinda* songs and is salient in certain genres of Yoruba singing, such as *apala* and *ese odu*.

7 Because many African languages are tonal, a spoken sentence can have only one fixed intonational curve. In order to maintain that curve, harmonizing voices have to imitate that melody at exact intervals. Any deviation affects a change in tonal contour and therefore in the meaning of the words of the song.

8 Cf. Mary Jane Hewitt, "An overview of Suriname", *Black Art* 5, no.1 (1981): 18.

9 Morton Kahn, *Djuka—the Bush Negroes of Dutch Guiana* (New York: Viking Press, 1931), 55.

10 M. Kolinski *in* Melville Herskovits and Frances Herskovits, *Suriname Folklore* (New York: Columbia Univ. Press, 1936), 522. There may be a common African term or series of cognate terms from which words like *kwaka* (Trinidad, Surinam) *kwekwe* (Guyana), and *kwaat* (Jamaica) have come. They all refer to wood-on-wood percussion, bamboo lengths in the case of Guyana, Jamaica, and Trinidad.

11 Cf. Akpabot, op. cit., 109.

12 The use of bells and other forms of rattling and vibrations—whether of vegetal matter such as straw or seeds or of musical instruments—is, in African tradition, indicative of mystic communication.

13 Price and Price, op. cit., 178.

14 Kofi Agorsah suggests the former, while in *Music of the Maroons of Jamaica* Notes to Folkways Records Album FE 4027 (1981), 3, Kenneth Bilby proposes the latter.

15 Bilby, op. cit., 7.

16 See Price and Price, op. cit., 179.

17 Kolinski, op. cit., 521. Kolinski's analysis and transcriptions of Suriname Maroon music occupy pp.491-527 of Herskovits and Herskovits, op. cit.

18 Kahn, op. cit., 54.

ten

Maroon Warfare: the Jamaica Model

Albert Edwards

Introduction

To discuss the history of the Maroons is to examine the life of a society whose entire life in the diaspora has been warfare. It was warfare of a special kind and that is the history of guerrilla warfare in the New World, beginning with the establishment of the first Maroon settlements in Hispaniola in 1503 or even earlier in some other places. Thomas Higginson, writing in 1889, has rightly observed that:

> The Maroons! It was a peril once; and terror spread along the skirts of the Blue Mountains of Jamaica when some fresh foray of those unconquered guerrillas swept down upon the outlying plantations, startled the Assembly from its order, General Williamson from his billiards and Lord Balcarres from his diplomatic ease—endangering, according to official statements, 'civil rights' and the 'prosperity, if not the very existence of the country', until they were persuaded to make peace at last . . .[1]

Susan Pierres has noted that they have been variously referred to as "desperate villains", "pernicious scum", as well as "sneaking and treacherous rogues".[2] But these were the people who embarked on a process of freedom fighting that pioneered liberation toward human dignity in the New World. Writing over two decades ago at the height of the Vietnam War, Robert Taber, who is highly respected for his "critical analysis of great guerrilla campaigns in history", set out to show by examples from Algeria, Cuba, China, Cyprus, Malaya and Greece that guerrilla warfare, when used as a political weapon, can be extremely potent and may even be used for other purposes far beyond politics.[3] But in all his analysis, no mention is made of one of the longest guerrilla campaigns in history—the Maroon guerrilla campaign against the English in Jamaica. The lessons of this great survival strategy of the Maroons constitutes the discussion of this chapter.

Guerrilla warfare

The word guerrillero was used to describe the Spanish or Portuguese insurgents who fought alongside the Duke of Wellington's armies to help drive the French, under Napoleon Bonaparte, from the Iberian Peninsula during the military campaigns which lasted from 1809 to 1814. Spanish records[4] also indicate that some members of the Yssassi family who settled in Jamaica were from the Basque Province of Guipuzcoa, northern Spain, a region which has prided itself on the fighting capabilities of its inhabitants. They functioned as mercenaries and sea captains to many expeditions which were sent to the New World as guerrillas. They were also said to have served in Roman armies as far back as 200 BC. So how can the term guerrilla warfare be applied in relation to the wars fought by the Maroons against the English from 1655 to 1796? Which comes first, the warfare or the name? To answer these questions one needs to examine the state of affairs in Jamaica just before the English invasion of 1655 and the events leading up to the peace treaties in 1739 and after.

Jamaica was a Spanish colony before the English invasion. The first Spanish settlers arrived around 1509, and brought with them black slaves from the west coast of Africa. It is claimed that at the time of the invasion, there were approximately 1,000 black slaves in Jamaica. Not all of these were brought to Jamaica by the Spanish, for there are reports of the French abandoning slaves off the coasts of Jamaica and also of slaves being washed ashore from vessels, following acts of piracy [Postma 1990]. Jamaica was then a kind of supply centre for expeditions going further east to Mexico and Santo Domingo.

There were extensive Spanish farms or *estancias* on which a wide variety of crops were grown. Cattle ranches dotted the island and in between large herds of wild cattle roamed the vast savannas on the south of the island. On the north coast cattle was raised and there was an abundance of wild pigs. In 1581 Francisco Lopez de Villalobos, an Abbot, wrote: "There is such a great quantity of pigs, so much so that very often the smaller ones are caught by hand". The Spaniards, who inhabited Jamaica at the time, were a hardy lot. There were the clergy, the laity and the common folk. In 1611 there was a population of some 1,510 persons, 103 of whom were described as "Free Negroes" in Jamaica [Wright 1924]. A cleric of the period said that the Spaniards were mostly from three large families, and among these families the names Yssassi and Leyba (Leiba) were very prominent and were to be later associated with the Maroons. Don Francisco Leyba de Yssassi (Yzazi), father of Cristobal Arnaldo de Yssassi, a leader in the Spanish resistance, is said to have cohabited with a coloured woman for more that sixteen (16) years, even though he was a married man [Wright 1924].

The Spanish records mention that in addition to the "Free Negroes" there were such groups as "Fifteen Negro Bowmen" who arrived in the island with a group of 130 soldiers who had firearm and lances. It appears, therefore, that in addition to the slaves and freemen there were blacks serving in the Spanish forces. Who were these other black people? They may have been second and third generation blacks who were taken as slaves and body servants to Jamaica. Many abandoned their masters to live a free life in remote and inaccessible settlements of their own, soon after arrival. Men like . . .

> a Negro belonging to Sargento Mayor Duarte de Acosta Noguera—
> although an Angola Black, this Negro was clever. He could read and write,
> knew ... conjunctions of the moon and tides as well as though he had studied
> them. He was a good sugar master and could give an excellent account of himself
> when necessary.

This may be an extreme example but it demonstrates that not all the blacks in Jamaica were "wild and unruly savages". Unfortunately, this prominent Negro, "despite many pleas for his life", was later hanged by the Spaniards who suspected that he had collaborated with the English against them.

When the English landed, many of the blacks were no strangers to arms or military discipline. Men under Lieutenant Don Cristobal included "skeleton companies of fifteen Spaniards and fifteen negroes" and "negroes who abandoned their masters and built stockades for themselves". There were blacks such as those whom Captain Julian Castilla wrote about in 1658 when reporting on a particular incident during which an English supply of wagons were captured: "The negroes of the stockade got their share, whether they returned very well satisfied offering the Lieutenant and Sargento Mayor to serve on any subsequent occasion in larger numbers".

The English had their "guides" and "fugitive negroes" who were to assist them in rounding up the "persons who had retreated to the bush". It was this struggle in the bush that was to bring to the fore men like, Diego Pimienta, whom Castilla described as "This slave, a Creole named Diego Pimienta, in these combats showed how greatly does virtue adorn the individual and how diversity of colour is no obstacle on nobility of blood and worth. He was a fine marksman and did not waste a shot. Whenever he fired he indicated his mark saying to his comrades: 'That English man drops now'" [Wright 1924]. It was men like these and others who passed on their military experience and skill to generations who were to be part of the Maroon struggle. The skill also came from men such as Captain Don Cristobal Leiba de Yssassi as leader of the Spanish resistance in Jamaica. He was not only a trained soldier, but "a brave and proven fighter against French and English pirates" [Wright 1924].

Strategy

Yssassi wrote to the Duke of Albuquerque, Viceroy of Mexico, concerning the English: "I will make him retire to his forts and prevent him doing any planting or benefitting from what planting he has already done". Out of this struggle came men and women whom Juan de los Reyes, a Spanish Commander, in a letter to the King of Spain (Phillip 1V) spoke about as: "Three settlements of two hundred and fifty black men and women who govern themselves". This may have been the nucleus of the guerrilla warfare against the English. The Spanish resistance against the English continued. It is reported that "a Mexican contingent" was to arrive in Jamaica with 31 captains of infantry, 31 ensigns, 28 sergeants and 467 infantrymen, including Negroes, mulattoes and Indians.

So the arrival of blacks with military skills continued. Unfortunately, many of these were to die at Rio Nuevo at the hands of Edward D'Oyley and the Buccaneers whom he brought in from Tortuga to hunt the Negroes in the bush. The Spanish capitulated in 1665 and many departed for Cuba, leaving behind many of their former slaves to fend for themselves. The groups of people who formed the Maroon societies, therefore, were already very conversant with the conditions of the environment in which they were to fight for centuries of survival.

The Maroons who took to the bush were practising one of the cardinal rules of guerrilla warfare, which was to fight on their terms in the terrain that was most familiar to their combatants. To retain their cultural identity was no doubt foremost in their minds. The first phase of their struggle was, as Mao Tse Tung[5] would put it, the period of "strategic withdrawal". During this period the Maroons retreated into the bush, only attacking where necessary to obtain arms and supplies. The next phase is referred to as the "strategic defense".

The slave rebellions during both the Spanish and English periods were blamed on the Maroons and many runaway slaves joined the Maroons. In addition, in September of that year, 1660, the English Governor was to report that a band of rebels in the mountains of St Mary, St George and St Thomas had established settlements in the hills. This shows that the Maroons were extending the range of their source of supply of arms and ammunition. In addition to planting their own crops and establishing themselves as a "settled" community, raiding for supplies was an important part of the fighting strategy to the Maroons. They also utilized the natural resources and land available to them at any time [Hart 1985]. In his writing on guerrilla warfare, Mao Tse Tung [1966] recognized three elements which were vital if a guerrilla campaign was to be successful. These he defined as *time, space* and *will*.

The location of Maroon strongholds were in three main areas of the island: the cockpits of the modern parishes of Trelawny, St James, northern Manchester and St. Elizabeth, the bush and scrubland of St Catherine and the Grand Ridge of the Blue Mountains in St Andrew, Portland and St Thomas, Juan de Bolas and surrounding areas. Familiarity with the terrain of these areas was an important asset of Maroon guerrilla warfare. The two principal groups chose the territory with which they were most familiar and dictated their tactics. The strategy of the English forces was to keep the various Maroon groups separate, except for small joint actions. Nonetheless the communication between the Maroon groups continued. The English had, soon after the invasion, opened the old Spanish roads across the hills of St Catherine to St Ann to get at the Spaniards hiding on the north coast of Jamaica.

This effectively cut the island in two. Consequently, both Maroon groups were to operate independently of each other. Terrain demanded this, but the guerrilla is an "improviser" and the Maroons were able to use such tactics as "hit and run" which was very effectively suitable in the kind of environment in which they had to fight.

Because of the nature of the terrain, the Maroons had more space than one would suppose. Mountainous country, packed within a defined geographical area, offered as in their case, several more times the surface area of land. Their number at peak is reported to be less than two thousand—a small number that probably allowed them more than enough space to live in security and to carry on their defence operations.

The second ally of the Maroons was the forest cover. In the case of the Blue Mountains, this was covered by virgin forests, native hardwoods and scrub. In most areas, sun does not touch the forest floor. Stories of soldiers climbing up trees to spy out the surrounding countryside have been told, indicating desperate enemy attempts even to locate the Maroon hideouts.

The cockpits, on the other hand, though without the same growth as that found in the Blue Mountains, offered more than enough cover for the purposes of the Maroons. Even today helicopter-borne troops would find it virtually impossible to spot settlements that are concealed within the trees and where the settlers have not cleared wide areas away from the tree cover. Fire, if kept to a minimum, would not be spotted from great distances. The Cockpit Country does not possess the abundance of rivers as are to be found in the Blue Mountains, but water in sufficient quantities may be found in sinkholes and acquifers.

Alan Eyre [1980] has conducted a geographical appraisal of the Maroon wars and appears to have come to the conclusion that geographical factors were more important in the direction of events of the war than anything else. Eyre explains that:

> The Maroon Wars from 1690 to 1796 in Jamaica were the only significant British colonial wars to be fought in the humid tropical forest environment. Not until World War II was there military conflict in such conditions. These wars have a nearly contemporary literature on the British side[6] and an interesting modern descriptive appraisal from the Maroon viewpoint.[7] Even a cursory review of the progress of these wars suggests that geography was more than usually significant, and was a critical factor affecting the strategies used by both sides. The tragic dénouement of the Second Maroon War in 1769 was clearly due more to the geographical constraints imposed upon the combatants than to great generalship or any unambiguous military victory . . .

The enemies which the British Army had to fight were three: the Maroons, the terrain and the climate. The terrain is the ultimate in tropical karst, *a classic land form through which J.V. Danes rode on horseback in 1906, subsequently presenting the pioneer study of* karst *to the Royal Bohemian Society of Sciences in 1914. Fully developed Jamaican* karst *is a spectacular landscape, a bewildering jumble of cones, cockpits and caverns. Viewed in one way, it can be conceived as* cockpit karst, *a complex pattern of star-shaped closed depressions averaging less than four hectares in floor area, with steep, often precipitous convex slopes. They vary from 20 to 200 meters in depth. Drainage is radially into the centre, where there is usually a sinkhole. The depression is floored with red or yellow ferruginous earth which after heavy rain may hold a small, temporary perched water table. This concentrated on the positive rather than the negative elements of topography. The landscape is thus seen as dominated by rounded forested limestone masses with convex slopes, the cockpit being simply the intervening space where vertical erosion had widened joints in the limestone. This terrain obviously favoured Maroon defence and baffled British commanders newly arrived in the tropics.*
. . . .

The climate also was kinder to the insurgents than to the British troops . . . The heat, humidity and daily downpours of the rainy season were a constant irritation to the heavily clothed British solders. Climate-related tropical fevers drained their strength. Affections of the lower alimentary tract were almost universal and, to put it very mildly, both inconvenient and debilitating. Robinson [1969] summarizes the overall results of the struggle with 'Maroons, mountains and malaria'.[8]

It appears that the Maroons, knowing the advantage of the terrain in which they were fighting, tried as much as possible to restrict the wars to the geographical area that was of advantage to them. This is supported by the tactics adopted by their leadership. For example, Dallas [1805] explains that Cudjoe displayed a keen geographical sense and shrewd judgement in choosing this position and himself describes its advantages with considerable perception: "It proved to be impregnable against infantry assaults, however well armed. It has access to a small perennial river".[9] Robinson [1969], writing from the Maroon viewpoint, describes a typical assault on Pettee River Bottom:

Whenever the lookouts sounded their abengs (conchshell horns), warning that an enemy force was approaching, the Maroons would climb into the ledges on either side of the passage (into the cockpit), and conceal themselves behind large rocks. From there they could bottle up an attacking force by rolling down large boulders at either end, and even without using their guns they could destroy such a force with rocks alone . . . The [British] troops, all wearied by the long march, by fear of imminent attack and by tension caused by constant vigilance, would suddenly find themselves fired upon from two or three sides. They would return the first, but the Maroons would simply disappear.[10]

Vietnam War veterans will recognize an all too familiar pattern in the last sentence! Eyre also explains that *several parties, seeking to penetrate the Cockpit Country from the British base at Vaughnsfield were badly mauled or dispersed in disorder. One force of three hundred infantrymen set off from Vaughnsfield to storm the Pettee River Bottom headquarters but got hopelessly lost in the jumble of forested karst and found themselves very red-faced in Colonel Fitch's advance base at Flagstaff, whereupon he called them 'a bunch of fools' and sent them back to barracks!*

Taking advantage of the terrain, however, did not last, as the British forces realized their difficulties and attempted a remedy, which worked. Names of places in the Maroon areas indicate to us how the Maroons used the terrain to the fullest. Land of Look Behind, Quick Steps, Me No Sen You No Come, First Breakfast Hill, Flagstaff, Horse Guards, Don't Come Back, Cun See—and many more peasant farming districts today tell us where long forgotten British soldiers once passed and left their mark. Space also incorporated geographical features such as caves, rivers, ravines, forest and clearings. All these features, if familiar to the guerrilla operating in that defined area, could be used to great advantage. Terrain determined Maroon tactics and tactics assisted in bringing war to the enemy. Sun Tzu, in *The Art of War* [1983], speaks of "generals who know terrain but fail to take it into consideration in determining tactics".

The coffee planters, spurred on by the Coffee Encouragement Act (Act 5 George 11, 1732) had by this time sought to extend their plantations over the slopes of the Blue Mountains into the former parish of St George on the north coast of the island. Land in the Buff Bay and Spanish River Valley brought the settlers once more into conflict with the Windward Maroons who considered the area as their hunting and fishing reserve. Although the Maroons were restricted to the hills, there is no evidence that the Maroons failed in this regard. The terrain was their greatest ally. Not only was the terrain exploited for warfare, but in the hunt for food, especially wild hogs. Terrain also played an important part in the selection of ambush sites. The site, if properly chosen, would lead the enemy into a ravine or river course. The Maroons would then close the trap, cutting off both ends then pepper the trapped enemy troops with musket fire.

Nicholas Plysham, a regular officer who accompanied an expedition in 1730, spoke of troops being caught in such an ambush near the "Rebels Plantation". The Maroons abandoned the town and sent the women and children up the mountain. The following morning an advance group of twenty soldiers tried to enter the town. They were beaten back by effective fire. As soon as this group returned to the larger body they realized they were surrounded and pinned down by Maroons. Some tried to retreat down the river only to find to their dismay that they were exposed to the accurate fire of the Maroons. They were able to escape only because the Maroons allowed them to do so. Lieutenants Thicknesse and Concannon who led groups of soldiers up the Spanish River Valley suffered a similar fate in 1739.

A naval lieutenant, Thomas Swanton, was to report on a similar type of ambush. The armed sailors were 200 in number and were accompanied by 200 baggage "Negroes". The sailors had tried to outsmart the Maroons by sending some of their number to high ground overlooking the route of the march. All this was of no use for they still fell into the ambush set by the Maroons. Seamen's Valley bears the name of the site of that battle. "The general who does not understand these [terrain and tactics] may be well acquainted with the configuration of the country, yet he will not be able to turn this knowledge to his advantage" [Sun Tzu 1983].

Nanny Town was reported taken by the British forces in December 1734 and kept until July 1735 [Hart 1985; Campbell 1988]. No mention is made of the hurricane which occurred in September 1734 and which "did unspeakable damage to the eastern end of the island" [*Gentleman's Magazine*, 1734-1738]. This would have robbed the Maroons of their best ally—the forest cover—as well as modified their lifestyle by forcing them to concentrate on rehabilitating their provision grounds and coming into direct confrontation with the enemy, a situation which combatants engaged in guerrilla warfare should always avoid.

The troops who occupied Nanny Town were in constant fear of attack by the Maroons. As if this was not enough, their supplies were constantly stolen from them along the trails leading to Nanny Town. Another tactic of the Maroons was the use of fire. In an area where rainfall is an ever-present phenomenon, shelter played no small part to both Maroon guerrilla and colonial soldier. As soon as the Maroon realized his settlement was threatened, he would set fire to the abandoned huts thus depriving the enemy of shelter and supplies left behind. This must have played on the minds of soldiers who, after a long march into the mountains, looked forward to some abandoned Maroon huts to rest their tired bodies. Sun Tzu [1983] has suggested that "there are five ways of attacking with fire: the first is to burn soldiers in their camp; the second is to burn stores; the third is to burn baggage trains; the fourth is to burn arsenals and magazines; and the fifth is to hurl dropping fire among the enemy". It appears that the Maroons often modified tactics in the use of fire. There were times when they left their huts standing, only to set them afire after they were occupied by the enemy soldiers.

The period 1733 to 1734 was an active time for campaigns against the Maroons. In August 1733 the Maroons captured Hobbies (Habbys), a fort near Shrewsbury and three other plantations near Port Antonio. The reaction was that sale of rum was forbidden at Port Antonio and all gunpowder was ordered lodged in the government store at Fort George (Titchfield). The purists would say that it was at this period that the Maroons should have enlisted the aid of the population to drive the English off the island. But such a move did not appear to be in the priorities of the Maroons, because all they were fighting for was to be free from bondage and to live in peace.

In October 1734 martial law was declared and the full weight of the war unleashed on the Maroons. This change of approach and seriousness on the part of the British administration is demonstrated by the fact that between 1664 and 1668, forty-four laws were enacted in its connection. In addition, making an expenditure in the sum of two hundred and forty thousand pounds further supports the importance of the Maroon activities to the plantation system and the British government. Fort George was designed to hold as many as twenty-two cannons and cost in the region of two thousand pounds. In 1728 much of the money was used to pay for regular English troops brought in from Gibraltar. It was clear at the time that the Maroons had not run out of space. However, they may have run out of time.

Time

Time, to the Maroon guerrilla, determined the direction of action. Time also influenced the strategy or tactics: how and when to start and where and when to stop. Could the Maroons have understood the meaning of the situation as is being analysed in this presentation? Time, to a highly mobile society, revolved around seasons of the environment which the Maroons knew very well. What the Maroon had to do depended on the season rather than fixed periods of weeks or months. To gain time, the Maroons avoided any direct confrontation, blocking off all possible routes of attack, for as Hart [1985] has pointed out, several of the British soldiers lost their lives at various isolated points to "hit and run" night attacks. Several observations may be made about Maroon strategy. Firstly, it appears that they knew that to fight the type of war they were fighting they needed to know their environment and make the best use of it. They appeared to have absolute respect for their leadership in fighting back or engaging in "hit and run" tactics. Points of escape and entry appear to have been controlled and monitored very well. The names mentioned above give support to this action.

"Surprise, treachery and secretiveness", to quote Che Guevara[11], appear to have been their watchwords. It is probably due to their secretiveness about their military struggle why many issues about the Maroons have not yet been uncovered. They watched constantly for spies and as oral traditions record, set not only sinkholes in the Cockpit country as traps for their enemies but also constructed misleading trails. They avoided excessive enlargement of their territories—this, perhaps, explaining why by the end of the wars they had little land for themselves. Most importantly, the Maroons made the best use of woman power which Kamau Brathwaite and Carolyn Cooper (this volume) have discussed in greater detail.

A guerrilla army in the field without time piece has to use nature's clock, day and night, to break down longer periods. The Maroon fighter was no different. His tactics depended on his objective. Did he want to gain time so that his women and children could escape? Was he concerned that a particular British monarch may reign for "x" number of years or was he more concerned about time for his sons and daughters to reach adulthood and live in freedom and peace? The year 1655 was of no concern to the Maroon, apart from the fact that the developments of that year interrupted his flow of time.

The Maroons did not set out in 1658 and after, to fight the British for a certain number of years and stop there. The fact that the eighty-four years to the peace treaty in 1739 were spent in conflict is measured more in terms of generations than in any other period. The fact that so soon after so many successful actions against the British the Maroons were at the point in time ready to make peace was not very clear. The Maroons wrote very little down, and therefore any clarification would require further reference to the colonial record. It is also interesting to note that the Maroons started their prolonged guerrilla campaign only after punitive action was taken against them. The time was thrust upon them.

The Maroon guerrilla chose time and nature but at that point, time was chosen for him. He made the best use of whatever time was left for them by withdrawing from direct conflict and taking refuge further into much more inaccessible areas of the hills. There they used time to consolidate, plan and develop [Hart 1985]. They also chose time to take action in search of supplies to hunt and to communicate with other blacks who worked as slaves on the various plantations. The Maroons appeared to have too much on their hands: they needed time to train, rest, consolidate and prepare for new attacks. For instance, timing in relation to the ambush was most critical. The use of time had to be effective, both from a strategic as well as a tactical point of view.

A concerted effort and a common goal was behind the strong will which served as the driving force of Maroon guerrilla fighters. It was what kept them going against the odds. This willpower came from many sources. According to experts in guerrilla fighting, in modern times such determination may be ideological, nationalistic or religious as one finds, for example, in ancient and modern times with fundamentalism, kumina or obeah in the New World.

The fight between the Spanish settlers and the English was to a large extent a fight between religions—Cromwell's Protestants against Spanish Catholics. The blacks no doubt retained their own religious beliefs. Kamau Brathwaite, writing about "The spirit of African Survival in Jamaica", speaks of the Spirit-Ancestor remaining close to the living; the possession of the living by the dead. ". . . In this achievement music and dance—locomotive energy—plays an essential role . . . The Priest . . . in whose company the community can be led most easily into a wholesome relationship with the ancient and the approaching past" [Brathwaite 1978].

It is well known that the African approached religion in a situation much closer to the ways of native American Indians, rather than to that of the Judeo-Christian. The African looked to nature, to his clan, to family as all integral parts of his religion. It is in the same way that the Maroons, consisting mainly of people of African descent, approached war.

Ethnographic evidence and oral traditions [Bilby 1985,1987] indicate that preparation for war always included the use of music, dance and libations. The drums, which were used in the dance, were ideal for focusing one's attention on the task at hand. During the ceremony instructions could be easily passed on to persons preparing for battle. Compare the war-dance ceremony of the American Indian. This type of activity, though in a different form, is carried out by all modern armies when troops are blessed and exhorted to perform valiantly, just before a battle, by stirring speeches and martial music. The priest/priestess was no doubt a central part of the Maroon community. It was their role to justify to the fighters the reason and importance of the struggle they were waging. It was to the priest or priestess that the community looked for inspiration and morale building.

It is interesting to note that in the period 1735-1739 the English began to use and obtain a lot of information from spies about the life and tactics of the Maroons. Much of this information may have been of increased significance, since the English were becoming more involved with the dynamics of West African society and so the information gleaned took on its true meaning. There are secrets behind the successes of the Maroons. Ease of movement, an effective communication system, the ineffectiveness of the sophisticated British military equipment in an unfriendly environment, procurement of supplies, effective use of spiritual powers such as is related to those of Nanny, the great warrior woman, and a determination to survive in the life-or-death circumstances of the time—all these circumstances sustained their struggle.

In any military confrontation, engagement is of two types: direct or indirect. Direct engagement is primarily the province of the main battle and aims at control and influence of the battle. Indirect engagement involves effecting an attack without necessarily coming into direct or face-to-face contact with the enemy. The aim is to restrict effective onslaught or manoeuvre. In both types of engagements technology—old and new—are important. The Maroons may have realized their technological weakness, knowing very well the superiority of the equipment of the British forces.

Sensibly and logically, the Maroons chose the indirect method which involved quick, effective, sudden "hit-and-run" engagements. Clumsy, heavily armed and unable to move swiftly and decisively, the British forces only recorded the attacks after they had happened. It was not until the eighteenth and nineteenth centuries that long-range arms came into use, so there was no opportunity to use such facilities against the Maroons. In addition, the terrain and the location of the Maroon settlements [Agorsah 1992b] indicate that the Maroons would have made considerable use of trenching and ditching as a method of besieging the enemy and staging surprise attacks. The technique of camouflage described in the traditions of the Maroons of Accompong and Moore Town, lends support to this proposition. It appears, from all indications of the events of the Maroon wars, that one can rightly apply the Chinese aphorism: "Know yourself and your adversary and you will be able to fight a hundred battles without a single disaster".

The ability of the British forces to withstand the power of Maroon warfare greatly depended on technological development of arms and ammunition. The first explosive device consisting of what came to be known as gunpowder was invented in China from where it spread to the West. Although it was mentioned as far back as 1044, its formulation was not made fully available until AD 1242, when Roger Bacon[12] disclosed it in the journal, *De Mirabili Potetate Artis et Naturae*. The following year, directions were given on how to manufacture such an explosive device by use of charcoal, saltpetre and sulphur.

The use of such explosive power did not become popular until the fourteenth century, when gunpowder was used to propel a projectile or shot. It was first used in the West by the English in 1346 at the battle of Crecy. By the seventeenth century, the use of the explosive device had become quite popular. During the voyages of exploration which took several European countries such as Portugal, Spain, Sweden, France and others to various parts of the world, weapons related to the use of explosives were carried along, not only for self-defence, but also for launching attacks on rival colonizers.

The musket, a military weapon fired from the shoulder, was the most popular of the arms brought to the Caribbean. Introduced in the mid 1500s by the Huguenots, it was a long barreled weapon which could fire a 203 ball some 300 metres. The firing mechanism was a "match lock", which was modified later into a "flint lock". This was an easier and more reliable method for discharging the weapon. This was well suited to the open battlefields of Europe but quite unsuited to the jungle warfare of Jamaica. In particular, its adaptation for the peculiar circumstances by the Maroons may have given them the edge over the English. Archaeological evidence from Nanny Town [Agorsah 1992c] points to the adaptation of the shorter barreled version of the "Brown Bess" flintlock musket which was the standard military weapon of English forces for over 200 years (1660-1860). By shortening the barrel one sacrifices range, but 150-200 metres would have been more than sufficient for the distances encountered. The "Brown Bess" was cheap and easily manufactured. A basic knowledge of metallurgy and forging would have enabled the Maroons to repair and refit this weapon. Records [Hart 1985] speak of the capture of large quantities of muskets. Therefore, apart from the need for adaptations of newer models, the Maroons may have been amply supplied with muskets in relation to the number of combatants in their ranks. By combining the qualities of marksmanship, good powder and ammunition with their encyclopaedic knowledge of the terrain, they could use a minimum of men to pin down large groups of English troops without the need for exposing themselves. They may have used sniper techniques to greater effect than had been heard of before.

On the battlefield, even in modern times, fast movement of soldiers is a priority. A system of linkages between various parts of a force thus becomes very important. Commanders must have not only continuous communication, so essential for operations, but must themselves be able to move very swiftly in a combat situation. In the terrain of the Maroons this was a difficulty for the British troops. The Maroons used the side-blown "cow horn", the *abeng*, a name derived from the Akan language of the then Gold Coast (now Ghana), to sound messages. Although the sound would be heard by the British troops, the content of the messages would not be understood. The *abeng* remains today as part of the cultural paraphernalia of the Maroons.

The ability to procure supplies of good quality food and water is a vital factor in the effective operation of any military group. The Maroons, as well as the British forces, relied on the destruction of each other's food supply in order to introduce weakness into the enemy camp. Water supplies were also poisoned. Maroon traditions relate that Maroons never drank from free flowing rivers, but from such waters as the Nanny Falls near the site of Nanny Town—the sources of which the British could not gain access in order to poison. Even if this particular situation did not arise, it is at least clear that the Maroons were aware of the possibility of river poisoning. Also, certain plants, such as the cocoon or black whiss[13] in the Blue Mountains, were depended upon for drinking water. This is an indication that the Maroons understood their environment and its resources, medicinal qualities, food yields and features it provided for defence or attack. Frequent shortages of certain critical supplies appear to have characterized the operation of the British forces, especially in their expedition against the stronghold of the Maroons in and around Nanny Town.

Conclusions

The Maroons were not the first people who won the battle only to lose the war. Today the Maroons do not accept that they were defeated by the British forces. It is thought that they forced the seemingly invincible British army to a military stalemate. The Maroons faced forces backed by the largest and most successful colonial power of the time. They knew their strength. They knew the strength of their adversary and planned all their strategies around that knowledge. Their strategy at the inception of the war was to maintain freedom and autonomy. This ultimately meant a stern test of their ability to retain their cultural identity. In the end they succeeded beyond their wildest imaginations.

This analysis is only a first step towards understanding the struggle and survival of one of the first freedom fighters in the New World and is only one example of many that have taken place over time. It should not be considered as being exhaustive of all the available evidence. Discussing this issue as an officer still in active service imposes certain restrictions, but the discussion should open the doors to further discussion and analysis. But one thing is clear: The Maroons deserve a Nobel Peace Prize with retrospective effect from the 1730s.

Notes

1 Thomas Wentworth Higginson, *Black Rebellion* (1899).

2 Susan Pierres, "Land of Look Behind", *Caribbean Travel and Life* (March-April 1993): 86-93 and 115.

3 Robert Taber, *The War of the Flea - Guerrilla Warfare Theory and Practice* (Paladin, 1970).

4 Irene Wright, Translations of the letters of Captain Julian Castilla. *Spanish Resistance to English Occupation of Jamaica, 1655-1660 (Diary of the Indies Collection: Institute of Jamaica, 1660)*.

5 Mao Tse-Tung, *Problems of War and Strategy* (Peking: Language Press, 1966); also, his *Selected Works*, Vols.1-4 (Peking: Language Press, 1966).

6 R.C. Dallas, *The History of the Maroons*, 2 vols. (London, 1803); G.W. Bridges, *The Annals of Jamaica, Vol. II* (London, 1828).

7 C. Robinson, *The Fighting Maroons of Jamaica* (Kingston, 1969).

8 Alan Eyre, "The Maroon Wars in Jamaica: A Geographical Appraisal", *The Jamaica Historical Review* XII (1980): 5-18.

9 R.C. Dallas, op. cit., 43-44.

10 C. Robinson, op. cit., 44.

11 Che Guevarra, *Guerrilla Warfare*. Translated from Spanish by J.P. Morray with prefatory note by I.F. Stone (N.Y.: Alfred A. Knopf, 1969).

12 In 1242 Roger Bacon, an English friar, in the technical journal, *De Mirabili Potetate Artis et Naturae* (see Compton's Encyclopaedia), disclosed the formulation of gunpowder/blackpowder as a mixture of saltpetre, charcoal and sulphur: 75-15-10. Saltpetre or potassium nitrate (KNO_2) is used not only in gunpowder, but also as an important ingredient in preserving pork today in rural communities. Did the Maroons understand the dual nature of this commodity at that time? Charcoal—from wood fires, especially dogwood or alder—the other important ingredient, was always available. Sulphur though occuring naturally in nature, is not known to be readily available in Jamaica. There may, however, be elements with similar properties which were available to the Maroons. Therefore, the ability to formulate one's own ammunition would have saved them the risk of raiding plantations or other stores for supplies. Even today the formula for mixing blackpowder is a matter largely of individual taste, and the important thing is that it works and is not detrimental to the user while it is being formulated. Keeping it dry would be most important, and the historical record shows that the powder horn was widely used by the Maroons. There is also evidence that the Maroons obtained gunpowder supplies from Jewish merchants in Kingston. The quality and quantity of the ingredients would have some effect on the projectile, but a 2oz. ball fired from such a weapon has a devastating physical and psychological effect.

13 See, for example, Olive Senior, *A-Z of Jamaican Heritage* (Kingston: The Gleaner Co., 1987); also Maroon guide to the 1991 Nanny Town expedition, who described "whiss" (also called by several other names, e.g. "black wiss", "water wiss", "withe", "wild grape") as Maroon traditional survival medicine.

eleven

Archaeology of Maroon Settlements in Jamaica

E. Kofi Agorsah

Introduction

The significance of Maroon heritage in Jamaica as an important link between the prehistoric and the historical periods, as well as the only major chain of cultural history that weaves through the whole of Jamaica's historical past introduces the subject of this chapter. A review of the location and distribution of Maroon communities in Jamaica in historical times is conducted and some of the outstanding features of the sites examined through archaeological reconnaissance, survey and excavation are described. A discussion of the material follows and some generalizations or interpretations are made in an attempt to identify the place and the heritage of the Maroons of Jamaica in a more objective cultural perspective, and the implications of the material available so far for the history and culture of Jamaica as a whole.

Archaeological excavations at the sites of Nanny Town in the Blue Mountains and Old Accompong Town in the Cockpit country are reviewed and used as the main basis for the generalizations.

It is generalized that finds such as the cowrie shells from Old Accompong Town (simply referred to as "Old Town" by Maroons of Accompong) as well as prehistoric and historical earthenware from the ancient site of Nanny Town, indicate that some issues of interpretations of the early history of Jamaica which claim the complete extermination of the prehistoric groups by the Spaniards need to be re-examined. Also, the true Amerindian and African elements in the heritage of the Maroons of Jamaica, need to be reviewed and revised if Thermoluminiscence and Carbon 14 dates turn out as expected. Archaeological evidence coming to light in the last few years is beginning to unravel some of the most exciting mysteries about the Maroons, placing it in its right position in the history of cultural development, not only in the Caribbean, but in the New World as a whole. Although the main evidence discussed in this chapter is archaeological, considerable reference is made to ethnographic and historical evidence.

A critical analysis of the history of Jamaica clearly demonstrates that Maroon society provided a cultural link between the indigenous societies of the island and the Spanish on one hand, and the English on the other [Blake 1898; Brathwaite 1977; Robinson 1969, 1987]. Historically, this is significant because it reconfirms that the history of the Maroons of Jamaica is not only a link, but has become and remains in its entirety a part of the historical period [Agorsah 1993]. The importance of Maroon heritage as a major cultural element that runs through the historical period in Jamaica, can therefore not be over-emphasized. A reconstruction of the cultural development of Jamaican society is thus incomplete without retracing the course of this major thread [Agorsah 1990, 1991]. Evidence regarding other aspects of Maroon heritage, such as their music, dance and religion [Bilby 1984, 1987; Beckwith 1969; Black 1983; Martin 1972] points to the availability of a substantial amount of background material with, and on which, to build a more complete picture of the Maroon heritage.

Many historical references portray the Maroons more as "rebels" than "freedom fighters". This attitude is criticized in this chapter as a one-sided way of presenting the cultural heritage of the Maroons [Eyre 1980; Furness 1965]. In addition, very few colonial writers have been bold enough to emphasize the point of the fight for freedom. But thanks to the spirits of their ancestors, the spirit of real freedom-fighting is still observable among Maroons and it continues to be very strong among them to this day [Bilby 1984,1987; Dalby 1971; Hall 1982; Carey 1970; Kopytoff 1973, 1978].

Archaeological research

Archaeological research in Jamaica that deals with Maroon heritage is limited to very few reconnaissance, survey [Teulon 1967], and minor excavation expeditions [Bonner 1974]. It was only recently that major excavations have been conducted by the University of the West Indies Mona Archaeological Research Project [Agorsah, 1992b, 1993a,b]. In 1967, a reconnaissance expedition led by Alan Teulon of the Survey Department made the first attempt to locate and identify the ancient site of Nanny Town and to conduct an environmental study of the area.[1] A ruined stone wall, a stone with engraved inscriptions as well as several surface artifacts such as fragments of bottles and crockery, and some botanical specimens were observed and some collected. The 1973 expedition led by a Lieutenant Harvey Nott, with Anthony Bonner as the scientific leader, appeared to be more serious and conducted a small-scale excavation.[2] Although not a large quantity, the range of artifacts was quite significant [Bonner 1974] and at least seems to confirm that military action took place at the site.[3] Since 1991, a series of planned reconnaissance, surveys and large scale excavations have been undertaken at the Nanny Town and Accompong Old Town sites in eastern and western Jamaica respectively, although work at the former has been more intensive and extensive.[4]

The amount of archaeological material assembled so far in no way compares quantitatively to the amount of ethnological and written data on the Maroons. However, the few finds made indicate that several new issues regarding Maroon heritage, particularly in Jamaica, have to be raised for reconsideration and discussion and review: the mysteries of Maroon survival; contribution to the achievement of freedom, human dignity and liberty in the New World; Maroon-Amerindian relationships; Maroon social, political and economic systems; Maroon women, specifically Nanny, the great woman warrior of all time; Maroon settlement and behaviour patterns; and history of guerrilla warfare. The main goal has been to determine the nature and mechanism of functional adaptation of Maroon communities in the New World over time—a search for a culture history rather than a history of "rebels" or a second-rate group of people. Tackling these new issues or elements in the history and archaeology of the Caribbean is not an easy task, especially since previous speculations or conclusions have become so well accepted as facts. It means that one really needs to approach the questions with absolute objectivity [Agorsah 1993a, b].

Although today Maroons occupy three main areas of Jamaica (Fig. 11.1), the total area under Maroon control in the past was quite substantial. The activities of the Maroons were geared solely towards maintenance of their hard-won freedom and for survival (economic, social and political) [Dallas 1803; Blake 1898; Robinson 1969; Brathwaite 1977; Campbell 1988]. Owing to the constant need to fight back against slavery and to maintain independence, many of the settlements would, as expected, be semi-permanent or even if permanent, destroyed during attacks by the British and rebuilt several times over.

Earliest Maroon settlements

The earliest Maroons in Jamaica may be traced to a mixture of prehistoric groups existing in the island before the Spaniards, Africans and possibly people of other origins. Many such runaways under the Spaniards or the British, seized the opportunity, presented by the war between the Spanish and the English who invaded the island in the early 1650s, and escaped from the estates to set up free communities in various parts of the hilly regions of the island [Dallas 1803; Morales 1952]. Although Spanish and British colonial documents provide figures of numbers of Maroons in some of the settlements of which they were aware, information on the exact location as well as their spatial extent and related data that would be relevant for identifying the individual settlements, was grossly neglected. For example, the

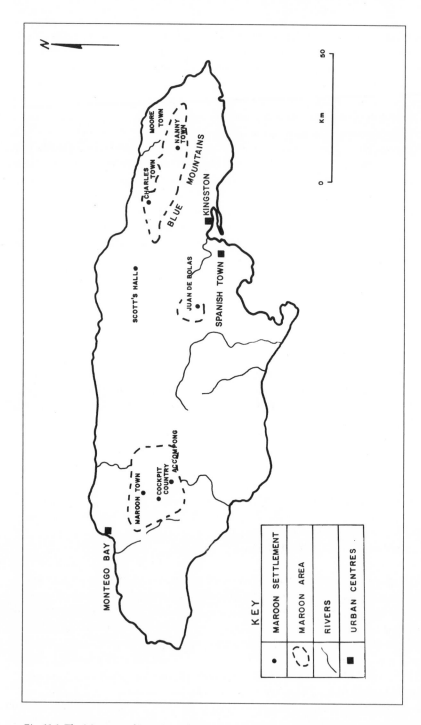

Fig. 11.1 The Maroons of Jamaica today

   Maroon Heritage

term "Negro village" [Hart 1980] became so very commonly used that one is unable to identify the particular settlement being referred to in any report. As a result of such unclear references and, also, owing to the fact that the Maroons did not possess a system of documentation of events, there is an almost absolute absence of the traditional names by which they referred to their individual settlements. Much more important to the Maroons may have been the need to keep information about their locations within closed circles, a situation one would expect in their circumstances.

The earliest known Maroon settlements were those established by Spanish slaves or aborigines enslaved by the Spaniards, but who escaped into the inaccessible parts of the island. In the Caribbean as in other parts of the New World, particularly Latin America [Bryan 1971], one of the main features of flight from bondage or captivity was that it was related to cultural contact between local Indians on one hand and between them and the various African ethnic groups on the other. This was the case with the establishment of the first Maroon settlements in Hispaniola in 1503, just a few years after the arrival of the Spaniards' first slave ships in the Caribbean.

In Jamaica, one of the known areas settled was Guanaboa Vale in the hilly Juan de Bolas area located in the modern parish of St Catherine. Generally, the Maroons of the Spanish period occupied and controlled the area between the modern towns of Linstead and Chapelton, including the Ginger Ridge, Pindars and Marlie Hill areas, which are dominated by the Rock River and Rio Cobre drainage systems.

Colonial records dating from about 1667-68 [5] also refer to another such settlement at Los Vermajales, a savannah area in the general vicinity of Guanaboa Vale, though said to be isolated from those in the Juan de Bolas mountain area. According to Mavis Campbell [1988], the group at the Vermajales settlement was led by one Juan de Sierras, then considered to be an outstanding fellow. Another early Maroon settlement is reportedly located south of Cave Valley, near the Clarendon/ St Ann border, in a grassland area lying between the Mocho mountains and the modern town of Porus. Its exact location is not known, but it is speculated that in addition to that one, there may have been several other temporary settlements.

The Spanish period Maroon settlements are not very well known, probably because of the fact that they may not have developed or may not have been established well enough by the time the English attacked and took over the island. Some Maroon groups who had at first sided with the Spaniards switched allegiance to join the English about 1633. However, others refused to change sides and consequently relocated in even more inaccessible parts of the mountain regions, mainly in the eastern portions of Jamaica away from their original locations. The groups were being reinforced continually by other slaves who escaped from the English plantations. Another group probably resettled in the Cockpit country, in the vicinity of modern Accompong in St Elizabeth and at Maroon Town in Trelawny. The Maroons continued to live in groups throughout their fight for freedom. The Accompong area became the main control point for the groups living in the adjoining modern St Elizabeth, St James and Clarendon parishes [Kopytoff 1973]. Meanwhile, New Nanny Town (Moore Town) controlled the Maroons in the Blue Mountain region. Many more Maroon settlements are referred to in colonial records of the eighteenth and nineteenth century or later, as the Maroon communities became more effective in their operations.

Eastern Jamaica sites

In eastern Jamaica, in the Blue Mountains in particular, many sites have been identified, some with features such as building foundations. Sites include Nanny Town, Pumpkin Hill, Mammee Hill, Watch Hill, Seaman's Valley, Marshall's Hall, Gun Barrel and Brownsfield. These sites are located in and around the Windsor, Ginger House and Comfort Castle area, as well as parts of John's Hall district in the parish of Portland. The environment is generally fragmented because of its mountainous nature and the deep gullies of the Rio Grande, Negro and Dry Rivers which cut through the region. The Blue Mountain region, like the El Cobre and El Cuzco of Cuba and the forest regions of Suriname, proved to be particularly suitable for runaway slave settlements. Documentary evidence indicates that several years before the British came in, the Spanish government had sent troops to flush out some "Arawak" escapees from the Blue Mountains [Morales 1952]. This confirms the speculation that some prehistoric groups enslaved by the Spaniards or others who escaped from the Spaniards had begun to establish settlements in the Blue Mountains at that time. This also supports the view that the earliest Maroons consisted of indigenous people who may have been enslaved by the Spaniards and possibly people of African descent who may have come with the Spaniards.

One of the interesting sites is Marshall's Hall located near Comfort Castle, close to the Dry River, in the parish of Portland. The site is interesting because of its structural features and, also, because of the fact that oral traditions link the site to the modern town of Moore Town, also in Portland. Surface finds consist mainly of eighteenth and nineteenth century ceramics, house platforms and steps leading up to rooms. The site overlooks the Jackmandoore, a spring which flows into the Dry River. The Marshall's Hall site appears to consist of many quarters, each probably housing groups of families. Identifying these quarters of the site should explain aspects of Maroon social network.

The Brownsfield Maroon site [Agorsah 1990] is located on the Snake River near Alligator Church Bridge in the parish of Portland, high on a hill overlooking the main road that skirts the modern town of Brownsfield. House foundations are the principal features, along with a few ceramic pieces and green glass wine bottles— mainly surface finds.

The locations of Brownsfield and Marshall's Hall appear to support the view that they may have been chosen for the defence needs of the Maroons. This is to be expected in periods of conflict and war such as the Maroons experienced during the early part of their history. A test excavation of the site was undertaken, but it turned out to be a very disturbed area. Sub-surface testing has been undertaken in a few areas as well, but features encountered are yet to be exposed and identified.

One problem about the Brownsfield site is that much of it is being farmed and a greater portion of it continues to appear to be disturbed. This disturbance is expected to become even more intense, as many more Maroons are moving back to settle in the area around the site.

Seventeenth to nineteenth-century maps were useful in the identification of territories occupied by Maroon groups, as well as locating dwelling sites, guerrilla war camps, hideouts, burial and battlegrounds, military tracks and fortifications [Agorsah 1991, 1992b]. Several of the maps indicate the changing locations of the settlements over time, a feature that was common to Maroon settlements in other areas of the New World, such as in Spanish Florida, Mexico and Suriname. By the beginning of the 1700s several Maroon settlements varying in size and composition are observed to have developed. Thicknesse [1788] mentions Quao's Crawford Town[6] and another camp, supposedly one of those under Cudjoe, the Maroon leader who signed the Peace Treaty of 1739, but not much information is given about it.[7] Other settlements mentioned include Quao's Town and "a fishing and hunting village near Quao's Town with seventy four huts", Nanny Town,[8] and Men's Town described as located on the way "going towards Nanny Town with a dancing place". It is not clear what the "dancing place" referred to could have been. It appears to suggest a place for some kind of community activity.

English reports observe that the main town (Nanny Town ?) was located in the ridge of the Blue Mountains with two smaller towns in the same area but fairly far apart.[9] Also reported is a large cave with "two great troughs to hold water" and considered to be an important Maroon hideout.[10] Guy's Town is mentioned as a refuge for Nanny Town Maroons after the British forces had taken control of the Nanny Town site in 1734. In a confession to the English authorities, one Seyrus[11] mentions "Hobby's", a "Negro Town", and settlements in the "Carrion Crow Hill". The locations of these sites have still not been clearly established.

One of the conditions of the peace treaties signed between the British and the Maroons called for grants of land as well as the survey of land occupied by Maroon groups. Consequently, Maroon settlements became more and more spatially defined. A square parcel of land situated on the Negro River, an eastern arm of the Rio Grande, was granted to Nanny, described as "a great Negro woman", and her followers in the parish of Portland.[12] This land is said to have been bounded on three sides by the "King's" land and on the other by land belonging to a John Stevenson. This land grant refers to the location of New Nanny Town, which is today's Moore Town in the parish of Portland, referred to in Harris (this volume, Fig. 2 .1). Other Maroon settlements that resulted from land grants and colonial survey include Bath, a splinter town to the south of Nanny Town surveyed in the 1760s; Scott's Hall[13] with the Wag Water River serving as the main boundary in that area; Crawford Town, relocated and documented in 1754;[14] Charles Town, which was a new settlement of Crawford Town, several kilometres from the latter and located on the Buff Bay River close to the south shore.[15]

Goucher [1990, 1991] suggests that artisans of African descent from nearby splinter settlements, engaged by a John Reeder to run a brass and iron foundry at Morant Bay in the 1770s, may have come from among the Maroon communities in the Bath and Hayfield areas. The British government had given its approval for John Reeder to tap iron ore in the area. In western Jamaica, the Maroon lands, like those of the east, became more clearly defined. Accompong was granted some 1,500 acres of land 1000 of which was for Accompong itself.[16] Trelawny Town was another such settlement near Accompong [Dallas 1803].

The examples noted above indicate that only vague information exists about the earliest Maroon sites. One difficulty faced in attempting to locate the earliest sites is the craggy or rugged nature of the terrain in which they were established. The location of some of these settlements was certainly known by the British forces, but they may have had difficulty gaining access to them. Similarly, many of the settlements may not have been known at all as it was not an easy task to enter these areas to search for them, and also because the Maroons, as guerrillas, may have been constantly on the move, changing bases and establishing misleading tracks or trails.

Place names such as Parade, Gun Hill, Watch Hill, Lookout Point, Kindah, Bathing Place, Petty River Bottom, Gun Barrel and Killdead, identified from historical records and oral traditions of the Maroons, have helped to obtain directions to and information about some of the sites [Agorsah 1990, 1992b]. Also, the Maroons possess oral traditions about historical and other events related to some of the sites and sometimes could point out features they may have noticed in the past at some of the sites.[17] Where settlements are identified, structural features may not be readily identifiable. But there are exceptions, especially in the case of some of the modern settlements. For example, a 1757 map marks out one thousand acres of land for Accompong Maroons.

The modern settlement of Accompong appears to be in the same strategic area with restricted access routes, although it has been shifting south and westwards away from the original location of Old Accompong Town, locally referred to as Old Town. The main historical structural features in modern Accompong Town include the old church and cemetery, and the monument dedicated to Colonel Cudjoe (Kojo) who signed the peace treaty witht he English in 1739. Today Accompong consists of several quarters that appear to represent those of related family units [Francis 1991]. It is not clear whether these units or quarters were established at the initial stages of the founding of the town and later continued at the new quarters or were developed later. Oral tradition records that these quarters do not represent any predetermined family relationships. The quarters include Hill Top, Parade, Middle Ground, Over Yonder, Gipson, Guinea Grass, Pondside, Cedar Valley, River Hole, River Pond, Out Yonder, Force Hill, Outer Road, to mention some (Fig. 11.2).

The main archaeological sites in the neighbourhood of Accompong include Kindah, interpreted to mean "We are a family". It is located just outside Accompong Town to the northeast and is the venue for the annual anniversary celebrations of the 1739 peace treaty. It is said to have been the camp for holding

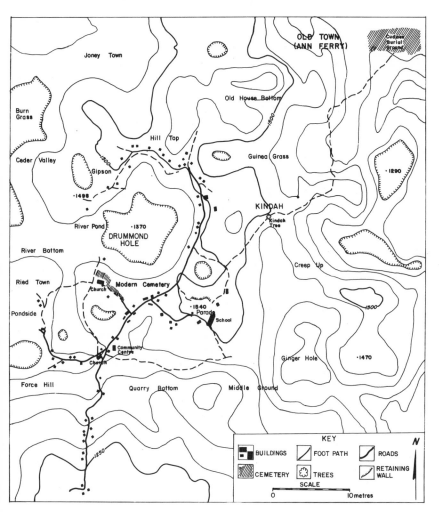

Fig. 11.2 Accompong Town quarters

consultations between Maroon military wing leaders during their encounter with the British forces. The site of the burial ground of Kojo is located on fairly level ground, about half a kilometre down a rugged slope north-east of Kindah. The only identifying mark consists of two large stones on a piece of slightly raised ground. There must be a reason for maintaining the burial ground of such an important historical personality in its very simple form. Big Ground Grass is another site. It is mainly an open area to the east of Kojo's burial ground. It has no apparent archaeological feature and is very bare and in the middle of a well vegetated area. The question to be examined is, why is that area so heavily deforested? Was it constantly sourced for timber or for burning coal? Could it have been that the area was inhabited only recently?

The Peace Cave site is located almost on the eastern border of the Accompong Maroon lands. The cave, also referred to as "Ambush" was, according to Maroon oral traditions, used as a hideout, as it was strategically located closest to the opponent's military camp, situated in the then Aberdeen Plantation to the east. The physical appearance of the cave appears to have changed over time and no longer fits the description in reported documents and photographs. The last battleground of the British/Maroon wars before the peace treaty of 1739 is said to have been located in the valley in front of the Peace Cave referred to as Pettee River Bottom [Eyre 1980]. Guthries Defile, an important point of access into Maroon lands in the Peace Cave area, is located in this vicinity.

The elementary school compound at Accompong also marks the location of the site referred to as Parade. A large quantity of imported ceramics, buttons, fragments of green glass bottle and nails were surface-collected from this site, and on the slopes leading up from the Peace Cave. Parade was what oral tradition refers to as "Lookout Point" because its strategic location enabled the Maroons to spy, or see in advance, any approaching person or army from all directions. Other sites to the north and west of Accompong include Gun Hill, Trelawny Town, Flagstaff and Vaughnsfield, where structural features such as burial ground and house foundations have been identified.

The fascination of the Cockpit country cuts across many scientific and historical fields. In such scientific fields as geomorphology, entomology and ornithology, the area ranks second only to the Gunun Mulu National Park as a potential heritage area.[18] With its tropical karst terrain and unique vegetation the Cockpit country was to be the scene of some of the wars in which the Maroons set an unprecedented example to the world, by successfully engaging the seemingly invincible British army to a military stalemate. It is speculated that a military track constructed across the Cockpit country from Windsor to Troy in 1796, a few kilometres east of Troy and popularly known as Robertson's Run, may have followed early Maroon military trails. The association of the Cockpit country with historical events can therefore be gleaned also from the special characteristics of the area, particularly from the star-shaped closed depressions within the rough and rugged terrain.

Archaeological evidence

Two sites which were of particular significance, Nanny Town and Accompong Old Town, were selected for site differentiation and excavation. The Nanny Town site (Fig. 11.3) is strategically located within the loop of the Stony River which marks its southern and eastern boundaries [Agorsah 1992b]. Blocking off the Stony River and standing steeply against it is Abraham Hill. To the north and west of the site is Nanny Hill from which Nanny Falls splashes down on to the open level ground and flows into the southeastern bend of the Stony River, marking the boundaries on that side of the settlement (Fig. 11.3).

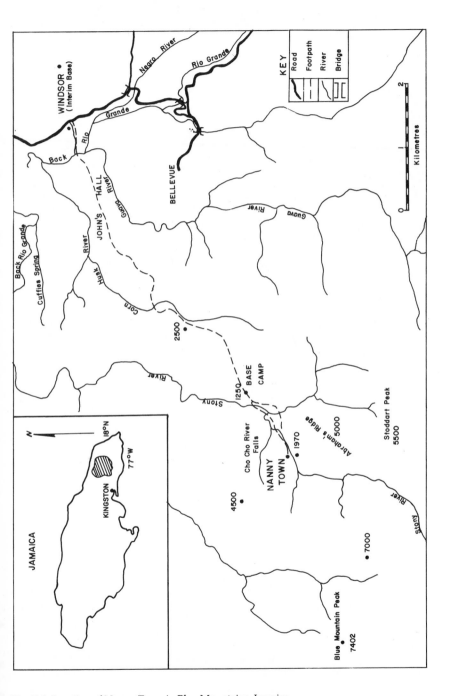

Fig. 11.3 Location of Nanny Town in Blue Mountains, Jamaica

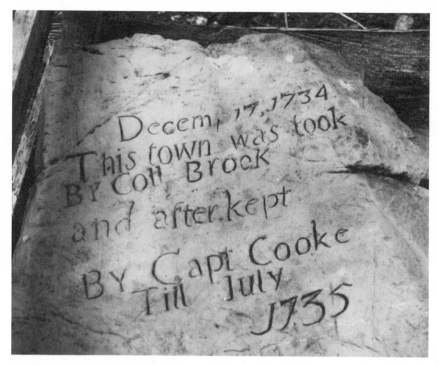

Rock with inscription at Nanny Town site. (Archaeological find.)

Recent archaeological investigations indicate that in fact there are five (three large and two small) rectangular stone structures and not only one, as noted from previous expeditions. They are considered and reported to be military fortifications built during the Maroon-British wars [Bonner 1974]. A large block of stone located near the stone structure is engraved with a message that the settlement was taken and briefly controlled by the British forces.[19] Another stone monument (slab) measuring 27 x 35 cm, which appears to be more recent, has the inscription "BERMUDA REGIMENT 1971"—clearly very recent.

The Nanny Town site

As indicated above, the Stony and Peters Rivers and their tributaries dominate the drainage pattern of the site and areas around it, while Abraham Hill to the south and Sugar Loaf to the north and northwest dominate the topography. Rocky and rugged, the Nanny Town site and the surrounding areas are engulfed in thick luxuriant green vegetation [Adams 1972]. Some of the plants identified during the pre-excavation surveying of the site include broomweed (*Sida acuta*); bully tree (*Bumelia nigra*); climbing cocoon (*Entanda gigas*); tea bush (*Ocimum gratissimum*); ashes bush (*Tetrazygla pallens*); bachelor's buttons (*Gonyshrena globosa*);

One of five rectangular stone structures (military fortifications?) at the Nanny Town site. (Archaeological find.)

common bamboo (*Bambusa vulgaris*); basket hoop (*Croton lucidus*); bitter aloe (*Aloe vera*); bitter wood (*Picrasma excelsa*); black sage (*Lantana luticifolia*); sweet wood (*Nectandra antiliana*); cow itch (*Mucuna pruviens*); gully bean (*Solanum torvum*); poisoned hogmeat (*Aristolochia grandifolia*); lablab tree (*Alchornea latifolia*); congo mahoe (*Hibiscus clypeatus*); cow foot (*Pothomorphe umbellata*); chew stick (*Gouania lupuloides*), among others.[20]

Until this day, the Maroons have very good knowledge of the medicinal and other traditional uses of many of these plants and claim that knowledge of the uses of the plants was handed down from their ancestors [Lang 1991]. Today many of the known plants in the area appear to include plants introduced into Jamaica from the very time the Spaniards introduced Africans into the island in 1517.[21] The Nanny Town site continues to be populated by wild hogs, as well some of the very few types of known snakes in Jamaica. Hunting and fishing are the normal occupations of people encountered in those remote areas of the Blue Mountains and, according to Maroon traditions, these were their occupations from ancient times.

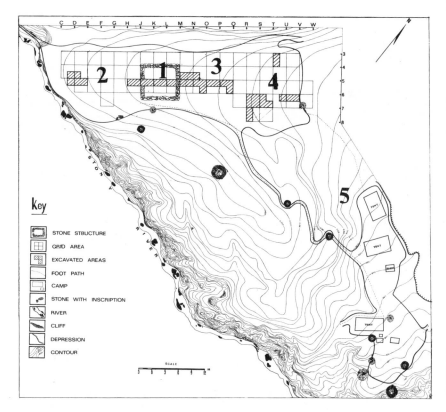

Fig. 11.4 Nanny Town site

Excavation

The site was differentiated into areas during the pre-excavation survey as Area 1, Area 2 through to Area 9 (Fig. 11.4) first, for logistical reasons as well as according to the distribution of artifacts and the general topography of the site and adjoining territories. The period 1991 to 1993 has seen three major excavations which appear to have covered approximately 40% of the total site of Nanny Town, and were based on a three-metre grid superimposed on the 10-foot grid of the 1973 excavation. Depth to bedrock or sterile layer of the 3 x 3 or 1.5 x 1.5 metre pits and sometimes 1.5 x 6 or 8 metre trenches ranged from 10 to 72 cm and only more than 1 metre in very few, especially in areas to the east and south of the site.

Several areas appear to have been disturbed by recent military activities at the site, but these were easily identifiable. The stratigraphy, particularly the texture and humus content of the soils varies from area to area, depicting differential site utilization which could be related to different periods of time or to the same period, but for different activities.

Considering the distribution of artifacts in the pits generally, one thing is clear: local ceramics (earthenware) are more common as one moves away from the west toward the east and southeastward of the site. Four more stone fortifications have been identified. Two of them are much the same in size as the only one known so far, and two smaller ones—one at the entrance to the site coming from the west and the other on top of the highest point of the site. One of the newly discovered large stone structures has been excavated and one side (which had completely collapsed) has been reconstructed. Much of the local earthenware were recovered from this particular stone structure, at depths that indicate that it had been built over a previous living floor which, obviously, would have been the Maroon level, dateable by a coin find in that level to approximately 1681. But this speculation must await a complete analysis of the finds. Results of soil chemical analysis and further dates are expected to also confirm the relationships of the levels.

Finds

Artifacts recovered from the site of Nanny Town consist of a wide variety of items such as local earthenware and teracotta figurines; imported ceramics such as Belarmine jars, tin glaze and delftware; glass including wine, alcoholic and medicinal or pharmaceutical bottles; metal implements; fragments of gun barrels and musket balls of various sizes and weights; nails, lead and other metal objects such as knives, spearheads and door hinges; crockery, red clay and kaolin (white clay) smoking pipe stems and bowls; grinding stones and other stone implements including fragments of worked and unworked flint; Spanish (*pieces of eight*) coins; glass and stone beads and buttons (see photographs below, pp.177-180).

Lower grinding stones with upper grinding stone, recovered 45cm away from it, placed on top. Scale in inches. (Archaeological finds from Nanny Town.)

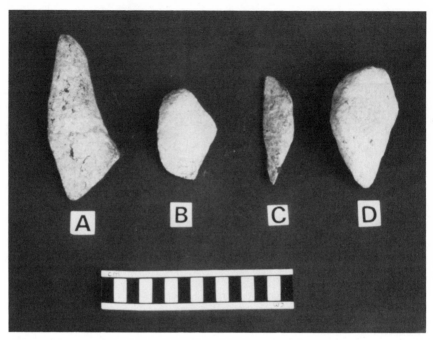

Stone tools (Amerindian-Arawak?). (Archaeological finds from Nanny Town.)

Ceramic fragments – handle and rim areas. (Archaeological finds from Nanny Town.)

178   *Maroon Heritage*

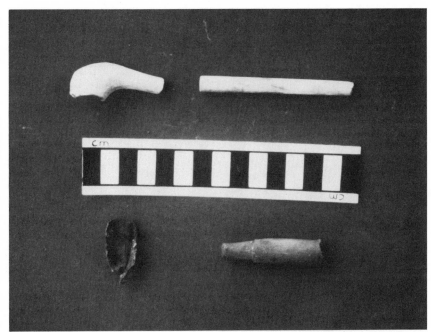

Kaolin smoking pipe stems (*top*) and bowl (*bottom left*) and fragment earthenware (local) smoking pipe stem (*bottom right*). (Archaeological finds from Nanny Town.)

Terracotta figurines (Amerindian-Arawak?). (Archaeological finds from Nanny Town.)

Spanish coin (peices of eight) dated early Maroon phase to 1668. (Archaeological finds from Nanny Town.)

Occupation levels

The 1993 excavation appears to indicate that there were two occupation levels, rather than three, observed during previous excavations. The lower level appears to have a combination of two different cultural features which, although clearly different, do not appear to represent one cultural entity. The terracotta figurines and the associated local thin but highly-fired earthenware at the bottom of the lower cultural level, appear, from all its features, to be typically Amerindian. This level changes as one comes up toward the upper level, into a combination of poorly fired ceramics mixed with imported European material.

The top sections of the lower cultural level, however, are completely devoid of any such material that can be referred to as Amerindian. Not a single clay figurine comes from that top part. Neither were there any such Amerindian material in the top cultural level containing European imported material. Thermoluminescence dates should confirm this relationship in cultural levels, as well as confirm the speculation that the "Arawaks" were still inhabiting parts of the island at the time that the British took over the island and had, therefore, not been exterminated as has often been asserted.

Phases of history at Nanny Town

Nanny Town is recognized as having seen three phases of occupation. The first appears to predate Maroon presence in the area and is represented by a mixture or local ceramics, shell and stone artifacts, such as beads and flint. The second phase, provisionally referred to as the Maroon Phase, contains ceramic (much of which is local), grinding stones and a considerable quantity of charcoal, gun flints, fragments of gun barrels, musket balls, iron nails, a red clay and several kaolin smoking pipe bowls and stems and green and clear glass bottle fragments. This phase probably lies between 1655 and 1734. One of the Spanish coins dates the lower section of this phase to 1668. The third phase, and the latest in time, is represented by the stone fortifications and an engraved stone. The main finds include kaolin pipe stems and bowls, buttons, fragments of gun barrels, medicine bottles, imported ceramics bowls, plates and cups, a large quantity of green glass bottle fragments, pairs of scissors, among other things. One of the several post holes observed appears to represent the location of a flag post erected at the site at the time of its brief occupation by British forces. The picture from Accompong is equally interesting, although the evidence is somewhat different.

Old Accompong

The Accompong settlement was surveyed and mapped in order to determine the boundaries of the Old Town and to relate it to other adjoining sites. An excavation was conducted near the burial ground of Kojo. Although not an extensive excavation, the finds were of great significance. Artifacts recovered include local earthenware, a bead (probably imported), a copper bracelet, fragments of green glass bottles, and a few musket balls. Three cowrie shells, identified as West African, where they were used as currency in ancient times, were also recovered. No specific period or date has been assigned to the excavated material, but many of the artifacts point to the late seventeenth or early eighteenth century, although occupation of the area could have been much earlier.

Discussion

Although no data are yet available from a study of Nanny Town and Accompong presentation, the results appear to be very interesting because they raise many issues that suggest the need to begin a rethinking of the interpretation of the history of Jamaica. That Nanny Town, for example, was a stronghold that has seen considerable military action, is clearly confirmed by the evidence. Evidence seems to suggest, also, that Nanny Town has been occupied for a fairly long period of time and that its occupation could date to periods long before and during colonial contact.

This speculation becomes even more attractive if the artifacts, suggested to be prehistoric or "Arawak", are confirmed. In this case, one could further suggest that Nanny Town was, certainly, a stronghold or a hiding place for freedom fighters during the Spanish period. These freedom fighters may have consisted of the traditional prehistoric groups (the people encountered by the Spaniards on their arrival) or slave crew men who came with them on their voyages to the New World. It also appears that some of the traditional groups who may have inhabited the island and who were already settled at Nanny Town or adjoining areas before the Spanish came in, may have eventually welcomed and accommodated escapees from the Spanish, and also the later English estates. If we assume that the prehistoric group were "Arawaks", it would suggest that the very first escapees (Maroons) were "Arawaks".

Association between material of the first two phases at Nanny Town, therefore, points to the suggestion that a few (even if a few scores) of the "Arawaks" who may have escaped into the inaccessible parts of the Blue Mountains and similar places, were still around, some at Nanny Town at the time the English drove the Spanish from the island. Although attempts to provide population figures for the prehistoric groups as well as for Maroons have been made, there is no indication of the areas covered by the counting. It is not known whether the inaccessible areas of the Blue Mountains were also covered, as there is no record that indicates that any person or persons visited the Blue Mountains to take a census. If there was anyone, how was the counting conducted? Extreme reliance on estimated figures has therefore become the basis of acceptance of historical interpretations. Should this be confirmed by the analysis of the material, books on the history of Jamaica would have to correct the erroneous impression that the "Arawaks" had all been exterminated by the Spanish. It appears from the evidence from Nanny Town, that prehistoric groups in hideouts on the island may have been gradually absorbed into the groups who later joined them.

Material associated with the stone structures at the site of Nanny Town clearly supports the view that the structure was built by the British forces when they briefly occupied the site in the 1730s. The feature may have been used later, after the Maroons took over the site, but only after the British had left Nanny Town.

As regards Accompong, the cowrie shell finds, now identified as West African, clearly establishes that connection. *Cyprae moneta*, as it is known, was used as currency in West Africa in ancient times. The context in which it was brought into the New World is not definitely known. Had it been in a large quantity, one would suggest that it may have been hoarded for use in West Africa for buying more slaves. It appears that the three cowrie shells were part of an ornament brought by a slave or a master from West Africa. Armstrong (personal communication) has also reported about a dozen cowrie shell finds of West African origin from excavations at the site of New Seville, the first Spanish settlement in Jamaica, located in the parish of St Ann. The Accompong excavation was too small and limited, and therefore any further generalizations should await additional work.

Archaeological evidence available so far appears to be identifying certain features of West African connections [Armstrong 1990; Agorsah 1992b, 1993a]. However, it is appropriate to begin to examine the material against the backdrop of the evidence related to the traditions from which the majority of Maroons were drawn. For an objective assessment and cross-cultural comparison, it is necessary to begin to examine evidence from both sides of the Atlantic at this initial stage when archaeological evidence is becoming available. This introduces the issue of West African connections.

The roots

Archaeologists and historians are now agreed that the slaves often referred to as *Kromantee* did not all come from or through Kromantse, a small fishing town of that name. When the English arrived on the coast of the then Gold Coast, the Portuguese and the Dutch had set up bases at various points along the West African coast from where they operated their trading activities with the local people. Kromantse, a small settlement of the Fante-speaking people, became the first location from which the British commenced their colonial economic operations, having built a small fort there for the purpose. It was from there that, beginning 1631, the English shipped out their first consignment of slaves.

Controlling the whole coastal area within which Kromantse was located, long before the arrival of the English, was the traditional Kingdom of Efutu (Fetu), whose kings were the first to be involved in trading activities with the English, as well as the Dutch and the Portuguese before them. Given the circumstances of their shipment, one would ask the question as to which cultural practices the slaves would have taken with them before making the long, long journey to their new home. Life at Fetu, their last stop on their way out of the native land, would leave a few memories on the minds of the slaves. Archaeological evidence indicates that early seventeenth century Efutu had become a well developed, typical coastal chiefdom with an advanced political system that is described in historical records [Meyerowitz 1952; Ward 1958; Birmingham 1966; Claridge 1915; Fynn 1975; Muller 1973; Ozanne 1962; Shinnie 1971].

It had come into contact with European traders and obtained such items as smoking pipes, wine, glass beads and possibly textiles in exchange for gold dust. By the end of the seventeenth century and the early eighteenth century, Efutu had absorbed some features of western culture through trade and politics. They began to bury their dead in coffins constructed with metal nails and handles imported from Europe.

As an important camp on the main military route coming from the powerful Asante area, it probably saw a large number of slaves coming from many different parts of West Africa. Evidence shows that by the end of the eighteenth and early nineteenth centuries, Efutu, like other kingdoms of the interior such as Begho [Posnansky 1972, 1976], Buipe and Gonja [Braimah and Goody 1967], Kitare [Davis 1967], Bonomanso [Effah-Gyamfi 1978] and others had declined as Asante power vigorously expanded and seemed to attack many states interested in the gold trade at the time [Ward 1958]. At the same time, the Sudanic states of the interior of West Africa had also turned their attention to the coastal trade and thus introduced more cultural elements into the system from or through which the slaves were to live for the last time before being shipped out into the New World. All these events have significant implications for the relationship between the traditions of the Maroons and those of the West African region.

The example of Efutu is only one of the many that need to be examined, although historical archaeology in West Africa is only just beginning to consider issues of such connections.

First, it is clear that considerable activity and interaction were taking place in the coastal area of the Gold Coast which brought together people who were shipped out from different backgrounds. Secondly, many of those shipped out seemed to have obtained considerable military experience, such as in the use of fighting equipment, local and imported, during their local wars, guerrilla tactics similar to that which later characterized the Maroon struggle in the West Indies, political organization obtained from their individual kingdoms, trade transactions and traditional technological knowhow such as metal working, textile production and other practices.

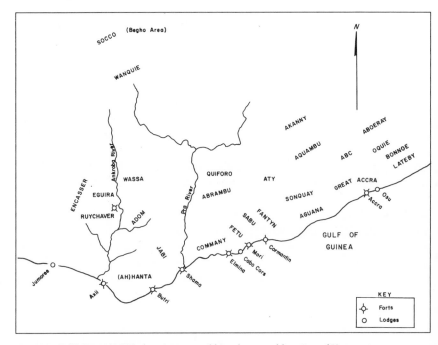

Fig. 11.5 Gold Coast (1655) showing coastal kingdoms and location of Kromantse

For example, in some areas fighting shields consisted of woven leaves of special trees and were strong enough to imbue fighters with what they believed to be physical and spiritual protection; they knew the use of musketry carried guns and gunpowder and leather belts. With very strong fighting skills and good knowledge of trading operations and given the wealth of the kingdoms from which they were coming, it is no surprise that the tendency to fight for their freedom should resurface after they had landed in the New World. Back in their West African homeland, prisoners of war were, for example, enslaved, sometimes for life and many of them were either sold or taken to other areas to provide labour. According to tradition, important personalities were sometimes ransomed for some debt or gold.

Plundering, burning of towns and villages, destroying granaries and food crops, were very characteristic of the wars and life of the people along the coast of West Africa, particularly during the period of European contact. Carey Robinson (this volume) describes the hassle which the slaves encountered, from the point of their departure from their homelands. Although not many of these past behaviour patterns on the West African coast are directly obvious from the archaeological record, ethnohistorical activities of the Maroons indicate that some aspects have been carried over to the New World (see Col. Harris, this volume). But such studies and comparisons are only one step towards the search for identification in archaeological records that are almost non-existent or just coming to light [Agorsah 1992b; Armstrong 1990; Goucher 1990].

Identification of West African cultural elements in the Caribbean also depends on the identification of the particular regions from which slaves were imported to different places and times. For example, there were preferences for slaves from particular areas. Postma [1990] mentions, for example, that the Dutch obtained their slaves, generally referred to as *Calabaris,* from the Bight of Biafra (the region extending from the Niger Delta to the Cameroons); the *Luango* or *Angola* slaves from the Congo region and the "slave coast", and the *Cormantin* slaves from the Gold Coast. The Dutch are reported to dislike *Calabari* slaves because they were considered to be "prone to run away or die more readily than other African slaves". On the other hand, the English were reputed to have preferred *Cormantins* although *Ardra* slaves, as those from the slave coast were called (also referred to as *Papas* in Suriname) were often rated above the *Cormantin* and the *Luango*—especially in the eighteenth century. Such preferences and related issues need to be examined, in any attempt to identify cultural links between the Maroons of African descent and their West African roots.

Similarly, evidence available so far is insufficient to enable conclusive generalizations about issues such as the relationship between Accompong and Nanny Town, and other known Maroon settlements in the vicinity of these sites, as well as those in other parts of the island during the period of their occupation, or to make speculations about the social network that may have bound them in any relationships.[22] It is also premature to speculate about the spatial pattern of the Maroon settlements because of the limited extent of excavation undertaken. With much more data on the physical nature of the settlements, as well as those of other Maroon sites, it should be possible to attempt serious generalizations, particularly on the perceived character and mechanism of the functional adaptation of the Maroons over time. There is the need also to come up with more generalizations as evidence becomes available later, to be able to write a cultural history about the Maroons.

There is a strong chance that the final results of ongoing archaeological studies will necessitate revision of some issues related to the history of Jamaica. The results of the excavations appear to have reopened the opportunity for the achievement of a better appreciation of the heritage of the Maroons within the general history of Jamaica. As the research programme continues with further excavations, it is hoped that more evidence will be obtained which will provide an expanded version of the generalizations made so far. It cannot be assumed that much has been achieved at this time. But one fact is clear, and that is that the true place of the history of the Maroons and their heritage is being gradually defined, a situation that makes the realization of a meaningful history of Jamaica imminent.

Notes

1 *The Daily Gleaner*, 17 August 1967, 3a, reported Alan Teulon had mentioned that in 1890 Mr Herbert Thomas, a police inspector, had reported visiting the site to search for the swivel gun reportedly used by Captain Stoddart, the commander of the military forces that reportedly destroyed the ancient town in 1734. Also, Mr Reginald Murray, a mountaineer and a former head of one of the leading high schools in Kingston, is also mentioned to have claimed that he visited the site several times in the 1920s and 1930s. It is not known exactly what the results of these trips were.

   Alan Teulon's 1967 party consisted of several Maroon guides from the Windsor and John's Hall areas of Portland; Mr Terrence Bennett, assistant supervisor of forests; Mr George Proctor, botanist at the Institute of Jamaica; Dr Henry Osmaston, geologist from Bristol University, England; Mr Neville McFarlane, geology undergraduate, Dr Michael Ashcroft, Mr David Lee, Mr Dennis Hendriks and Mr Franklyn St Juste, a cameraman from the Jamaica Information Service. The Jamaica Defence Force assisted with transportation to the site. The location of the site was described as 42o1"N and 71o1"E using compass bearings to recognizable topographical features on valuation index sheet 115 in the 12,500 series map published by the Survey Department of Jamaica.

2 Anthony Bonner, "The Blue Mountain Expedition", *Ja Jour* 8, nos.2 & 3 (1974): 46-50.

3 The figures used to make this graph were derived from the 1973 expedition report available at the Archaeology Museum at Port Royal. Thanks to Mr Roderick Ebanks for making the report available to me.

4 The University of the West Indies (UWI) Mona Archaeological Research Project (UMARP) has benefitted from the support of various kinds from the Research and Publications Fund Committee of the University, The Jamaica National Heritage Trust (JNHT), The Wenner-Gren Foundation for Anthropological Research, USA, The Archaeological Society of Jamaica (ASJ), Earthwatch and Centre For Field Research, Watertown, MA, USA, Helitours (Jamaica) Ltd and the Jamaica Defence Force (JDF). Providing further support have been student volunteers of the University of the West Indies.

5 This settlement is also probably one of the early ones established by a separate group of Spanish escapees and probably did not last as it may have been located in a lowland area with no ecological protection. The founding of this settlement *palenque* is dated to about

1668 [Kopytoff 1973]. When the British took the island from the Spaniards in 1655, some of the slaves who had been working on the Spanish plantation took to the more protective hills, some into the Blue Mountains of the east to join those who had escaped earlier, and others into the craggy Cockpit country in the parish of Trelawny where they were well sheltered from attack.

6 Ayscough, Board of Trade, May 1911, 1734, CSP 41, 103-4 and 15-116.

7 Lamb's Journal, enclosure in Hunter/Board of Trade, 18 November, 1732, CO/ 137 and 154.

8 *Ja Jour* 3: 62.

9 Lamb's and William's Journal, encl. in Hunter/Newcastle, 27 March 1733, CSP 40, 61-63; Allen's and Peter's Journals, encl. in Hunter/Newcastle, 28 March 1732, CO 37/54.

10 Extracts Campbell/Hunter, encl. in Hunter/Board of Trade, 23 January 1730, CO 137/47.

11 Confession of Seyrus, encl. in Hunter/Board of Trade, 25 August 1733, CO 40, 173.

12 STA, Patents 22, 16-17.

13 *JAJ* 4: 288, 315.

14 *JAJ* 4: 507, 517, 1754.

15 *JAJ* 4: 517. The land was purchased for the Maroons in 1770.

16 Laws of Jamaica 1758 and 1791. JAJ 4: 602, 644-45.

17 For example, locating the Nanny Town site would not have been possible for the 1967 expedition had they not been directed or guided by the Maroons of Windsor and Moore Town.

18 According to the Geographical Society of Jamaica in its regular field trip pamphlet issued each year, "it was in the Cockpit country that the geomorphology of tropical karst was first investigated in detail by geographers". Of the 106 species of vascular plants of 43 families found in the area, many of them endemic, many of them are confined to a very small percentage of the total area. The Cockpit area is also renowned for over a hundred species of ferns, orchids, land snails, frogs and live bromeliads (wild pines), lepidoptera (moths and butterflies) and others. See pamphlet, "Cockpit Country Field Trip 1991", Geographical Society of Jamaica.

19 The engraving read [Hart 1985]: DECEM 17, 1734 THIS TOWN WAS TOOK BY COL. BROOK AND AFTER KEPT BY CAPT COOK TILL JULY 1735. It appears that the stone monument has been tampered with in recent times as additional names can now be read. This stone slab is mentioned by the 1967 and 1973 expeditions.

20 The local names were collected from Maroon guides Leopold Shelton, Windsor, Garcia West, Clinton West and Wooley West of Cooper's Hill, all in the parish of Portland, Jamaica and may not be the same in other localities of the island.

21 J. Ashford, "Arawak, Spanish and African contributions to Jamaica's settlement vegetation", *Ja Jour* 24, no. 3: 17-23.

22 Other settlements mentioned as associated with Nanny Town or possibly as parts of it include Molly's Town, Dinah's Town and at least one other. These were sites supposedly captured by attacking British forces en route to the seizure of Nanny Town in 1734 [Hart 1985: 52-53, 55-56, 82]. The exact location of these sites is not known but, using the routes taken by the British troops to Nanny Town, they are most likely to be located between Nanny Town and back of the Rio Grande.

 *Bibliography*

The bibliography includes all references cited in the text as well as others of relevance to the issues addressed in the volume, particularly those related to Maroon heritage.

Abbreviations

Add Mss – Additional manuscripts, British Museum
AJ – Archaeology Jamaica
BT – Board of Trade
CO – Colonial Office Papers in the Public Records Office
CSP – Calendar of State Papers, Colonial America and West Indies
JAJ – Journals of the Assembly of Jamaica
JJ – Jamaica Journal
JNWA – Journal of New World Archaeology
WAJA – West African Journal of Archaeology

Adamson, Alan H. 1972. *Sugar without Stores: Political Economy of British Guiana, 1838-1904.* New Haven and London: Yale University Press.

Agorsah, E. Kofi. 1990. "Archaeology of Maroon Heritage in Jamaica", *Archaeology Jamaica* (Newsletter of the Archaeological Society of Jamaica) new series, 2: 14-19.

――――. 1991a. "Archaeology of Maroon Heritage", *The Daily Gleaner* (February 24): 23.

――――. 1991b. "Evidence and interpretation in the Archaeology of Jamaica", *Reports of the Archaeological-Anthropological Institute of the Netherlands Antilles* 9, Part 1: 2-14.

――――. 1992a. (ed.) *Archaeology Jamaica* (special journal issue) 6: 2-14.

――――. 1992b. "Archaeology and Maroon Heritage in Jamaica", *Jamaica Journal* 22, no. 1: 2-9.

――――. 1992c. "A Report on Archaeological Expedition to Nanny Town", *Newsletter of the African-Caribbean Institute of Jamaica* 16-20: 11-17.

――――. 1993a. "Archaeology and Resistance History in the Caribbean", *African Archaeological Review* 11.

――――. 1993b. "An Objective Chronological Scheme for Caribbean History and Archaeology", *Social and Economic Studies* 42, no. 1: 119-48.

――――. 1993c. "Nanny Town Excavations: Rewriting Jamaica's History", *Jamaican Geographer* (Newsletter of the Jamaican Geographical Society) 8, no. 1: 6-8.

――――. 1993d. "Jamaica's Freedom Fighters" (Preliminary Report on Nanny Town Excavation 1993). University of the West Indies, Mona.

Aguirre Beltrán, Gonzalo. 1944. "The Slave Trade in Mexico", *Hispanic American Historical Review* 24: 412-31.

———. 1956. "Los pobladores del Papaloapan". Pre-edición mimeo #19. México: Instituto Nacional Indigenista.

———. 1958. *Cuijla, esbozo etnográfico de un pueblo negro.* México: Fondo de Cultura Económica.

Akpabot, S. 1986. *Foundation of Nigerian Traditional Music.* Ibadan: Spectrum Books.

Alegria, R.E. 1980. "El Rey Miguel: Héroe puertorriqueño en la lucha por la libertad de los esclavos", *Revista de Historia de America* 85: 9-26.

Alleyne, Mervyn. 1988. *Roots of Jamaican Culture.* Kingston: Pluto Press.

Allison Judy, and Col. C.L.G. Harris. 1982. White is a part of Maroon. Kingston: Kingston Publishers.

Almeida, B.W. de. 1972. *Negros e quilombos em Minas Gerais.* Belo Horizonte.

Alvares, R.F. (Dir.). N.d. *Enciclopedia de México,* Vol. IX.

Aptheker, H. 1943. *American Negro Slave Revolts.* N.Y.: Columbia University Press.

Arcaya, P.M. 1949. *Insurreción de los negros en la serranía de coro.* Caracas: Instituto Panamericano de Geografía y Historia, Comisión de Historia.

Armstrong, D. V. 1982. "The 'Old Village' at Drax Hall Plantation: An Archaeological Process Report", *Journal of New World Archaeology* 5, no. 2: 87-103.

———. 1985. "An Afro-Jamaican Settlement: Archaeological Investigation at Drax Hall". In *The Archaeology of Slavery and Plantation Life,* edited by T.A. Singleton. New York: Academic Press.

———. 1990. *The Old Village and the Great House: An Archaeological and Historical Examination of Drax Hall Plantation, St. Ann's Bay Jamaica.* Urbana: Univ. of Illinois Press.

———. 1992. "African-Jamaican Housing at Seville: A Study in Spatial Transformation", *Archaeology Jamaica* (new series) 6 : 51-63.

Arrazola, R. 1970. Palenque, primer pueblo libre de América. Catrtegena: Ediciones Hernández.

Arrom, J.J., and M.A.G. Arevalo. 1986. *Cimarrón.* Ediciones Fondación García-Arevalo Inc.

Ashcroft, Curtis. 1938. "These Men are Maroons", *The Jamaica Standard* (February 26).

Ashdown, P. 1979. *Caribbean History in Maps.* New York: Longmans.

Augier F.R., et al. 1960. *The Making of the West Indies.* Kingston: Longman Caribbean.

———, and S.C. Gordon. 1962. Sources of West Indian History. London: Longman Green & Co.

Baily, B. L. 1966. *Jamaican Creole Syntax.* Cambridge: Cambridge University Press.

Barhan, H. 1722. "The Most Correct and Particular Account of the Island of Jamaica", unpublished. British Museum, H. Sloane MS 3918.

Barker, D., and B. Spence. 1988. "Afro-Caribbean Agriculture: A Jamaican Maroon Community in Transition", *Geographical Journal* 154: 198-208.

Barnet, Miguel. 1980. *Biografía de un cimarrón.* London: Allison & Busby.

Barrett, W. 1977. *La hacienda azucarera de los Marqueses Valle.* Siglo XXI.

Barroso, E. 1984. *Yan el cimarrón.* Havana: Ed. Gente Nueva.

Bastide, R. 1967. *Les Amériques noires.* Paris: Payot.

———. 1971. *African Civilizations in the New World.* New York: Harper & Rowe.

Beckford, W.A. 1796. *A Descriptive Account of the Island of Jamaica.* 2 vols. London.

Beckles, Hilary. 1986. "From Land to Sea: Runaway Slaves and White Indentured Servants in 17th Century Barbados". In *Out of the House of Bondage: Runaways, Resistance and Marronage in Africa and the New World,* edited by G. Heuman. London: Frank Cass & Co. Ltd.

———. 1988. Afro-Caribbean Women and Resistance to Slavery in Barbados. London: Karnak House.

Beckles, H., and V. Shepherd. 1992. *Caribbean Freedom: Society and Economy from Emancipation to the Present. A Student Reader.* London: James Curry.

Beckwith, Martha Warren. [1929] 1969. *Black Roadways: A Study of Jamaican Folklife.* New York: Negro Universities Press.

Beer, G.L. 1968. *The Old Colonial System 1660-1754.* Reprint. Peter Smith.

de Beet, Christoffel. 1980. "People in Between: The Matawai Maroons of Suriname", Ph.D. diss., University of Utrecht.

Bennett, Louise. 1983. *Selected Poems,* edited by Mervyn Morris. Kingston: Sangsters.

Bilby, Kenneth M. 1979. "Partisan Spirits: Ritual Interaction and Maroon Identity in Eastern Jamaica", Master's thesis, Weslyman University.

———. 1981a. "The Kromanti Dance of the Windward Maroons of Jamaica", *Nieuwe West Indische Gids* 55, nos. 1 & 2: 52-101.

———. 1981b. *Music of the Maroons of Jamaica*. New York: Ethnic Folkways Records.

———. 1983a. "How The 'Older heads' Talk: A Jamaica Maroon Language, Spirit Possession and its Relationship to the Creoles of Suriname and Sierra Leone", *New West Indian Guide* 57, nos. 1 & 2: 37-88.

———. 1983b. "Black Thoughts from the Caribbean: Ideology at Home and Abroad", *Nieuwe West-Indische Gids (New West Indian Guide)* 57, nos. 3 & 4: 201-14.

———. 1984a. "The Treacherous Feast: A Jamaican Maroon Historical Myth", *Bidjdragen tot de Taal, Land-volkenkunde* 140: 1-31.

———. 1984b. "'Two Sister Pikini': A Historical Tradition of Dual Ethnogenesis in Eastern Jamaica", *Caribbean Quarterly* 30, nos. 3 & 4: 10-25.

———. 1985a. "Caribbean crucible". In *Repercussions: A Celebration of African-American Music*, edited by G. Haydon and D. Marks, 128-51. London: Century Publishing Co.

———. 1985b. "The Half Still Untold: Recent Literature on Reggae and Rastafari", *New West Indian Guide* 59, nos. 3 & 4: 211-17.

———. 1987. "Religious Change among the Jamaican Maroons: The Ascendance of the Christian God within a Traditional Cosmology", *Journal of Social History* 20, no. 3: 463-84.

———. 1989a. "Divided Loyalties: Local Politics and the Play of States among the Aluku", *New West Indian Guide* 63 : 143-73.

———. 1989b."The Aluku and the Communes: A Problematic Policy of Assimilation in French Guiana", *Cultural Survival Quarterly* 13, no. 3.

Bilby, K., and E. Leib. 1983. *From Congo to Zion: Three Black Musical Traditions from Jamaica*. Cambridge, MA: Heartbeat Records.

Bilby, K., and D.B. N'Diaye. 1992. "Creativity and Resistance: Maroon Communities in the Americas", *1992 Festival of American Folklife*. Washington, D.C.: Smithsonian Institute, 54-61.

Birmingham, D. 1966. "A Note on the Kingdom of Efutu", *Ghana Notes and Queries* 9: 30-32.

Bishop, P. 1970. "Runaway Slaves In Jamaica 1740-1807". (A thesis based on newspaper advertisements published during that period.)

Black, Clinton V. 1966. *History of Jamaica*. London: Collins Educational.

———. 1973. *Jamaica Guide*. Kingston.

———. 1983. *History of Jamaica*. London and Glasgow: Collins Educational.

Blake, Lady Edith. 1898. "The Maroons of Jamaica", *North American Review* (November): 558-68.

Bleby, H. 1868. *Death Struggles of Slavery*. 3d ed. London.

Bonner, T. 1974. "The Blue Mountain Expedition", *Jamaica Journal* 8, nos. 2 & 3: 46-50.

Bowdich, T. E. 1821. *Mission from Cape Coast to Ashanti*. London: Griffith and Farran.

Brathwaite, E. K. 1968. "The Development of Creole Society in Jamaica 1770-1820", Ph.D. diss., University of Sussex.

———. 1970. *Folk Culture of the Slaves in Jamaica*. London: New Beacon.

———. 1971. *The Development of Creole Society in Jamaica*. Oxford: Clarendon Press.

———. 1974. "The African Presence in Caribbean Literature", *Daedalus* 103, no. 2: 73-109.

———. 1977. *Wars of Respect*. Kingston: Agency for Public Information.

———. 1977. *Nanny, Sam Sharpe and the Struggle for People's Liberation*. Kingston: Agency for Public Information.

———. 1978. "The Spirit of African Survival in Jamaica", *Jamaica Journal* 42: 50.

———. 1983. *Third World Poems*. Harlow: Longman.

Brereton, B. 1981. *A History of Trinidad 1783-1962*. London: Heinemann.

Bridges, G. W. 1828. *The Annals of Jamaica*. Vol II. London.

Brown, E. 1966. "A visit with the Maroons", *Gleaner Sunday Magazine* (October 2): 4.

Bryan, P. 1971. "African Afinities: The Blacks of Latin America", *Caribbean Quarterly* 17, nos. 3 & 4: 45-52.

Brymner, D. 1895. "The Jamaican Maroons: How they came to Nova Scotia - How they left it", *Transaction of the Royal Society of Canada* (second series) 1: 81-90.

Bullen, R P. 1964. "The Archaeology of Grenada, West Indies", *Contributions to the Florida Museum of Social Sciences* 11.

Bums, Sir Alan. 1954. *History of the British West Indies*. London: George Allen and Unwin.

Busia, K.A. 1951. *The Position of the Chief in the Modern Political System of the Ashanti*. London: Oxford Univ. Press.

Bustamante, Miguel García. 1988. "Dos aspectos de la esclavitud negra en Veracruz". In *Jornadas de Homenaje a Gonzalo Aguirre Beltrán*. Veracruz: Instituto Veracruzano de Cultura.

Campbell, M. 1973. "Maroons in Jamaica: Imperium in an Imperio", *Pan African Journal* 6, no. 1: 45-56.

———. 1977. "Marronage in Jamaica: Its Origins in the 17th Century". In *Comparative Perspectives on Slavery in New World Plantation Societies*, edited by V. Rubin and A. Tuden, 389-419. New York: Annals of the New York Academy of Sciences 292.

———. 1988. *The Maroons of Jamaica 1655-1796: A History of Resistance, Collaboration and Betrayal*. N.J.: Africa World Press.

———. 1992. "Early Resistance to Colonialism: Montague James and the Maroons in Jamaica, Nova Scotia and Sierra Leone". In *Peoples and Empires in African History* (Essays in Memory of Michael Crowder), edited by J.F. Ade Ajayi and J.D. Peel. N.J.: Africa World Press.

———. 1993. *Back to Africa: George Ross and the Maroons from Nova Scotia to Sierra Leone*. Trenton: Africa World Press.

Candler, J. 1840-1841. *Extracts from the Journal of John Candler Whilst Travelling in Jamaica*. 2 pts. London: Harvey & Darton.

Capitaine, F. W. 1988. "La vida de los cimarrones en Veracruz". In *Jornadas de Homenaje a Gonzalo Aguirre Beltrán*. Veracruz.

Careri, C.F.G. 1983. *Viaje a la Nueva España*. México: UNAM.

Carey, B. 1970a. "On the Maroons of Portland: Port Antonio Visitor's Guide". Port Antonio: Chamber of Commerce Ltd.

———. 1970b. "The Windward Maroons after the Peace Treaty", *Jamaica Journal* 4, no. 4: 19-22.

———. 1970c. "Portland and the Rio Grande Valley". Montego Bay Public Relations Advisory Service.

Carley, M. M. 1963. *Jamaica: The Old and the New*. New York: Frederick A. Praeger.

Carneiro, E. 1946. *Guerras de los Palmares*. México: Fondo de Cultura Económica.

Carter, E.H., G.W. Digby, et al. 1959. *History of the West Indian Peoples*. Bks. III & IV. London: Nelson.

———. 1969. *History of the West Indies from the Earliest Times to the Seventeenth Century*. Bucks: Hazell Watson and Viney Ltd.

Cassidy, F.G. 1971. *Jamaica Talk: Three Hundred Years of the English Language in Jamaica*. London: MacMillan.

Claridge, W.W. 1915. *A History of the Gold Coast and Ashanti*. London: Frank Cass & Co.

Clarke, M.B. 1976. "Maroons of Jamaica: a Socio-legal Exposition", *Caribbean Law Review* 1, no. 1: 7-21.

Clerk, A. 1974. "The Music and Musical Instruments of Jamaica", *Jamaica Journal* 9, nos. 2 & 3: 59-67.

Coelho, R. 1955. "The Black Carib of Honduras", Ph.D. diss., Northwestern University, Evanston.

Conniff, M., and T.J. Davis. 1994. *Africans in the Americas: A History of the Black Diaspora*. New York: St Martin's Press.

Coon, F.S. 1958. "A day with the Maroons", *The Gleaner* (May 25).

Cooper, T. 1824. "Facts Illustrative of the Conditions of the Negro Slaves in Jamaica", *The Weekly Jamaica Courant*. (First published 1718, this is the first survivng example of a Jamaican newspaper. It contains advertisements for runaway slaves.)

Corro, O. 1951. *Los cimarrones en Veracruz y la fundación de Amapa*. Xalapa, México: Veracruz Commercial.

Cousins, P.M. 1967. *Queen of the Mountain*. (Illustrated by Gay Golsworthy) London: Ginn & Co.

Craton, M. 1982. *Testing the Chains: Resistance to Slavery in the British West Indies*. Ithaca: Cornell University Press.

Craton, M., and J.A. Walvin. 1970. *A Jamaican Plantation: the History of Worthy Park 1670 to 1970*. London and New York: W.H. Allen.

Cumper, G.E. 1956. "Population Movements in Jamaica", *Social and Economic Studies* 5: 261-80.

———. 1962. "The Maroons in the 18th Century: a Note on Indirect Rule in Jamaica", *Caribbean Quarterly* 8: 25-27.

Cundall, F.C. 1937. *The Governors of Jamaica in the First Half of the Eighteenth Century*. London: The West India Committee.

Cundall, F.C., and J. Piertesz. 1919. *Jamaica under the Spaniards*. Kingston: Institute of Jamaica.

Curtin, P.D. 1968. "Epidemiology and the Slave Trade", *Political Science Quarterly* 83: 190-216.

———. 1969. *The Atlantic Slave Trade: A Census*. Madison: University of Wisconsin Press.

Dakubu, M.E. 1976. *West African Linguistic Data Sheets*. Vol.1. Accra: African Linguistic Society.

———. 1980. *West African Linguistic Data Sheets*. Vol.2. Accra: African Linguistic Society.

———. "The Peopling of Southern Ghana: A Linguistic Viewpoint". In *Archaeological and Linguistic Reconstruction of African History*, edited by C. Ehret and M. Posnansky, 245-55. Berkeley: University of California Press.

Dalby, D. 1971. "Ashanti Survivals in the Language and Traditions of the Windward Maroons of Jamaica", *African Language Studies* XII: 31-51.

Dallas, R. C. 1803. *The History of the Maroons*. London: T.N. Longman and O. Rees/London: A. Strahan.

Dalton, M. 1967. "Los depósitos de los cimarrones en el siglo XIX", *Etnológica y Folklore* 3 (enero-junio): 5-29.

Danger, R.Z. 1977. *Los cimarrones del Santiago de Cuba*. Oriente: Emporia Editorial.

Dark, P.J.C. 1970. *Bush Negro Art: An African Art in the Americas*. London.

Davidson, B. 1965. *Black Mother: The African Slave Trade*. London: Longman.

Davies, D.B. 1970. *The Problem of Slavery in Western Culture*. London: Pelican Books.

Davies, O. 1967. *West Africa Before the Europeans*. London: Methuen.

Davis, K. 1993. "Maroon Archaeology in Jamaica". *Krik Krak* : 1 & 4.

Dawes, N. 1975. "The Jamaica Cultural Identity", *Jamaica Journal* 9, no. 1: 34-37.

D'Costa, J., and B. Lalla, eds. 1989. *Voices in Exile: Jamaican Texts of the Eighteenth and Nineteenth Centuries*. Tuscaloosa: Univ. of Alabama Press.

Debbasch, Y. 1961. "Le marronage: essai sur la désertion de l'esclave antillais", *L'année sociologique* 3: 1-112.

Decorse, C. 1987. "Historical Archaeological Research in Ghana 1986-87", *Nyame Akuma* 29: 27-32.

———. 1991a. "West African Archaeology and the Atlantic Slave Trade", *Slavery and Abolition* 12, no. 2: 92-96.

———. 1991b. "Culture Contact, Continuity and Change on the Gold Coast, A.D. 1400-1900", *African Archaeological Review* 10: 163-96.

———. 1993 "The Danes on the Gold Coast: Culture, Change and the European Presence", *African Archaeological Review* 11: 149-74.

Debien, G. 1965. "Les marrons autour du Cap en 1790 à 1791", *Bulletin de l'Institut Français d'Afrique Noire* 23 série B: 363-87.

———. 1966. "Les esclaves marrons de St Domingue en 1734", *Jamaican Historical Review* 612, nos 1 & 2: 755-99.

———. G. 1970. "Un Nantais à la chasse des marrons en Guyana, 1808", Reprint from: *Enquêtes et documents. Centre de Recherches sur l'Histoire de la France Atlantique*. Vol 1.

Debien G., and W.I. French. 1966. "Le marronage aux Antilles Françaises au XVII siècle", *Caribbean Studies* 6, no. 3: 3-44.

Debien G., J. Houndaille, et al. 1961. "Les origines des esclaves des Antilles", *Bulletin de l'Institut d'Afrique Noire*.

Diez, C.L.A. 1968. *Los cimarrones y la esclavitud en Panamá*. Panamá: Editorial Litográfica.

Dougherty, R. 1973. "Rediscovering the Land of Look Behind", *Miami Herald Sunday Magazine* (March 4): 18-20 & 38-40.

———. 1971. *Jamaican Maroons*. Leningrad Academy of Sciences of the USSR. Institute of Ethnography. (Text in Russian.)

Drewet, P. 1991. *Prehistoric Barbados*. Cambridge: Cambridge University Press.

Dridzo, A.D. 1967. *The Maroons of Jamaica in the Second Half of the Eighteenth Century*. Leningrad Academy of Sciences of the USSR. Institute of Ethnography.

———. 1972. "The Origin of the Second Maroon War 1795-1796 (A Planters' conspiracy)", *Jamaica Journal* 6, no. 1 (March): 21-25.

Dunham, K. 1946. *Journey to Accompong*. New York: Henry Holt & Co.

Edwards, B. 1793. *History of the West Indies*. London.

———. 1795-1796. *Proceedings of the Governor and the Assembly in regard to Maroon Negroes*. The Minutes of the Council of the Jamaican Assembly. 1895-99 (Public Records Office CO 140/84). London: John Stockdale.

———. 1796. *Observation on the Disposition, Character, Manner and Habits of life of the Maroons*. London: John Stockdale.

———. 1819. *History, Civil and Commercial, of the the British West Indies*. 5 vols. London.

Effa-Gyamfi, E. 1978. "Bonomanso: An Archaeological Investigation into Early Akan Urbanism", Ph.D diss., University of Ghana, Accra.

Escalante, A. 1979. *El palenque de San Brasilio: una comunidad de ascendientes de negros cimarrones*. Bogotá: Ediciones Editorial Mejoras.

Evans, C., and B.J. Meggers. 1960. "Archaeological Investigations in British Guiana", *Bureau of American Ethnology Bulletin* 15: 46-47.

Eyre, L. A. 1980. "The Maroon Wars in Jamaica: A Geographical Appraisal", *Jamaica Historical Review* XII: 5-18.

Fortune, A. 1958. Corsarios y cimarrones en Panamá", *Lotería* II época 3, no 33: 77-97.

Foster, D. 1970. "Captain Cudjoe of the Maroons and the Independence in the West Indies". In *Banjo's Notebook*.

Fouchard, J. 1972. *Les marrons de la liberté*. Paris: Edition de l'Ecole.

———. 1981. The Haitian Maroon: Liberty or death. (Translated from the French by A. Faulknor Watts.)

Francis, A. 1991. "A Preliminary Report on Ethnographic Analysis of the Accompong Maroon Family System", *Archaeology Jamaica* (new series) 4: 22-23.

Franco, J.L. 1968. "The Palenques: Runaway Slave Settlements", *Granma* (Nov. 15).

Frederici, G. 1960. *Amerikanistisches Worterbuch und Hilfswortebuch fur den Amerikanisten* 2, Hamburg: Auflage, Gruyter & Co.

Furness, A. E. 1965. "The Maroon War of 1795", *Jamaican Historical Review* V, no. 2: 30-49.

Fynn, J.K. 1975. *Asante and its Neighbours 1700-1807*. London.

Gabb, W. 1872. "On the Topography and Geology of Santo Domingo", *Memoirs of the American Philosophical Society* 15: 46-47.

Galloway, E.R. 1981. "Religious beliefs and practices of Maroon children of Jamaica", Ph.D. diss., New York University, USA.

Garcia, A. 1965. *A History of the West Indies*. Harrap.

Gardner, W.J. 1873. *A History of Jamaica*. London: Elliot Stook.

———. 1909. *A History of Jamaica from its Discovery by Christopher Columbus to the year 1782*. London: T. Fisher Unwin.

Gaspar, D.B. 1979. "Runaways in the Seventeenth Century Antigua, West Indies", *Boletín de Estudios Latino Americanos y del Caribe* 26 (June).

———. 1985. *Bondsmen and Rebels: A Study of Master-Slave Relations in Antigua with Implications for Colonial British America*. Baltimore: The Johns Hopkins Press.

Genovese, E.D. 1979. *From Rebellion to Revolution: Afro-American Slave Revolts in the Making of the Modern World*. Louisiana State University.

Gibbons, C. 1945. "A Letter to Mrs Mathews" (Typed copy in Maroon file). Kingston: Institute of Jamaica, West Indies Reference Library.

Giddings, J.R. 1858. *The Exiles of Florida or the Crimes Committed by our Government Against the Maroons who Fled From South Carolina and Other Slave States Seeking Protection Under Spanish law*. Columbus (Ohio): Follet, Foster & Co.

Givens, S.M. 1984. "An Ethnographic Study of Social Control and Dispute Settlement among the Aluku Maroons of French Guiana and Surinam, South America", Ph.D. thesis, University of California, Berkeley.

Glave, T. 1949. "Colonel and New Leader of Maroons named", *The Gleaner* (February 7): 11, 13.

Gleaner [The]. 1938. "Maroons Celebrate Two Hundred Years of Freedom" (March 4, 5 and 7).

———. 1938. "Treaty for Maroons" (September 10).

———. 1938."Maroons Meet" (October 8): Clipping in Files of C.L.G. Harris, Moore Town, Jamaica.

———. 1938. "Young Maroon Hotheads Caused Resignation of Colonel H.A. Rowe" (October 16).

———. 1938. "Maroon issue pretty near to settlement" (October 21).

———. 1939. "Chief of Maroons sees the Governor" (April 20).

———. 1939. "Maroons prefer grant to bigger life tenancy" (June 30).

———. 1944. "Noted Maroon dies" (April 17).

———. 1946. "Colonel Rowe repudiates 'General Quaco'" (October 9).

———. 1946. "Bail refused Quaco" (October 9).

———. 1946. "'Quaco' and aides before court" (October 10).

———. 1946. "Witnesses allege forced labour imprisonment" (October 24).

———. 1946. "Maroons resentful over Quaco's fate" (November 11).

———. 1949. "Deputation to see Governor on Maroon Land" (April 1).

———. 1949. "Maroons see Governor on land claims" (April 8).

———. 1952. "A warning from the Maroons" (March 20).

———. 1953. "Governor tells Maroons: let's make a fresh start" (October 6): 1, 11.

———. 1953. "Maroons would like to welcome the Queen" (November 3).

———. 1954. "Improved government for Maroons" (March 19).

———. 1954. "Development plans for Maroons" (March 19).

———. 1954. "No conflict over Maroon leadership" (April 10).

———. 1954. "Maroon Leader dies suddenly" April 10.

———. 1954. "Maroon Privy Council meets" (May 18).

———. 1956. "Are Maroons exempt from Jamaican Law? 'No' says R.M." (March 13): 1, 12.

———. 1956. "The Maroons" (March 16).

———. 1957. "Robertson against Maroon Town Chief" (June 22).

———. 1958. "The Maroon's gift" (March 5).

———. 1958. "Maroon's gift to Queen" (June 4).

———. 1959. "Maroons bar land valuators" (September 4).

———. 1959. "Maroon land: department insists on valuation" (September 10).

———. 1960. "Maroons meet to draft memo" (January 19).

———. 1960. "Maroons plan celebrations" (March 23).

———. 1962. "The Song of Jamaica" (May 17).

———. 1962. "The Origins of the Maroons" (July 14): Independence Supplement.

———. 1964. "Maroon Colonel resigns" (February 27): Clipping from the files of C.L.G. Harris, Moore Town, Jamaica.

———. 1964. "Maroons at Accompong" (May 24): 3, 25.

———. 1964. "The Maroons and their treaty" (November 18): 3.

———. 1967. "Accompong Maroons at odds over election of Colonel" (13 October).

———. 1967. "Maroons elect Colonel" (November 16).

———. 1967. "Maroons pick new Colonel" (November 17): 1.

———. 1968. "Accompong Maroons celebrate treaty anniversary" (12 January): 1.

———. 1971. "History of Maroons in Russia" (28 July): Photocopy from the Embassy of Jamaica, Washington, D.C.

————. 1972. "Manley seeks closer link with Maroons" (4 June): 2.

Goucher, C. 1981. "Iron is Iron 'til it's Rust: Trade and Technology in the Decline of West African Iron Smelting", *Journal of African History* 22, no.2: 179-89.

————. 1984. "The Iron Industry of Bassar: An Interdisciplinary Investigation of African Technological History", Ph. D. diss., University of California at Los Angeles.

————. 1990. "African Hammer, European Anvil: West African Ironmaking in the Atlantic Trade Era", *West African Journal of Archaeology* 20: 200-08.

————. 1990. "John Reeder's Foundry: A Study of Eighteenth Century African-Caribbean Technology", *Jamaica Journal* 23, no. 1: 39-43.

————. 1993. "African Metallurgy in the Atlantic World", *African Archaeological Review* 11: 197-216.

Gouron, M. 1971. "The Maroons", *Gleaner Magazine* (October 3): 3.

Goveia, E. V. 1965. *Slave Society in the British Leeward Islands at the end of the Eighteenth Century.* Yale.

Graham, I. W. 1918. *A Maroon Legend: Nanny Pepperpot.* Kingston.

————. 1977. *Africans Abroad. A Documentary History of the Black Diaspora in Asia, Latin America and the Caribbean During the Age of Slavery.* Columbia University Press.

Groot S. W. de. 1969. "Djuka Society and Social Change: History of an Attempt to Develop a Bush Negro Community in Surinam 1917- 1926", Ph.D. diss., University of Amsterdam.

————. 1986. "Maroon Women as Ancestors, Priest, and Medium", Slavery and Abolition 7: 160-74.

Guevarra, Che. 1969. *Guerrilla Warfare.* Translated from Spanish by J.P. Morray with prefatory note by I.F. Stone. New York: Vintage Books, Alfred Knopf.

Gutiérrez, A.M.A. 1991. *Nabor Ojeda Caballero: El batallador del sur.* México: CEHAM.

Hall-Alleyne, B. 1980. "Language and Dialect in Jamaican Issues", *African-Caribbean Institute Newsletter* 5: 5-18.

————. 1982. "Asante Kotoko: The Maroons of Jamaica", *African-Caribbean Institute Newsletter* 7: 3-40.

Hall, D. 1938. "Lost in the Blue Mountains". Kingston.

Hall, D.G. 1954. "Background to Sugar in Slave Days", *The Caribbean Historical Review* III/IV (Historical Society of Trinidad and Tobago).

————. 1987. *The Caribbean Experience: An Historical Survey 1450-1960.* London: Heinemann Educational Books.

Hamilton, J. C. 1890. "Maroons of Jamaica and Nova Scotia", *Proceedings of the Canadian Institute* XXV, no. 153 (April).

Hancock, I. 1987. "A Preliminary Classification of Anglophone Atlantic Creoles". In *Pidgins and Creoles,* edited by Glen Gilbert. Honolulu: University of Haiwaii Press.

Harault, J. 1972. "The Guiana Maroons: Changing Perspectives in Bush Negro Studies", *Institute of Caribbean Studies* II, no. 4: 82-100.

Harcourt, S.S. 1964a. "The Maroons: Their Quiet Self-Assurance and Pure English", *The Gleaner* (7 May): 3.

————. 1964b. "Roar of Pleasure from a Thousand Maroons", *The Gleaner* (8 May): 3 & 10.

Harris, C.L.G. 1951. "'Nanny': The Maroon" (letter to the editor), *The Gleaner* (30 October) /*C.L.G. Harris files* (Moore Town).

————. 1958. "The Maroons" (letter to the editor), *The Gleaner* (13 October) /*C.L.G. Harris files* (Moore Town).

————. 1964. "Nanny Town we know" (letter to the editor), *The Gleaner*/*C.L.G. Harris files* (Moore Town).

————. 1964. "The truth about Maroons and taxes", *The Star* (16 October): 16/*C.L.G. Harris files* (Moore Town).

————. 1966. "The Maroons of Jamaica", *History Today* 16, no. 1 (January).

————. 1967. "The Maroons praised and condemned", *The Gleaner* (23 July): 7.

————. 1967. "The treaty is not abolished", *The Gleaner* (30 July): 7 & 11.

————. 1967. "The spirit of Nanny", *The Gleaner* (6 August): 11.

————. 1970. "Selfish fight" (letter to the editor), *The Gleaner*/*C.L.G. Harris files* (Moore Town).

————. 1971. "No surrender" (letter to the editor), The Gleaner/ C.L.G. Harris files (Moore Town).

————. 1992. "The Maroons of Moore Town". In *1992 Festival of American Folklife*. Washington D C: Smithsonian Institute.

Harris C.L.G., and C. Aarons. 1988. *On My Honour: A Tale of Two Maroons*. Kingston.

Harris, J. T. 1968. "A Tale of the Maroons", *The Bell* (8 November): 2 & 7.

Harris, P. 1924. "Archaeology of the Virgin Islands", *Proceedings of the International Congress of Americanists* 1: 29-42.

Hart, R. 1952. "Cudjoe and the First Maroon War". Kingston.

————. 1970. "Out of the House of Bondage. (A Brief Account of Some of the Principal Events in the Struggle Against Slavery in Jamaica)". Kingston.

————. 1971. "The Maroon treaties" (letter to the editor), *Jamaica Journal* 5, nos. 2 & 3.

————. 1977. *Black Jamaicans' Struggle Against Slavery*. Kingston: Institute of Jamaica.

————. 1980. *Slaves who Abolished Slavery*. Vol. 1: *Blacks in Bondage*. Mona: ISER, University of the West Indies.

————. 1985. *Slaves who Abolished Slavery*. Vol. 2: *Blacks in Rebellion*. Mona: ISER, University of the West Indies.

Hatt, G. 1924. "Archaeology of the Virgin Islands". In *Proceedings of The 21st International Congress for Caribbean Archaeology*: 129-42.

Haviser, J., and C. Decorse. 1991. "African-Caribbean Interaction: A Research Plan for Curaçao Creole Culture", *Reports of the Archaeological-Anthropological Institute of the Netherlands Antilles* 9, part 1: 326-37.

Helms, M.W. 1969. "The Cultural Ecology of a Colonial Tribe", *Ethnology* 8: 74-84.

Henderson D., and E. Henry. 1925-1927. "Visit to the Historic Settlement of Maroons at Accompong", *The Jamaica Mail* (15 September 1925).

————. 1927. "Maroons at Accompong", *The Gleaner* (28 & 29 March).

Herbert, E., and C. Goucher. 1987. *The Blooms of Banjeli: Technology and Gender in West African Ironmaking*. Watertown: (Documentary Educational Resource).

Herskovits, M.J. 1934. *Rebel Destiny among the Bush Negros of Dutch Guiana*. New York: McGraw Hill.

————. 1958. *The Myth of the Negro Past*. Boston: Beacon Press.

Herrera y Tordesillas, A. de. 1934-1957. *Historia general de los hechos de los Castellaños en las islas y tierra firma del Mar Octaño*. Madrid.

Heuman, G.J., ed. 1986. *Out of the House of Bondage: Runaways, Resistance and Marronage in Africa and the New World*. London: Frank Cass.

Hewitt, M.J. 1981. "An overview of Suriname", *Black Art* 5, no. 1: 18.

Higginson, T.W. 1889. "Travellers and Outlaws: Episodes". In *American History*. Lee & Shepard.

————. 1969. "Black Rebellion". (A selection from *Travellers and Outlaws*: Introduction by James M. McPherson). New York.

Higman, B.W. 1974. "A Report on Excavations at Montpelier and Roehampton", *Jamaica Journal* 8, no. 2: 40-45.

————. 1979. "African and Creole Slave Families in Trinidad". In *Africa and the Caribbean: Legacies of a Link*, edited by M.E. Graham and F.W. Knight. Baltimore: Johns Hopkins University Press.

————. 1986. "Plantation Maps as Sources for the Study of West Indian Ethnohistory", *Ethnohistory: A Researcher's Guide* 35: 107-36.

Hostos, A. de. 1919. "Prehistoric Puerto Rican Ceramics", *American Anthropologist* 21: 376-99.

Howard, G.D. 1943. "Excavation at Ronquin, Venezuela", *Publications in Anthropology* (Yale University) 28.

————. 1947. "Prehistoric Ceramic Styles of Lowland South America: Their Distribution and History", *Publications in Anthropology* (Yale University) 37.

Hurault, 1972. "The Guiana Maroons: Changing Perspectives in Bush Negro Studies", *Institute of Caribbean Studies* II, no. 4: 82-100.

Irvin, W.G. 1977. *Africans Abroad. A Documentary History of the Black Diaspora in Asia, Latin America and the Caribbean During the Age of Slavery*. New York: Columbia University Press.

Israel, J. 1980. *Razas, clases sociales y la vida política en el México colonial, 1610-1670*. México: Fondo de Cultura Económica.

Jacobs, H.P. 1950. "The Cave Valley Banditti", *The West Indian Review* 11.

Jamaica House of Assembly. 1796. *Proceedings of the Honourable House of Assembly Relative to the Maroons*. London: Alexander Aikman.

———. 1796. *Proceedings of the Governor and Assembly of Jamaica in Regard to The Maroon Negroes*. London: Stockdale.

Jennings, J.D. 1974. *Prehistory of North America*. New York: McGraw Hill.

Jones, R.S. 1976. "White Settlers Black Slaves: Jamaica in the Era of the First Maroon War 1655-1738", Ph.D. diss., Brown University.

Keegan, W.F. 1984. "Columbus and the City of Gold", *Journal of Bahamas Historical Society* 6: 34-39.

———. 1985. "Dynamic Horticulturalists: Population Expansion in the Prehistoric Bahamas", Ph.D. diss., University of California, Los Angeles.

———. 1986. "The Ecology of Lucayan Arawak Fishing Practices", *American Antiquity* 51: 816-25.

———. 1987. "Archaeology and Christopher Columbus' Journey Through the Bahamas: 1492", *American Archaeology* 6: 102-08.

———. 1988. "New Directions in Bahamas Archaeology", *Journal of Bahamas Historical Society* 10: 3-8.

———. 1989a. "The Columbus Chronicles", *The Sciences* (Jan-Feb): 47-55.

———. 1989b. "The Evolution of Avunculocal Chiefdoms: A Reconstruction of Taino Kinship and Politics", *American Anthropologist* 91, no. 3: 613-30.

Keegan, W., and M.D. MacLaughlan. 1982. "Lucayan Cave Burials from the Bahamas", *Journal of New World Archaeology* 5:57-65.

Keegan, W.F., A.V.Stokes, and L.A. Newson. 1990. *Bibliography of Caribbean Archaeology*. 2 vols. University of Florida: Bullen Research Library.

Kidder, A.V. 1944. "Archaeology of Northwest Venezuela", *Papers of the Peabody Museum of American Archaeology and Ethnology* 26, no. 1.

———. 1948. "The Archaeology of Venezuela", *Handbook of South American Indians* 143, no.4: 413-38 (edited by J.H. Steward).

Kipple, K.E. 1984. *The Caribbean Slave: A Biological History*. Cambridge: Cambridge University Press.

Knight, F.W. 1978. *The Caribbean: The Genesis of a Fragmented Nationalism*. N.Y.: Oxford University Press.

Knibb, W. et al., eds. N.d. *Facts and Documents Connected with the Insurrection in Jamaica*. Tower Hill, London: Teape & Son Printers.

Knight, J. N.d. *The Natural Moral and Political History of Jamaica . . . to the Year 1742*. (Unpublished). Add Mss 12419.

Kopytoff, B.K. 1971. "Ancestors as Elders in Africa", *Africa* 42: 128-42.

———. 1973. "The Maroons of Jamaica: An Ethnohistorical Study of Incomplete Polities", Ph.D. diss., Univ. of Pennsylvania.

———. 1976a. "The Development of Jamaica Maroon Ethnicity", *Caribbean Quarterly* 22, nos. 2 & 3: 35-50.

———. 1976b."Jamaica Maroon Political Organisations: The Effects of the Treaties", *Social and Economic Studies* 25, no. 2: 87-105.

———. 1978. "Early Political Development of Jamaican Maroon Societies", *William and Mary Quarterly* 35: 287-307.

———. 1979. "Colonial Treaty as Sacred Charter of the Jamaican Maroons", *Ethnohistory* 26: 45-64.

Kozlowski, J.K. 1974. "Preceramic Cultures in the Caribbean" (Zespyty Naukowe, Universytetu Jagiellonskiego 386), *Prace archaeologiczne Ze* 20.

———. 1980. "In Search of the Evolutionary Patterns of the Preceramic Cultures of the Caribbean", *Boletín del Museo del Hombre Dominicano* 13: 61-79.

Kushner, G. et al. 1865. "The Maroons of Jamaica", *Once a Week*. (December 16): 707-09.

Lalla, Barbara. 1979. "Sources for a History of Jamaica Creole", *Carib* 1: 50-66.

———. 1981. "Quaco Sam: A Relic of Archaic Jamaican Speech", *Jamaica Journal* 45: 20-29.

Lang, K. 1991. "Traditional Maroon Medicine and the Survival of Nanny Town", *Archaeology Jamaica* (new series) 4: 12-15.

Las Casas, B. 1552-1553. *Historia de la Indias*. 6 vols. Seville.

Laxalt, R. 1985. "The Indomitable Basque", *National Geographic* 168, no. 1.

Leante, Cesar. 1979. *Los guerrilleros negros*. Siglo XXI.

Lee, J.W. 1978. "Current Archaeological Activity in Jamaica", *Archaeology Jamaica* 78, no. 4: 1-4.

Leeson, R. 1978. *The Cimarrones*. London: Collins.

Lenoir, J.D. 1975. "Suriname National Development and Maroon Cultural Autonomy", *Social and Economic Studies* 24: 308-19.

LePage, R.B., and D. DeCamp. 1960. *Jamaican Creole*. London: Macmillan.

Lewin, O. 1967. "Arawak Song", *Jamaica Journal* 1, no. 1: 88.

———. 1969. "Cult Music", *Jamaica Journal* 3, no. 2: 14-15.

———. 1970. "Jamaica Folk Music", *Jamaica Journal* 4, no., 2: 68.

Lichtveld, L., and C.F.A. Bruijning. 1959. *Suriname: A New Nation in South America*. Paramaribo: Radhakishun & Co.

Long, E. 1774. *The History of Jamaica*. 3 vols. London: T. Lowndes.

Loven, S. 1935. *The Origin of Tainian Culture, West Indies*. Goteberg.

MacPherson, Pamela. 1971. "To Cudjoe", *Savacou* 3-4: 81.

Maggiolo, M.V., and B.Vega. 1982. "The Antillean Preceramic: An Approximation", *Journal of New World Archaeology* 5, no. 2: 33-44.

Mann, R.W., B.W.M. Meadows, and D.R. Watters. 1987. "Description of Skeletal Remains from Black Slave Cemetery from Montserrat, West Indies", Annals of Carnegie Museum 56: 319-36.

Mannix, D.P. (with Malcolm Cowley). 1963. *Black Cargoes: A History of the Atlantic Slave Trade 1518-1865*. London: Longmans.

Manoukian, M. 1950. *Akan and Ga-Adangme Peoples of the Gold Coast*. London: International African Institute.

Marshall, B.A. 1976. "Maronage in Slave Plantation Societies: A Case Study of Dominica 1785-1799", Ph.D. diss., University of California, Los Angeles.

Martin, L. 1972. "Why Maroons", *Current Anthropology* 13: 143-44.

———. 1980. "Maroon identity: Processes of Persistence in Maroon Town", Ph.D. diss., University of California.

Martin, N. 1957. *Los vagabundos en la Nueva España: siglo XVI*. México: Editorial Jus.

Mathews, Mark. 1971. "For Cuffee", *Savacou* 3-4: 151-52.

McDowell, R. 1963. "The Myth of the Maroons". In *Jamaica Annual*. Kingston.

McFarlane, M.C. 1949. *A Treasure of Jamaican Poetry*. London: University of London Press.

———. 1977. *Cudjoe the Maroon*. London: Allison & Busby.

McKussick, M.B. 1960. "The Distribution of Ceramic Styles in the Lesser Antilles, West Indies", Ph.D. diss., Yale University.

McMillan, M. 1957. *The Land of Look Behind*. London: Faber & Faber.

Metcalf, George. 1965. *Royal Government and Political Conflict in Jamaica 1729-1783*. London: Longmans.

Meyerowitz, E. 1952. *Akan Traditions of Origin*. London.

Mintz, S.W., and S. Price. 1985. *Caribbean Contours*. Baltimore: Johns Hopkins University Press.

Mitchell, H. 1957. "The Maroons of Accompong", *Geographical Magazine* 23, no.1: 2-5.

———. 1967. *Caribbean Patterns*. London: Chambers.

Montejo, E. 1968. *The Autobiography of a Runaway Slave*. The Bodley Head.

Moore, J. G. 1953. "Religion of Jamaican Negroes: A Study of Afro-Jamaican Acculturation", Ph.D. diss., University of Pensylvania, Philadelphia.

Morales, P.F. 1952. "Jamaica Español". Sevilla: Escuela de Estudios Hispano-Americanos de Sevilla.

Moran, M.H. 1986. "Using Census Material in Ethnohistorical Research: An Example from South Carolina", *Ethnohistory: A Researcher's Guide* 35: 61-76.

Moreno, E.H. 1959. *El cantón de Córdoba*. Vol. I. México: Ed. Citlaltpetl.

Moret, N.B. 1984. *Esclavos prófugos y cimarrones, 1770 - 1870*. Rio Piedras, P.R.: Editorial de la Universidad de Puerto Rico.

Moreton, J.B. 1793. *West India Customs and Manners*. London: J.Parsons.

Morris, Mervyn. 1984a. "Strange picni - Namba Roy's Black Albino", *Jamaica Journal* 17, no. 1: 24-27.

———. 1984b. "Nanny Town", *Jamaica Journal* 17, no. 2: 46-48.

Moure, R.D. 1984. "Arqueología aborígen de Cuba", *Manuel Rivero de la Calle*. Habana Viejo: Orelly 4.

Mueller, H. 1973. *Die Africanische auf Guineischen Gold Coast. Gelegene Landschaft Fetu*. Hamburg.

Murray, R. 1951. "A Visit to Nanny Town", *The Gleaner* (October 28).

———. 1951. "Description of the way to Nanny Town", *Sunday Gleaner* (October 28).

———. 1962. "Shades of Nanny Maroon, Amazon", *The Gleaner* (January 14).

Nadel, S.F. 1952. "Witchcraft in Four African Societies: An Essay in Comparison", *American Anthropologist* 54: 18-29.

Nevada, A. 1980. "La lucha de los negros en las haciendas azucareras de Córdoba en el siglo XVIII", In *Anuario II*. Universidad Veracruzana: Centro de Estudios Históricos.

———. 1987. *Esclavos negros en las haciendas azucarers de Córdoba, Veracruz, 1690-1830*. Xalapa: Universidad Veracruzana.

Nodine, B.K. 1990. "Interaction Spheres in the Caribbean". Paper presented at the Symposium of Americanist Archaeologists, Las Vegas, Nevada.

Nuñez, A. 1948. *Hueves descubrimientos arquelógicos en Punta del Este, Isla de Piñas*. Universidad de la Habana, Revista.

———. 1963. *Cuba con la mochilla hombre*. La Habana.

Ogilby, J. 1851. *Description and History of the Island of Jamaica*. Kingston: George Henderson.

Osofsky, G., ed. 1969. *Puttin' on Ole Massa*. N.Y.: Harper.

Ozanne, P. 1962. "Notes on the Early Historical Archaeology of Accra", *Transactions of the Historical Society of Ghana* VI: 51-70.

Pares, R. 1936. *War and Trade in the West Indies 1739-1763*. Oxford: Oxford University Press.

Parry, J.H., and P.M. Sherlock. 1956. *A Short History of the West Indies*. London.

Patterson, H.O. 1969. *The Sociology of Slavery: An Analysis of the Origins, Development and Structure of Negro Slave Society in Jamaica*. New Jersey: Rutherford.

———. 1970. "Slavery and Slave Revolts: A Socio-historical Analysis of the First Maroon War, Jamaica 1655-1740", *Social and Economic Studies* 19: 289-325.

Pereira, J. 1988. "The Maroon as Apolitical Motif in Contemporary Poetry". In *West Indian Literature and its Political Context* (Special Issue). Rio Piedras: Sargasso.

———. 1990. "The Maroon in Cuban and Jamaican Literature". In *Caribbean Literature in Comparison*, edited by J.R. Pereira, 9-30. University of the West indies: Institute of Caribbean Studies Series 1.

Phillips, U.B. 1914. "A Jamaican Slave Plantation", *American Historical Review* XIX, no. 3 (April).

Phillipson, D.W. 1985. *African Archaeology*. Cambridge: Cambridge University Press.

Pierres, S. 1993. "The Land of Look Behind", *Caribbean Travel and Life* (March-April): 86-93 & 115.

Pinckard, G. 1806. *Notes on the West Indies*. London: Longmans, Hurst Rees & Orme.

Posnansky, M. 1972. "Introduction", *Journal of New World Archaeology* V, no. 2: 12.

———. 1984. "Towards an Archaeology of Black Diaspora", *Journal Black Studies* 15, no. 2: 195-205.

Postma, J.M. 1990. *The Dutch in the Atlantic Slave Trade 1600-1685*. Cambridge: Cambridge University Press.

Price, R. S. 1973. *Maroon Societies: Rebel Slave Communities in the Anericas*. N.Y.: Anchor Press.

———. 1975. *Saramaka Social Structure: Analysis of a Maroon Society in Surinam*. Univ. of Puerto Rico: Institute of Caribbean Studies.

———. 1976. *The Guiana Maroons: A Historical and Bibliographical Introduction*. Baltimore: Johns Hopkins.

———. 1983. *Afro-American Arts of the Suriname Rain Forest*. Museum of Cultural History. Los Angeles: Univ. of California.

Price, R., and S.W. Mintz. 1992. *The Birth of African-American Culture: Anthropological Perspectives*. Boston: Beacon Press.

Price, S. 1993. *Co-wives and Calabashes*. Ann Arbor: University of Michigan Press.

Price, S., and R. Price. 1980. *Afro-American Arts of the Suriname Rain Forest*. Berkeley: Univ. of California Press.

Radcliffe, J. (Rev.). 1884. *The Maroons, Handbook of Jamaica for 1884-1885*. Kingston: Government Printing Press.

Rainey, F. 1940. "Puerto Rican Archaeology", *Scientific Survey of Puerto Rico and Virgin Islands* (New York Academy of Sciences) XVIII, pt. 1.

Rashford, J. 1993. "Arawak, Spanish and African Contributions to Jamaica's Settlement Vegetation", *Jamaica Journal* 24, no. 3: 17-24.

Rattray, R. S. 1923. *Religion and Art in Ashanti*. Oxford: Clarendon Press.

Reckord, M. 1968. "The Jamaica Slave Rebellion of 1831", *Past and Present* 40 (July).

Reid, M. 1883. "The Maroon", *Beadle'd Dime Library* XXIII, no. 28.

Reid, V. 1967. *The Young Warriors*. London: Longman.

———. 1978. *The Jamaicans*. Kingston: Institute of Jamaica.

———. 1983. *Nanny Town*. Kingston: Jamaica Publishing House.

Renny, R. 1807. *An History of Jamaica*. London.

Roberts, M. 1927. "Maroons at Accompong", *The Gleaner* (March 28 & 29).

Roberts, W.A. 1955. *Jamaica: A Portrait of an Island*. N.Y.: Coward-McCann.

Robinson, C. 1969. *The Fighting Maroons of Jamaica*. Kingston: William Collins & Sangster.

———. 1987. *Fight for Freedom*. Kingston: Kingston Publishers.

———. 1992. *The Iron Thorn*. Kingston: Kingston Publishers.

Robinson, P. 1898. "A Dress Rehearsal of Rebellion", *Contemporary Review* 22, item 34 (November): 746-50.

———. 1898. "The Maroons", *Harpers Weekly* (October 29).

Robotham, D. 1980. "Anthropology and Archaeology in Jamaica", *América Indígena* XI, no. 2: 355-65.

Robotham, J., and C. William. 1980. *Caribbean Story*. Bk 1. Foundations.

Rodney, Walter. 1970. *A History of the Upper Guinea Coast 1545- 1800*. Oxford: Clarendon Press.

Rogers, P. 1940. "Letter to the Maroons of Accompong" (published at the request of T. G. Cawley, Major of Accompong), *The Gleaner* (March 5).

Ross, W. 1935. "The Maroons", *The West Indian Review* 1, no. 8.

Rouse, I. 1939. "Prehistory of Haiti: A Study in Methods", *Yale Publications in Anthropology* 21.

———. 1941. "Culture of the Ft. Liberté Region", *Yale Publications in Anthropology* 24.

———. 1948. "The Arawak", *Handbook of American Indians* 143, no. 4: 507-46.

———. 1951."The Circum-Caribbean Theory: An Archaeological Test", *American Anthropologist* 55: 94-111.

———. 1960. "The Entry of Man in the West Indies", *Yale Publications in Anthropology* 61.

———. 1976. "The Saladoid Sequence in Antigua and its Aftermath". In *Proceedings of the 6th International Congress for the Study of PreColumbian Cultures of the Lesser Antilles*, edited by P. Bullen, 35-41. Pointe Noire.

———. 1982a. "Ceramics and Religious Development in the Greater Antilles", *Journal of New World Archaeology* 5, no. 2: 45-55.

———. 1982b. "The West Indies: An Introduction". In *Handbook of South Indians*, edited by J.Julian Steward, Vol.4. Washington D.C.: Government Prtg. Office.

———. 1986. *Migrations in Prehistory*. New Haven: Yale University Press.

————. 1992. *The Tainos*. New Haven: Yale University Press.

Rouse, I., and L. Allaire. 1978. "The Caribbean". In *Chronologies in New World Archaeology*, edited by R. Taylor and C. Meighan. N.Y.: Academic Press.

Rouse, I., and J.M. Cruxent. 1963. *Venezuelan Archaeology*. New Haven: Yale University Press.

Rouse, I., J.M. Cruxent, and R. Roosevelt. 1976. "Ronquin revisited". In *Proceedings of the 6th International Congress For the Study of PreColumbian Cultures of the Lesser Antilles*, edited by P. Bullen, 117-22. Pointe Noire.

Rowe, K.D. 1956. "The Maroon Treaty" (letter to the editor), *The Gleaner* (March 28).

————. 1964. "Maroons will fight to protect rights", *The Star* (October 17).

Rowe, M.O. 1949. "On Cudjoe's land", *The Gleaner* (April 7).

Roy, N. 1961. *Black Albino*. London: New Literature.

Russel, S.I.N. 1959. *Maroons of Jamaica: A Short Historical Sketch*. Kingston: Up Park Camp.

Ryman, C. 1969. "Jonkonnu: A Neo-African Form 1", *Jamaica Journal* 17, no. 1: 13-27.

————. 1970. "Jonkonnu: A Neo-African Form 2", *Jamaica Journal* 17, no. 2: 50-70.

Sanoja, and Vargas. 1983. "New Light on the Prehistory of Eastern Venezuela", *Advances in World Archaeology* 2: 205-44 (Academic Press).

Schafer, D.L. 1973. "The Maroons of Jamaica", Ph.D. diss., University of Minnesota.

Schuler, M. 1966. "Slave Resistance in the Caribbean During the Eighteenth Century", Ph.D. diss., University of the West Indies.

————. 1970. "Ethnic Slave Rebellion in the Caribbean and the Guianas", *Journal of Social History* 3: 374-85.

————. 1979. "Myalism and the African Religious Tradition in Jamaica". In *Africa and the Caribbean: The legacy of a Link*, edited by M.E. Crahan and F.W. Knight, Baltimore: Johns Hopkins University Press.

Scott, Clarissa, S. 1968. "Cultural Stability in the Maroon Village of Moore Town, Jamaica", M.A. thesis, Florida Atlantic University.

Senior, B.M. 1835. *Jamaica As It Was, As It Is And As It May Be Comprising . An Authentic Narration Of Negro Insurrection In 1831 By A Retired Military Officer*. London.

Sertima, I. van. 1990. *They Came Before Columbus*. N.Y.: Academic Press.

Sherlock, P.M. 1973. *West Indian Nations*. London: MacMillan.

Sherman, G. 1954. "A Morning with the Maroons", *Jamaica Mirror* 2: 14, 33.

Shinnie, P. 1971. *The Iron Age of Africa*. Oxford: Oxford University Press.

Singleton, T.A. 1985. *The Archaeology of Slavery and Plantation Life*. N.Y.: Academic Press.

Smith, Norval. 1984. "The Epithetic Vowel in the Jamaican Maroon Spirit Possession Language Compared with that in the Suriname Creoles", *Armsterdam Creole Studies* 44: 13-19.

————. 1987. "The Genesis of the Creole Languages of Suriname", Ph.D. diss., University of Armsterdam.

Southey, T. 1827. *Chronological History of the West Indies*. London.

Spence, B. 1985. "The Impact of Modernisation on Traditional Farming Communities: The Case Study of Accompong Maroon Village", M.Phil, University of the West Indies.

————. 1989. "Predicting Traditional Farmers' Responses to Modernisation: The Case of A Jamaican Maroon Village", *Caribbean Geography* 2, no. 4: 217-28.

Standard, The Jamaica. 1939. "Maroons deny they refused land" (July 6).

————. "Governor offers the Maroons of Accompong grants of more land"(July 19).

Star, The. 1964a. "Maroons and land tax: lost their case in court".

————. 1964b. "Teacher of Maroons: Colonel" (*C.L.G. Harris Files*, Moore Town).

————. 1972a. "Maroons did not sell Bogle, says Chief" (February 23).

————. 1972b. "Message from Colonel to Maroons" (*C.L.G. Harris Files*, Moore Town).

Steady, F.C., and K. Bilby. 1981. "Black Women and Survival: A Maroon Case". In *Black Women Cross-culturally*, edited by F.C. Steady, 451-67. London: MacMillan.

Stephen, J. 1969. *Slavery of the British West Indian Colonies*. 2 vols. N.Y.: Krauss Reprint Co.

Steward, J. H. 1808. *An Account of Jamaica and its Inhabitants*. London: Longman.

Sun Tzu. 1983. *The Art of War* (edited by James Clavell). New York: Delacorte Press.

Taber, R. 1970. *The War of the Flea: Guerrilla Warfare - Theory and Practice*. Paladin.

Tabio, E. 1970. "Arqueología de Cuba", *Serie Espeleológica* 27.

———. 1979. *Prehistoria de Cuba*. La Habana: Editorial de Ciencas Sociales.

Tabio, E., and J.M. Guarch. 1966. *Excavations en Arroyo del Palo, Mayari, Cuba*. Havana: Dept of Anthropology, Academy of Sciences.

Tanna, L. 1983a. "Anansi, Jamaica's Trickster Hero", *Jamaica Journal* 16, no. 2: 27-31.

———. 1983b. "Yoruba and Kikongo Songs in Jamaica", *Jamaica Journal* 16, no. 3: 47-52.

———. 1984. *Jamaican Folktales and Oral Histories*. Kingston: Institute of Jamaica.

———. 1987. "Dinki Mini", *Jamaica Journal* 20, no. 2: 27-31.

Taylor, A.C. 1954. "The Maroons", *The Gleaner* (June 7).

Taylor, D. 1963. "The Origin of West Indian Creole Languages: Evidence from Grammatical Categories", *American Anthropologist* 65: 800-14.

Taylor, J. 1688. *History of his Life and Travels in Jamaica*. 2 vols. London.

Taylor, S.A.G. 1963. "The Diary of Sir Henry de la Beche", *Jamaican Historical Society Bulletin* III, no. 4: 52-56.

Terborg-Penn, R. 1986. "Black Women in Resistance: A Cross-Cultural Perspective". In *Resistance: Studies in African, Caribbean and Afro-American History*, edited by G.Y. Okihiro. Amherst: University of Massachusetts.

Teulon, A. E. N.d. "Report on the Expedition to Nanny Town (July 1967)". (Mimeo pamphlet). Kingston: Institute of Jamaica.

———. 1973. "Nanny, Maroon Chieftainess", *Caribbean Quarterly* 19, no. 4: 20-27.

Thicknesse, P. 1790. *Memoirs & Anecdotes*. Dublin: William Jones.

Thomas, Herbert T. 1890. *Untrodden Jamaica*. Kingston.

———. 1927. *The story of a West Indian policeman (Forty-seven years in the Jamaican Constabulary)*. Kingston: The Gleaner Co.

Thompson, I.E. 1938. *The Maroons of Moore Town (Anthropological Series)*. Boston College, Graduate Studies.

Thurloe, J. 1742. *A collection of State papers of John Thurloe*. 7 vols. London.

Thybony, S. 1991. "The Black Seminoles: A Tradition of Courage", *Smithsonian* 22, no. 5.

Tse-Tung, Mao. 1966. *Problems of War and Strategy*. Peking: Foreign Language Press.

———. 1966. *Selected Works of Mao Tse-Tung*. 4 vols. Peking: Foreign Language Press.

Vanderwal, R.L. 1968. "Problems in Jamaican Prehistory", *Jamaica Journal* 2, no. 3.

Vansina, J. 1988. *Art History of Africa*. New York: Longman.

Vassel, L. 1991. "A Report on the Workshop of the Nanny Town Expedition", *Newsletter of the African-Caribbean Institute of Jamaica*, nos. 16-20: 18-24.

Velazquez, M de C. 1961. *Colotlan: doble frontera contra los bárbaros*. México: UNAM.

Vivianco, M.J.L. 1975. *Breve historia de Veracruz*. Xalapa: Edta del Gobiernno de Veracruz.

Voorhoeve, J. 1970. "Varieties of Creole in Surinam: Church Creole and Pagan Cult Languages". In *Pidginization and creolisation of Languages*, edited by Dell Hymes. Cambridge: Cambridge University Press.

Voss, L. 1976. *Seashore Life in Florida and the Caribbean*. Miami: Banyan Books Inc.

Wadell, D.A.G. 1967. *The West Indies and the Guianas*. New Jersey: Prentice Hall.

Waddell, H.M. 1863. *Twenty-nine Years in the West Indies and Central Africa*. London.

Wallace, A.F.C. 1961. *Culture and Personality*. N.Y.: Random House.

Wanderlust, S. 1938. "A Visit to Accompong", *The Gleaner* (March 16).

Ward, W.F. 1958. *A Short History of the Gold Coast*. London.

Warner-Lewis, M. 1986. "The Kikuyu Spirit of Messengers of Kumina", *Savacou* 13: 57-86.

Watson, J.B. 1979. *The West Indian Heritage: A History of the West Indies*. London: Cox & Wyman Ltd.

Watson, K. 1988. "Amerindian Cave Art in Jamaica: Mountain River Cave", *Jamaica Journal* 21, no. 1: 13-20.

Watters, D.R. 1982. "Relating Oceanography to Antillean Archaeology: Implications for Oceana", *Journal of New World Archaeology* 5, no. 2: 3-13.

————. 1987. "Excavations at the Hearney Site Slave Cemetery, Montserrat, West Indies", *Annals of Carnegie Museum* 56: 269-318.

Willey, G.R. 1956a. "Prehistoric Settlement Pattern in the New World", *Viking Fund Publications in Anthropology* (New York) 23.

————. 1956b. *An Introduction to American Archaeology (North and Middle America)*. New Jersey: Prentice Hall.

Willey, G.R., and G. Phillips. 1958. *Method and Theory in American Archaeology*. Chicago.

Williams, E. 1944. *Capitalism and Slavery*. USA: Chapel Hill.

————. 1970. *From Columbus to Castro: The History of the Caribbean 1492-1969*. London: Deutsch.

Williams, I. 1962. "Maroon settlement in St Elizabeth", *The Gleaner* (September 6): 8.

Williams, J. J. 1934. *Psychic Phenomena of Jamaica*. N.Y.: The Dial Press.

————. 1938. *The Maroons of Jamaica*. Chestnut Hill: Boston College Press.

————. 1938. "The Maroons of Jamaica", *Anthropological Series of the Boston College Graduate School* 3: 318-471.

Williams, W.R. 1891. "A Letter concerning Herbert Thomas' Book", *Victoria Quarterly* IV, no. 1: 1-2.

Williamson, K. 1962. "Changes in the Marriage System of the Okrika Ijo", *Africa* 32: 53-60.

Wilson, C.E. 1992. "Texas Seminole Scouts", *1992 Festival of American Folklife* (Smithsonian Institution): 80.

Wing, E.S., and E.J. Reitz. 1982. "Prehistoric Fishing Economies of the Caribbean", *Journal of New World Archaeology* 5, no. 2: 13-32.

Wiseman, H.V. 1950. *A Short History of the West Indies*. Univ. of London Press.

Wright, Irene A., ed. and trans. 1923. "The English Conquest of Jamaica", *Camden Miscellany* (London: Royal Historical Society) 13, no. iv-vi: 1-32.

————. 1970. "War and Peace with the Maroons 1730-1739", *Caribbean Quarterly* 16, no. 1: 5-27.

Wright, P. 1976. "Jamaican Political Organisation: The Effects of the Treaties", *Social and Economic Studies* 25, no. 2: 87-104.

————. 1981. "The Kromanti Dance of the Windward Maroons of Jamaica", *Nieuwe West Indische Gids* 55, nos. 1 & 2.

Wright, M-L. 1992. "The Accompong Town Maroons: Past and Present", *1992 Festival of American Folklife* (Smithsonian Institution): 74.

Index

Charles Town, 39, 49, 169
Christianity: impact of, on Africa, 23
Chorkie: use of, 56
Churches: in Accompong Town, 70
Climate: effect of, on British troops, 154
Clothing: use of as metonym in resistance science, 111
Cockpit country: association with historical events, 172
Cocoon soup, 57
Coffee Encouragement Act (1732), 155
Combolo machete, 116
Community cooperation, 45-46
Córdoba, Mexico: establishment of, as garrison to control maronage, 98
Cornwall Barracks, 39
Coromantins: reputation of, 90
Costa Chica: and retention of African cultural heritage, 104
Cowrie shells: at Accompong Town, 163; identification of, 182
Cowshut boots, 52
Craton, Michael, 121
Crawford Town, 169
Cuba: Maroons in, 128, 128n
Cudjoe, 46, 90; burial site of, 171
Culture: intangible aspects of Maroon, 73; of Maroons, as Jamaican culture, 79-83
Cupping, 62

De Bolas, Juan (Juan Lubola), 89; desertion of, to British invaders, 89
De la Matosa, Francisco, 99
De Serras, Juan, 89
Dispute resolution: among Jamaican Maroons, 60-61
Djuka music: use of large and small scale in, 140
Djuka songs: melodic structure of, 140
Dominica: final confrontation between Maroons and whites in, 130-131; intermixing of Caribs with slaves, 127, and Maroons at *Morne Nègre*, 129-130
Drums: function of, in Maroon ritual setting, 144-147
Dual ethnogenesis: in eighteenth century Jamaica, 82-83; in Suriname, 82
Dukunu: preparation of, 57

Earthenware: find of, at Nanny Town site, 163
Efutu, kingdom of: 30; archaeological finds at, 183; implications of find for relationships between Maroons and West African traditions, 184
Elmina, 30
Ethnic groups: effect of colonial intervention on, in West Africa, 15
Ethnicity; concept of, 15

Europeans: and establishment of colonial administration in West Africa, 28
Eyre, Alan, quoted, 153-154

Family systems: similarity to West African, in Accompong, xv-xvi; in West Africa, 15
Family traditions: among Jamaican Maroons, 42
Feedback: problems of, in written documents, vii
Fernandez, Andres: and proposal of formation of free village in Mexico, 102
Festival, annual: at Accompong, 68-70
Festivals: effect of European influences on, in West Africa, 18; military element in, 18
Fete-man., *See* Fettehman
Fettehman, 49; function of, 76
Fighting Maroons the, Robinson, Carey , x
Fire: use of in warfare by Maroons, 153, 156
Fish pots: making of, 56-57
Fishing: methods of, among Moore Town Maroons, 53
Fishing lances: types of, 52-53
Food preparation: among Maroons, 57
Fort George, 156
Foundry: at Morant Bay, using Maroon labour, 170
Freedom: concept of, 86-87, 92
French Revolution, 131
Funeral traditions: of Maroons, 46

Garifuna, the: and ties to St Vincent, 129
Geographical conditions: advantages of, in Maroon wars, 153
Ginger House, 39, 168
Ginger Ridge, 167
Gold: importance of, in trans-Saharan trade, 29
Goodison, Lorna, *Nanny*, 113-114
GrandeeNanny, See Nanny
Grandy Nanny. *See* Nanny
Griot, 110, 112; defined, 118; Vic Reid as, 117
Guanaboa Vale: Maroon settlement at, 167
Guerrilla: derivation of, 150
Guerrilla warfare: techniques used by Maroons in, 159, 160; terrain as asset in, 153-154; use of, by Maroons, 152; value of, 159
Gumbey drumming, 70
Gun Barrel, 37, 168
Gunpowder: development of, 159-160
Guthrie's defile, 66, 172
Guy's Town: refuge for Nanny Town Maroons, 169

Haitian Revolution, 2, 127, 131
Harrison, James (Colonel), 38-39
Historical period: in Africa, 10-14, archaeological reconstruction of,8; in Caribbean chronology, 8; Maroons of Jamaica as part of, xiv; proposed sub-periods, 8
History: writing of, 109
History of the Maroon Peoples of Jamaica, Beverley Carey, 121-122

Contributors

E Kofi Agorsah, associate professor in the Departments of Black Studies and International Studies, Portland State University, Oregon, teaches courses on African and Caribbean cultures and international studies, mainly cultural or heritage. Formerly appointed Edward Moulton Barrett lecturer in Archaeology at the University of the West Indies, Mona he has also served on the board of directors of the Jamaica National Heritage Trust and the African-Caribbean Institute of Jamaica, among others. Current projects include Archaeology of Maroon Heritage in the Caribbean and the Volta Basin Archaeological Research Project (VBARP), Ghana.

Kenneth Bilby, research associate in the Center for Folklife Programs and Cultural Studies at the Smithsonian Institution in Washington, D.C., has carried out extensive ethnographic research in Jamaica and French Guiana, focusing on contemporary Maroon societies. He has produced several ethnomusicological recordings, and written numerous articles on Caribbean folklore, expressive culture, and history. In 1992 he curated (with Diana Baird N'Diaye) a programme at the Smithsonian Festival of American Folklife, entitled "Creativity and Resistance: Maroon Culture in the Americas".

Kamau Brathwaite, professor of Comparative Literature & Caribbean Cultural Expression at New York University, is also poet & cultural historian, with some 50 publications to his credit. Formerly on staff at the University of the West Indies, Mona (1962-1991), he is co-founder & secretary, Caribbean Artists Movement (CAM) and editor of its journal, *Savacou*.

Carolyn Cooper is senior lecturer in the Department of English, University of the West Indies, Mona. She teaches Caribbean, African and African-American literature, and is developing a research specialization in Cultural Studies. Her study of Jamaican popular culture, *Noises in the Blood*, was published in 1993 by Macmillan Caribbean.

Albert Edwards, Detective Inspector of Police, and member of the Jamaica Constabulary Force since 1974, has been an avid student of Portland history for several years. His interests also extend to the areas of archaeology and photography. He has participated in two archaeological digs at Nanny Town (1991, 1992), and is a member and treasurer of the Archaeological Society of Jamaica.

Collin Lloyd George Harris, born in Moore Town (Portland, Jamaica), was elected Chief of the Moore Town Maroons in 1964, remains one of the leading authorities on Maroon history and culture in Jamaica. He is a member of the Executive Committee of the International Maroon Organization and chairs one of the committees of that organization. He has thrice been elected president of the Portland chapter of the Jamaica Teachers Association, and has also served as senator. He is also a Justice of the Peace.

Joe Pereira, senior lecturer in the Department of Spanish at the University of the West Indies, Mona, has focused his research interests on Maroons in Caribbean literature and the literature of the Cuban Revolution, and has published various articles on both areas. Former head of the Department of Spanish and dean of the Faculty of Arts & General Studies, he is currently director of the Institute of Caribbean Studies, Mona (ICS). He also continues to be very active in the academic staff union, the West Indies Group of University Teachers (WIGUT).

Carey Robinson, historian and former outstanding journalist and broadcaster, has studied and published on resistance history of Jamaica. Having written *The Fighting Maroons of Jamaica* (1969) and its expanded version *Iron Thorn* (1992), as well as *Fight for Freedom* (1987), he continues to take an active part in the search for an authentic history of Jamaica with the conviction that through such studies the true character and needs of the Jamaican people will be better understood.

Maureen Warner-Lewis, reader in African-Caribbean Language and Orature, Department of English, University of the West Indies, Mona lectures on African and Oral literatures. She has co-edited *Garvey. Africa, Europe, the Americas* and has written, among others, *Nkuyu: Spirit Messengers of the Kumina*. Her forthcoming publications include *Yoruba Songs of Trinidad* and *Trinidad Yoruba: From Mother Tongue to Memory*.

Marjorie Whylie, practising musician, composer, music educator and musicologist, is consultant on Caribbean music and culture. She leads her own band, Whylie Wrythm, and is a member of the Jazzmobile and the Big Band. Formerly on staff at the Jamaica School of Music where she directed the Folk Music Research Department for fourteen years, she is now also musical director of the National Dance Theatre Company of Jamaica (NDTC), and part time tutor in Caribbean musics at the Phillip Sherlock Centre for the Creative Arts, University of the West Indies, Mona.

Martin Luther Wright, born in Accompong Town (St Elizabeth, Jamaica) has been Colonel of the Accompong Town Maroons for twenty years, having been elected and re-elected for three consecutive five-year terms (1967-1982) and again in 1988, retiring in 1993. He has also been a deacon and local preacher of long standing, as well as a very successful farmer and businessman.